C. G. JUNG AND LITERARY THEORY

C. G. Jung and Literary Theory

The Challenge from Fiction

Susan Rowland
Senior Lecturer in English
University of Greenwich

palgrave
macmillan

Published by PALGRAVE MACMILLAN
Houndmills, Basingstoke, Hampshire RG21 6XS and
175 Fifth Avenue, New York, N. Y. 10010
Companies and representatives throughout the world

PALGRAVE MACMILLAN is the global academic imprint of the Palgrave Macmillan division of St. Martin's Press, LLC and of Palgrave Macmillan Ltd. Macmillan® is a registered trademark in the United States, United Kingdom and other countries. Palgrave is a registered trademark in the European Union and other countries.

Outside North America
ISBN 0–333–74720–8

In North America
ISBN 0–312–22275–0

This book is printed on paper suitable for recycling and made from fully managed and sustained forest sources.

A catalogue record for this book is available from the British Library.

Library of Congress Catalog Card Number: 98–55202

Transferred to digital printing 2002

Printed and bound in Great Britain by
Antony Rowe Ltd, Chippenham and Eastbourne

To my father, K.T. Rowland (1925–93), a writer

Contents

Acknowledgements

All the errors in this book are of my own creation and responsibility but there are many people whose help has been incalculable. I am particularly grateful to my doctoral supervisor, Judie Newman of Newcastle University, for her unflagging encouragement and assistance during the early stages of this work. This book would never have been completed without her invaluable support. I owe a great deal to Gerard Livingstone for philosophy and patience. Hazel Davis, a retired Jungian analyst, has been very helpful in discussing Jungian theory and contemporary analytic practice with me and in reading early versions of Chapter 1. Colleagues at Liverpool University English Department sustained this work during revisions, in particular Jocelyn Wogan-Browne, Val Gough and Nick Davis. Greenwich University has assisted my research both materially and by providing supportive colleagues and congenial teaching. Special mention should be given to the Theory and Contemporary Writing class of 1997/8 for lively comments on the subjects discussed in the following pages. I thank all my family and friends for their good humour, nourishing meals, computer advice and practical help.

Abbreviations

CW for *The Collected Works of C.G. Jung, vols. 1–20, A and B*, edited by Sir Herbert Read, Michael Fordham MD, MRCP, Gerhard Adler PhD, translated by R.F.C. Hull (London: Routledge & Kegan Paul, 1953–91).

Introduction: Beyond Traditional Jungian Literary Criticism

The purpose of this book is to bring together the psychology of C.G. Jung and modern theories of literary representation in an era of poststructuralist literary criticism. My aim is to initiate the process of absorbing Jungian theory into modern critical discourses such as deconstruction, feminism, postmodern spirituality, reader-response and postcolonialism in ways that have been achieved with great perspicacity and thoroughness for the theories of Sigmund Freud. One of the most significant gifts of poststructuralist practice to literary theories is the possibility of reversing and renegotiating the customary power relationship between the theory and the body of material it seeks to explain. Both Freud and Jung assumed that their theories could give an adequate account of the psychological dynamics of literary production and consumption: theory had priority over literature and indeed such a superiority was a guarantee of the status of the theory. The poststructuralist dissection of the authoritative claims of discourses has enabled a critical experimentation in which conventional priorities are swapped to allow literature to be read as illuminating, and even contesting, the precepts of Freudian theory. The resulting criticism constructs a more complex and intimate bond between the literary corpus and the discourse of psychoanalysis. In such a project the literary text becomes the site of the testing and challenging of psychological writing. Fictions function as the arena in which competing literary theories such as feminism and postcolonialism may productively encounter psychoanalytic doctrine. None of this has yet taken place for C.G. Jung and literary theory despite Jung's profound influence on twentieth-century culture.

I would like to employ the metaphor of romance to describe the aims and methodology of this book. The following chapters attempt to stage a romance between Jungian psychology and modern poststructuralist critical theories where 'romance' implies a relationship in which neither Jung nor the literary theories remain the dominant partner. I will argue that Jungian psychology can make positive contributions to modern literary theory in ways hitherto unsuspected. Simultaneously, poststructuralist literary approaches can supply an important critique both of Jungian theory's empirical claims and of its cultural biases. These biases are particularly acute in the areas of gender, politics and colonialism. After two chapters introducing Jungian theory in deconstructive, feminist, occult, historical and political contexts, my method will be to work from literary texts outwards to Jungian theory. By scrutinising novels which have deliberately imported Jungian ideas into their scheme of representation, the book will outline the challenge from fiction to both Jungian theory's cultural authority and to poststructuralist literary theory's neglect of this resource.

It must be emphasised that I am not suggesting that the literary establishment's omitting of Jung is merely an oversight. The first two chapters will also consider the very real problems with Jungian discourse in its misogynistic drives and Jung's culpable personal career, which gave him a role in Nazi Germany. By providing an historical context for Jungian theory, arguments built upon a feminist or new historicist critiques of Jung gain effectiveness and resonance.

It would also be wrong to imply that a valuable body of Jungian literary criticism does not already exist.[1] Beginning, naturally, with Jung's essay on literature 'Psychology and Literature',[2] what I would like to call 'traditional Jungian literary criticism' has developed a large following consisting of a variety of practices linked by the assumption of Jungian theory's superior powers to explain literature. My work marks a complete break with traditional Jungian literary criticism in treating Jungian texts as 'writing' in the poststructuralist sense. This book is predicated upon the necessity of deconstructing Jungian writings and thereby reconstructing a Jung not restricted to humanism and its influence on older forms of literary practice. In effect, by examining Jungian theory in contemporary fiction, it is possible to evade the limitations of traditional Jungian literary criticism (which cites Jungian ideas as unproblematically authoritative), by treating Jungian writings as texts open to deconstruction and reimagining. Jungian theory opens its borders to the field of fiction. First of all, it would be useful to be more specific about traditional Jungian literary criticism and its humanist Jung.

TRADITIONAL LITERARY JUNGIAN CRITICISM AND HUMANIST JUNG

Unsurprisingly, Jung himself was one of the first to apply his psychological theories to the production and criticism of literature. In his essay, he distinguished two types of fiction: the psychological, pertaining to the conscious mind and its complexes, and the visionary. For the visionary artist, creation is a form of unconscious possession where one or more of the archetypes of the collective unconscious will seize the mind of the artist, shape the work and may be communicated directly to the reader. Jungian theory will be described in detail in the next chapter and in the glossary. Nevertheless, it is worth stating now that traditional Jungian literary critics follow the master's lead in seeking transhistorical archetypes in literary texts. These critics seek in literature a powerful psychic image (often related to a myth), which can be identified in more than one literary work. Examples could include a mythological representation of mothering, frequently termed 'the Great Mother', a young hero embarking on a quest, devouring dragons and frail, flower-like heroines. My reservation would be that such critics usually assume that what is represented in literature can be unproblematically identified with Jung's notion of the collective archetype. The collective unconscious is every human's biological inheritance of archetypes which offer potentials for meaning and image formation. An archetype can never be fully manifest in the conscious mind, let alone a literary text. What critics are really searching for are archetypal images which will inevitably be affected by culture even if they bear the numinous stamp of the antecedent archetype. Jungian critics tend not to make a rigid distinction between the unrealisable archetype and the culturally influenced derivative, the archetypal image. By characterising powerful literary symbols as archetypes, it enables critics to postulate a constant human essence free of historical determinism, although most critics would acknowledge a minor effect of local cultural inscription. This facilitates a criticism of culture from a posited 'outside' of archetypal powers. Belief in archetypal images as transcultural constants provides an ideology against the very notion of ideology itself for it claims to be a common human 'ground' outside culture and history. From such a position, traditional Jungian criticism feels licensed to criticise culture and all other ideologies as inferior discourses. It can have an interesting effect when traditional Jungian criticism is applied to such movements which consider themselves deeply embedded in culture and history such as feminism.

An example of how a quite subtle traditional Jungian criticism remains mired in essentialism and humanism can be found in an article reprinted in the very useful collection edited by Richard P. Sugg.[3] Evelyn J. Hinz and John J. Teunissen argue that feminism demonstrates the rise of the Great Mother archetype but leave open the question of whether this is the scorned feminine 'in her creative or destructive phase'.[4] Such an orientation works as a pro-feminist statement in their belief that neglect of the feminine in culture has *caused* the archetypal eruption. However the equivocation about a destructive or creative Great Mother offers no means of evaluating feminism except against the rather unfortunate language of Jung's writings on 'the feminine', which will be scrutinised in Chapter 1. Is feminism a 'good' thing because it signifies the return of the Great Mother archetype to cultural power, or is it an ideological betrayal of her (and all women's) essential femininity? The increased participation of women in culture and society is not grounds for judging the appropriateness of feminism because these archetypal critics are working on the assumption of a transhistorical archetypal feminine essence. Traditional Jungian criticism quickly lapses into essentialism on gender which enables some Jungian critics to attack feminism for betraying the essential feminine nature of women. The criterion for the 'essential feminine nature' is taken both from the meta-narrative of Jung's texts (as the master theorist) and what is posited as the 'pure' expression of the archetype in literature. It is worth noting that traditional Jungian literary criticism thus forms a distinct branch of liberal humanist literary theory. It exploits the concept of the collective unconscious to theorise a human essence independent of history and culture, and it tends to essentialist notions of gender. Traditional Jungian literary *practice* is liable to construct Jung as rather more of a liberal humanist than his writings necessitate. This is because of the habit of regarding archetypal images in literary texts as 'archetypes' and so transhistorical human constants.

A certain if somewhat marginalised resistance to humanism in Jungian theory will be elaborated in Chapter 1 in relation to structuralism and deconstruction. Suffice to say here, it remains correct to associate Jung with the broad spectrum of humanism in a number of ways. His psychology does describe the formation of a privatised self which is autonomous and takes a detached attitude to cultural forces. In his dealings with religion, Jung stresses its importance as a psychological phenomenon and provides a narrative of the numinous which permits wide variations of faith from orthodox Christian, through 'new age' type beliefs and even atheism. All the while, Jung retains spirituality as an authentic manifestation of unconscious powers. However, unlike the usual position of humanism, Jung does not privilege reason. Instead, he designates as supremely important forms of knowledge dependent upon the collective unconscious. Such immediate psychic knowledge is, at least in part, accessible to the conscious self, if never completely comprehensible. However, it is the well-known Jungian trope of the collective unconscious itself which most promotes the attachment of the humanist label because it can be read as relatively insulated from cultural forces if the distinction between unrealisable archetype and culturally inflected archetypal image is not conscientiously maintained. I have already suggested that that traditional Jungian critics tend to do this.

My own position, as elaborated in future chapters, is that such cultural insulation is a neither a necessary nor a sustainable conception of Jungian theory. The collective unconscious does not entail inherited forms of society, inherited images or an inherited form of human 'being'. Archetypes in the mind are potentials for image formation but formless in themselves. Any archetypal expression (in dreams or in art) must therefore require material from the subject's personal history and culture for anything to be represented at all. Therefore, although it is not incorrect for an intentionalist reading of Jung to classify him in association with humanism, there reside traces of a resistance to humanist philosophy which may promote a romance with poststructuralism. It is Jung's tendency to collapse unrepresentable archetypes into their derivative and culturally inflected archetypal images which allow his absorption into traditions of unchanging human essences and social characteristics.[5] Traditional Jungian literary criticism builds upon this practice (never substantiated in Jungian theory) to create a specific but enclosed type of literary criticism, opaque to influence from modern poststructuralist, feminist or postcolonial theories. Indeed, traditional Jungian criticism flourishes upon the margins of literary study as one refuge from the deconstructive rigours of 'theory'. A traditional Jungian critic and a deconstructive, postmodern, postcolonial or feminist literary critic can have no dialogue: the former believes in the humanist Jung who can demolish Derrida with an authentic logos and defeat Marx with a transhistorical human essence while the latter knows that such humanist logocentrics as Jung have been exploded by the exciting detonations of modern theory. In short, traditional Jungian critics accept Jung as authoritative; modern theoretical critics will not even read him. The approach of this book is different in that it neither uses Jungian theory as unproblematically authoritative nor constructs him on the humanist model where the ideas can be easily dismissed by the important current philosophies in literary studies. It is contemporary fiction which provides the opportunity to deconstruct Jungian theory as authority and reinstate it as textuality. Humanist Jung may give way to Jungian writings in a post-structuralist context. Fiction's display of and challenge to Jungian theory enable a dialogue to be staged between modern theoretical approaches and Jungian ideas. As a consequence, it is possible to foresee an expanded role for Jungian discourse in the future developments of literary theory. In turn, literary theories and contemporary fictions produce an important critique when they encounter Jungian writings.

JUNG AND THE CHALLENGE FROM FICTION

This book will make use of works by four British writers and concentrate on novels published between 1978 and 1990. All the texts chosen are literary novels using Jungian theory as a one source of an oppositional discourse to 1980s British culture, although Nicholas Mosley's *Hopeful Monsters* is set in the interwar years. All the novelists are rooted in the realist tradition, although they make departures from it, particularly Doris Lessing (whose science fiction will be considered). I have chosen two female and two male writers in order to examine any gender differences in approaching a powerful male theorist. Although valuable objects of study in themselves, the literary texts are considered here principally as the site of a collision between Jungian ideas and modern literary theories. My aim is to reformulate the collision into a romance which will be productive for both Jungian discourse and literary theory.

Chapter 1 is a philosophical introduction to the major Jungian theories in relation to literary studies. It deconstructs humanist

Jung in favour of looking at Jungian writings as permeable to both theoretical and fictional challenges. It then aligns Jungian ideas with structuralism, deconstruction, postmodernism and crucial aspects of feminist theory as well as critiquing Jungian writing of the feminine. Jung in historical and political context is the focus of Chapter 2 which will examine both the occult and contentious role of cultural politics in the discourse. Its implications for an historicist criticism of a Jungian fiction is developed in Chapters 5 and 6.

Chapter 3 considers a Jungian conception of reader-response theory and Lindsay Clarke's novel, *The Chymical Wedding*. This text uses Jung to represent religious and psychic experience, esotericism and alchemy. It attempts to employ Jung to recover a sense of the feminine lost to patriarchal culture and to structure a pervading fear of the 1980s: the threat of nuclear destruction. In the novel's naive faith in Jungian ideas of the feminine, it is revealing of distinctive esoteric discourses such as spiritualism inhabiting Jung's work.

For Michèle Roberts in Chapters 4 and 5, Jung's meaningful unconscious is also central to her creative beliefs. Her novels are explored in order to examine Jung further in relation to feminist theory and to suggest the viability of Jungian feminist narrative practices. Roberts' fiction pursues feminist goals and uses Jung to represent and value the Other. Additionally, Jungian ideas are constructed to authenticate female religious experience and presence in the sacred. Furthermore, her novels explore gender using Jung's fictional psyche to deconstruct bodily difference, to undo any hierarchy based upon it and to promote plurality of meaning. These texts detect a postmodern Jung in relation to both spirituality and possibilities for meaning. Later works take Jungian fictionality into the challenging and rewriting of religious and historical traditions. Chapter 5 concludes with Roberts' most critical and illuminating critique of Jung in *In the Red Kitchen*. This novel investigates a seminal Jungian text to examine patriarchal, fictional and erotic structures to be found at the genesis of Jungian theory while still asserting the value of the concept of the creative Jungian unconscious. *In the Red Kitchen* explores the discourse of spiritualism in relation to Jungian ideas in an effective contrast to the less innovative, *The Chymical Wedding*. Roberts' novel exemplifies a poststructuralist feminist and new historicist engagement with Jungian theory.

Nicholas Mosley in Chapter 6 uses Jung in *Hopeful Monsters* to reformulate Christianity as psychology, a drive that is so energising in Jung's own works that it produces problems of power and authority in the novel. *Hopeful Monsters* supplies a narrative of salvation through the construction of a group identity. It attempts to integrate artistic discourses of power and love but remains politically flawed. Chapter 2 details some of the political flaws in Jung's own life and works which become replicated in *Hopeful Monsters'* production of an elite group. The resulting text seeks to colonise the reader with an overwhelming authority. Issues of colonialism, the body, gender and history form the theoretical context to this chapter.

For Doris Lessing, Jung is a way into a larger esoteric system and she is politically acute about Jungian theory's possible use as an imperialist discourse appropriating the Other. Chapter 7 does more than merely locate a colonial Jung, it explores the possibility of a Jungian postcolonial literary theory. The book concludes with a chapter bringing together the various arguments detailed in the romance of Jungian ideas and modern poststructuralist literary theory. By summarising the critical developments, it seeks to outline the new relationship sought by this work between Jungian discourse and literary theory.

All major Jungian concepts are additionally explained in the Glossary at the back of this book for convenient reference.

1

Jung for Literature and Literary Theory

JUNGIAN THEORY AND LITERARY STUDIES

The wide-ranging discipline of literary studies has neglected the potential of Jung for literary theory. Such neglect becomes acute in an age when meta-narratives such as those of Freud and Marx are tested, reconfigured and reinscribed for a postmodern era. Where is the interrogation of Jung which can also diagnose the 'otherness' of his writings? Could a powerful contemporary critique such as feminism detect a textual hysteria in Jungian theory? Could such a project as this offer a contribution to still pertinent debates about psyche, gender, power, history and discourse? My argument rests upon the contention that what has been previously undervalued in Jung is what Doris Lessing has called his sense of the 'double face' of truth,[1] the ability of his theory to be one capable of disputing its own authoritative claims. Such a theory may be said to problematise or even to 'deconstruct' the boundaries between theory and fiction. In this chapter I shall present Jung's most important concepts in the context of some of the most significant modern literary theories. The aim, as always, is twofold: to employ techniques such as post-structuralism, postmodernism, feminism (and in later chapters new historicism, reader theory and postcolonialism) to critique the humanist Jung, while at the same time exploring the potential for Jungian ideas to contribute to these modern literary discourses in a productive and non-hierarchical manner.

Jungian psychology is notable for offering a theory of religious experience which can be divorced from traditional faith and constructions of that treacherous phrase, 'the feminine'. Perhaps most strikingly, he provides a valid fictional space in fantasy and imaginary worlds since his theories rest on the premise that psychic experience is primary: the mind witnesses nothing that is outside the psyche so that there is no category of knowledge to be privileged above the psychic.[2] Given the importance Jung assigns to the unconscious and its structuring powers, archetypes, it is unsurprising to discover that his psyche is distinctively creative. The psyche frames and organises the perception of reality, giving the term 'fantasy' a significant twist. Fantasy is not a category rigidly separable from the ordinary comprehension of reality.

> The psyche creates reality every day. The only expression I can say for this activity is *fantasy*.[3]

Jung's term 'unconscious' resembles Freud's in that it both describes mental contents not apprehended by the ego and designates a psychic place with its own functions and laws. However, unlike Freud, Jung believed that the unconscious exerted a creative force upon the ego, was the space or origin of meaning and value, and he generally tried to give the unconscious priority over consciousness. He considered that the unconscious was distinguished by its independence from the ego, containing potent elements beyond structures formed by the ego's repression of inadmissible material. The unconscious is an autonomous entity independently capable of organising a compensatory relation to conscious attitudes or personality. Within the unconscious is to be found the 'personal unconscious' – repressed material from everyday life and the 'Collective Unconscious', the strata of archetypes that are inherited and represent a phylogenetic layer. Archetypes are not inherited images: they are content-free but are inherited potentials for image-formation and meaning. They are unrepresentable and can manifest themselves only as archetypal images which are subject to the cultural and personal input through the personal unconscious. Therefore, a dream image of a maternal figure may be constellating inherited potentials for mother images but is crucially 'coloured' by the dreamer's own cultural perceptions of mothering. Archetypes themselves can be ascribed to the tradition of Platonic Ideas which exist in the minds of the gods and function as the blueprints for entities in the human dimension. When defining archetypes, Jung is clear that they are not inherited mental contents: he uses the imagery of crystallisation.

> Its form ... might perhaps be compared to the axial system of a crystal, which, as it were, preforms the crystalline structure in the mother liquid, although it has no material existence of its own.[4]

Jung does not help his case for archetypes which make up the Collective Unconscious by constantly referring to archetypal images as archetypes elsewhere in the *Collected Works,* but the general principle is clear: structuring potentials are inherited; contents are not. Given that archetypal images can never exhaust the multiple possibilities of the archetype and are refracted through the personal, they can be described as fictional, metaphorical versions of an unrepresentable reality. That is, archetypal images are fictional and metaphorical, not because they are arbitrary but because they are the partial and imaginative expressions of fundamentally plural potentials for meaning. All psychic imagery partakes of the archetypal to a greater or lesser extent and archetypes give an impersonal dimension to Jung's psyche.

Jung believed that mental existence was a continual dialogue with archetypal forces in the unconscious; that subjectivity was the result of unconscious processes shaping the ego. This continual psychic narrative he called 'individuation'. To use a modern term, individuation is a deconstructive process, privileging the ungraspable unconscious over the limitations of the ego as it continually reshapes identity and perceptions of reality. Individuation is teleological since Jung held that after mid-life the ego needed to discover and become subjected to the most important archetype of the 'self'.

> [T]he self designates the whole range of psychic phenomena in man. It expresses the unity of the personality as a whole.[5]

The self is both close to Jung's definition of the psyche – 'by psyche I understand the totality of all psychic processes, conscious as well as unconscious'[6] – and is the goal towards which the psyche travels. Usually represented in dreams by circular motifs or the mandala, it contains all opposites and is the source of all meanings and values for the ego. The teleological nature of individuation is the requirement for the ego to become a subordinate part of the self's structure. Since it remains largely unconscious, the self is experienced as numinous and transcendent. There is an ambiguity in the *Collected Works* as to how far individuation is a 'natural' process of the psyche and how far it can or needs to be initiated through analysis. If 'true' individuation is the analytic kind, then are there any limits on the type of personality? Could individuation become a restricted or even an elitist concept? This will be considered in Chapter 2. What appears to be more promising in the concept of individuation is the privileging of Otherness in the construction of subjectivity. Since the Other within, the unconscious, can be constructed as the Other without, the Other gender or simply Other people, then Jungian theory could form a flexible ethical model that counteracts the model of ego psychology as heroism. In the heroic narrative, the ego is constructed as opposite (so usually gendered male) to the terrible (m)Other, the unconscious, and is endlessly battling to conquer and suppress Otherness. Jungian theory would suggest this to be a dangerous fantasy of literalism. If the unconscious is the source of meanings and values, then the ego's construction of reality, formed by suppressing Otherness, is inauthentic. Instead, individuation offers unions or conjunctions with the unconscious often articulated in the structure of a 'marriage'. Such a 'marriage' can be expressed as a 'sacred marriage' due to the numinous nature of the unconscious which may manifest itself as divinity. So the Other in Jungian theory is the ethical Other which can never be authentically appropriated or colonised. This is the sense in which the Jungian 'Other' will be used in theoretical arguments throughout this book. I cite the 'Other' in upper case to indicate my precise and particular formulation here rather that any theorised 'other' structured from non-Jungian materials. If the Jungian Other is ever constructed as a fantasy of the Same, then that is a distortion of the fundamental privileging of the unconscious as meaningful Other in Jungian ideas. This point will be returned to when considering Jung in a feminist context.

In fact, Jung suggests three sorts of conjunctions in his teleological narrative of individuation. First, there may occur a 'marriage' with the Other gender in the psyche; second, one of psyche with body; and third, that of psyche experiencing a numinous encounter with the outer world. Jung liked to posit the third type of conjunction in the language of the alchemists; the *mysterium conjunctionis* links the human subject to the *unus mundus* forming a mystical union of Being.[7]

Unus mundus, as the term suggests, reflects Jung's belief in the fundamental unity of the cosmos, of matter with soul and spirit. In a sense, the body is the node that connects psyche and matter since for Jung, bodily impulses are connected to, but certainly do not simply cause, fictional archetypal images.[8] Jung asserted that any 'causal connections' could run from the psyche to the body, but not as a simple determining factor. Body and psyche also exist in a deconstructive relationship in that neither pole of the opposition operates a simple hierarchy over the other. On the one hand, archetypal reality is fundamental, and on the other, Jung never denied importance to Freud's Oedipus complex with its theorising about infantile sexuality and bodily pleasure. The role of the body as meaningful participant in psychic identity but never a governing principle has particular resonances for gender and feminist theory, as I will detail later.

The fact that 'spirit' can also be a part of the underlying unity of the cosmos for Jung brings in his theological discourse. For Jung, religious intuitions are by definition manifestations of the archetypal unconscious. In a bold move, he located transcendence in the unconscious as part of the archetypal potentials of the self. This means that psychology and theology become uncanny doubles of each other, for words about experiences of divinity, *theos logos*, are by definition in the Jungian scheme of primary psychic reality, also words about psyche. Consequently, to Jung, religious intimations are an authentic mode of experience in themselves: religious feeling need not be a fantasised version of bodily or sexual experience and it can be manifested without an external accompanying theological system to sustain its definition. To Jung, religious experience is an authentic psychic event which does not necessarily imply a transcendent reality *external* to psyche. Of course, Jung did try to reconcile his psychology with Christianity by calling images of the self the God-image in the psyche and Christ as a projection of the self. Since as a self-image this Christ must contain opposites such as both genders and darkness as well as light (the anti-Christ), this attempt to integrate psychology and traditional Christian theology still leaves radical disjunctions. Nevertheless, Jung remains a boon to artists who want to take spiritual experience seriously but do not want to reframe traditional religious systems. Essentially, Jung's autonomous psyche offers a wider canvas for competing forms of reality to be represented.

Dreams are likewise communications from an autonomous entity. Jung defined a dream broadly as 'a spontaneous self-portrayal, in symbolic form, of the actual situation in the unconscious',[9] and they could be seen in the Freudian way as creatures of causality, pointing to repressions from ego existence or construction, or they could be viewed in a distinctively Jungian frame as purposeful. The value of considering dreams as primarily about unconscious teleological processes rather than ego concerns is that dreams become a way of understanding what is happening in a person's unconscious now. Dreams do not require a kind of psychic archaeology. Interpretations of dreams are directed towards future development rather than uncovering a cache of symbols referring back to the ego's history.[10]

Jungian theory itself tends towards balancing concepts so that the creative side is met by the archetype of its opposite, the shadow. This archetype realises itself as 'the thing a person has no wish to be',[11] and it is the opposite or undoing of conscious personality. It forms the inferior complement of conscious personality and may be imaged as darkness, evil or chaos. Individuation demands a coming to terms with the shadow lest the ego's complete 'unconsciousness' of it lead to an inflation of the shadow's destructive and psychotic powers.[12] If this is true of the individual then what about a theory or the psychic processes of writing itself? Might it be possible that Jung's own theories or *Collected Works* are haunted by a shadow? Such traces of chaos, darkness or inability to signify securely may be detectable not only in the more deconstructive aspects (the undoing of its ostensible structures), to be detailed below, but also in the elements of cultural contamination. Such contamination, I will now argue, shadows to the point of disfiguring Jung's writings on gender and particularly 'the feminine'.

JUNG'S FEMININE OR 'HYSTERIA' IN THE THEORY

Jung considered that the main unconscious image signifying Otherness would be the Other gender and he called the male's feminine contrasexual image the *anima*, and the female's masculine image for the unconscious the *animus*. Psychic gender is fluid and archetypes can manifest themselves equally as female or male. Jung usually called them androgynous, but he suggested that individuation would centre on a romance with the other gender in the psyche culminating in a conjunction, or 'sacred marriage'. These balanced concepts are somewhat problematized by the introduction of two principles, another pair of opposites, Eros/Logos. Jung aligned the anima with Eros for men, the principle of relatedness that men must access in their unconscious, and the animus with Logos for women, the principle of spiritual meaning and reason. He considered that masculine consciousness was already oriented towards Logos, powers of analysis, separateness and reason, and feminine consciousness aligned with Eros, relatedness, feeling and love. Jung neither justifies these depictions by a bodily model, based on female bearing of and bonding to infants, nor on a cultural model, such as that offered by Nancy Chodorow,[13] who suggests that exclusive female care of infants results in the female gender constructed on principles of likeness and relating. Boys, by contrast, are forced into a sense of opposition and separation. Jung neither provides a biological nor a cultural justification for his Eros-dominated female consciousness because his theories do not allow the body or culture to govern meaning, although he concedes that these factors intervene in it. On other occasions Jung refers to Eros and Logos as capable of coexisting in individuals of either gender, which is how many in the current British school of Analytical Psychology regard these ideas.[14] Andrew Samuels, the eminent post-Jungian theorist, describes anatomy as a metaphor for Otherness in the formation of anima and animus images.[15]

However, any recent recuperation of animus/anima or Eros/Logos should not obscure the way Jung's writings allow the theory to slide into essentialism and damaging cultural prescriptions. In women, Jung wrote, Eros 'is an expression of their true nature while their Logos is often only a regrettable accident'.[16] By giving women an indirect access to Logos, Jung and his immediate disciples even cite this construction of the female psyche supposedly to legitimate the spiritual authority of men over women. As Jung's follower Linda Fierz-David wrote of the Logos-animus in *Women's Dionysian Initiation*:[17]

> Especially concerning their spiritual development, women are dependent upon men. In the first place, they receive spiritual instruction through their fathers and through the men in their circle of life.[18]

This cultural slippage of authoritative image in the unconscious to external rule by men is powerfully suggestive of its own opposite, that the cultural dominance of men, patriarchy, has been naturalised in this aspect of theory. Nowhere does Jung suggest that, for men, coming to terms with the anima means submitting to the authority of women. On the one hand, Jung's insistence that the feminine has been disastrously suppressed in modern culture, religion and the psyches of the ruling gender, is a powerfully resonant theory for feminism. On the other hand, his theory is possessed by an ambiguous treatment of essentialism. It refuses essentialism in locating the feminine in the psyches of males and yet betrays a cultural slippage into essentialism when he generalises from his concept of his own masculine subjectivity. In the masculine psyche the feminine is unconscious and, therefore, by projecting from this, women are condemned as innately more unconscious than men. The anima exercises a hypnotic power in Jungian texts: expanding from its definition as a male's unconscious femininity into material forming an outmoded cultural prescription for all women. We may say that Jungian writings contain a powerful misogynistic drive to collapse women into animas. Such theoretical hysteria significantly threatens to appropriate 'the feminine' rather than to allow the Other a voice. Women become doubly marginalised, first as animas and then because animas are valued only when resident in the masculine unconscious. The treasured 'feminine' becomes subordinated into an ingredient of a reconstructed masculine identity. A typical comment by Jung excluding women from meaningful cultural signifying follows:

> It is a woman's outstanding characteristic that she can do anything for the love of a man. But those women who can achieve something important for the love of a thing are most exceptional, because this does not really agree with their nature.[19]

What might construe this lapse as 'shadow' in the theory is its contradiction of Jung's more coherent proposition that men can never say anything objective about women because their own fantasies or anima images will result in distortion.

> What men say about feminine eroticism, and particularly about the emotional life of women, is derived from their own anima projections and distorted accordingly.[20]

The feminist Archetypal theorist, Carol Schreier Rupprecht, has anatomised Jung's weaknesses on gender. There are:

> [F]our critical limitations in Jung's thought that bear particularly on his views of the nature of woman: the tendency towards dualism; the sanctifying ontology accompanying archetypal

> images ascribed to the female; confusion of enculturated social roles with actual gender identity; and the tendency to define the female predominantly through her relation to the male.[21]

She also suggests that the female as depicted in Jung's writings tends to be not a contrasexual Otherness but the shadow to male subjectivity.[22] The anima-equals-woman projection stalks the text as a patriarchal fantasy: not the Other comprehended in the theory, but an Otherness to the objective claims of the theory. It is an uncanny return of the Same, denying Jung's claim to have constructed an empiricist discourse of sexuality. Jung's erotic anima is dangerous when substantiated into fantasies of female deviousness and power. This literalising of contrasexual archetypal images into essential 'mythical' differences between women and men is still prominent in the mythopoetic men's movement in the United States inspired by the poet Robert Bly.[23] This movement promotes 'male initiations' to wean boys from the dangerous contaminations of maternal influences. It is implicitly and sometimes explicitly anti-feminist. Andrew Samuels, in *The Political Psyche*, criticises Bly under the heading 'Delusions of Sexual Difference' for discounting the importance of cultural influences upon gender.[24] Samuels' ability to distance his post-Jungian approaches from Bly's regressive fantasies does not pretend to obscure the genuine links between Jung's misogyny and this particular cultural movement. It remains to be seen whether other aspects of Jung's ideas might be more useful in remaking the contemporary, one which might include positive contributions to feminism.

JUNG AND THEORY: STRUCTURALISM AND DECONSTRUCTION

The humanist construction of Jungian theory requires that the quest for the Jungian 'self' becomes collapsed into the liberal search for self-authenticity. The self that is the quest-object of individuation as the centralising principle of the entire psyche is an archetype of the unconscious. It therefore can never be wholly present to consciousness, can never be unambiguously represented, and remains a theoretical and unattainable goal. In effect, the Jungian self declares humanist identity, predicated upon rationality and self-presence, to be an impossible fiction, only culturally supported.

To perceive in Jungian theory a challenge to the metaphysics of presence and logocentrism is to manoeuvre Jungian discourse into a relationship with deconstruction, especially that practised by Jacques Derrida.[25] To do so is not to argue that a deconstructive Jung is a more accurate version of Jungian theory than the humanist constructions which have resulted in traditional Jungian literary criticism. Instead, it is to detect 'another Jung'[26] haunting the writings. Such a shadowy and fragmented figure has been evoked by post-Jungian theorists whose characterisation indicates both an adherence to, and a critical distance from, the master's texts. I want to argue for 'another Jung' in relation to deconstruction in the same way that Derrida offers 'another Freud' – one who crucially questions his topological fable of psyche.[27] First of all, it would be useful to comment upon Jung and structuralism.

Structuralism is a theory which argues for fundamental structures governing perception, language and human culture. Ultimately, such structures have to do with the workings of the mind. In psycholinguistic terms, Noam Chomsky described a common system of language acquisition in children which referred to 'universals'.[28] Just as Jung distinguished between the empty 'universal' of the archetype and the culturally inflected archetypal image, so Chomsky has formal and substantive universals in similar categories. The structuralist anthropologist Claude Lévi-Strauss believed that myths could be interpreted as transformations of earlier structures of thinking.[29] Similarly, Jacques Lacan's sophisticated theory of a tripartite psyche can be shown to resemble Jung's personal, archetypal and psychoid unconscious.[30] Lacan's Symbolic Order which structures the unconscious like a language has some affinity with a collective unconscious of empty but functional archetypes. The Imaginary order of psychological reality, fantasy and projection containing psychic residues of trauma and separation can be compared to Jung's personal unconscious where can be found the traces of a person's particular psychic history. Lastly, Lacan's concept of the Real, the repressed pre-verbal, inaccessible realm of reality can correspond to Jung's psychoid unconscious. If traditional Jungian literary critics openly reject structuralism as some do,[31] they miss structuralism's insistence upon primary mental structuration and assume that the structuralist critic is merely looking for repeating patterns. It is also to assume that Jungian theory necessarily offers a human essence outside history which is to imply that archetypes offer ahistorical *content* to succeeding generations. They do not: archetypes are inherited structuring principles and cannot be condensed into archetypal images which are their culturally influenced derivatives.

JUNG AND DECONSTRUCTION

Christopher Norris defines deconstruction as an activity that 'seeks to undo both a given order of priorities and the very system of conceptual oppositions that makes that order possible'.[32] Derrida proposes that western thought is dependent upon a metaphysics of being as presence and that this results in the privileging of one term over another in a series of hierarchical binary oppositions. Traditionally, one term of the pair is considered to be superior and originative, the other to be inferior and derivative, or, in Derrida's terms, 'supplementary'. Deconstruction seeks to undo the logic of oppositions reliant upon the supplement. Also, deconstruction combats logocentrism, the idea that the meaning of a word can be immediately and entirely present. Not only are linguistic signs arbitrarily related to the referent, but signifiers have no stabilising bonds to their signifieds. For Derrida, signifiers operate on a principle of *différance*, a word combining the 'difference' of Saussure on signs (that the crucial factor is their difference from each other), and a notion of 'deferral'. Signifiers differ from one another and infinitely defer the choice of transcendental signified which would limit the process of signification by an arbitrary act of closure. A deconstructive critic exposes *différance* at work in all kind of texts, an act which undermines the system of oppositions and structures which operate as arrests upon the signifying process. It remains to be seen whether deconstruction is an activity which can only be imposed upon the body of Jungian writing or whether Jungian theory can contribute deconstructive in-sights upon itself.

First of all, Jung shares with Derrida a suspicion of metaphysical language when discussing psychological concepts.[33] Indeed, Jung goes further in rejecting the totalising tendency of metaphysics as being appropriate for his psychology. Psyche is too 'variegated in form and meaning'[34] to be comprehended by any one system. Such hints of fragility in Jung's own mythology of psyche need to be borne in mind when considering logocentrism. Where Derrida associates logocentrism with the longing for a centre or authorising presence that spawns hierarchised oppositions, Jungian theory provides the self as the unconscious governing logos, source of meaning as the guarantor of psychic signifiers. Jung's self is what the Derrida of *Of Grammatology* would call a supplement that purports to originate. To complete the profile of a masquerading logos, archetypal images of the self are often described as god-images. This does not mean that the self is a derivative of an external god (it may or may not refer to an exterior god-head). In Jung's psychology the unconscious archetype itself *is* god within; the authorising location of self-presence and being. As Derrida writes:

> God is the name and the element of that which makes possible an absolutely pure and absolutely self-present self-knowledge.[35]

Also, like Derrida's Logos, the Jungian self does function as the authorising ground of a system of oppositions. All the major Jungian concepts are arranged in pairs: ego/self, image/instinct, individual/collective, anima/animus, extroversion/introversion, conscious/unconscious, and more. Jung described the structure of the psyche as an 'energic system ... dependent on the tension of opposites'.[36]

However, despite the metaphysical logocentrism of the self, archetypal images already operate upon a principle of difference and deferral. Since Jung regarded the psyche as essentially autonomous, then psychic images are signs within their own system utilising a semiotics of difference. The psychic image is not wedded to a referent in the exterior world but gains its being by its difference from other images in manifesting the ungraspable autonomous psyche. Most importantly, an archetypal image can bear only a metaphorical relation to its originating archetype. This is because archetypes are plural in nature, possess negative and positive poles and contain oppositions within themselves. An archetype can never be fully present in any dream and an archetypal image goes beyond a metonymic relation to its source to the difference of metaphor. In effect, psychic images in Jungian theory are what Derrida would call a kind of writing when he describes, 'the "literal" meaning of writing as metaphoricity itself'.[37] Although Jungian archetypes are conceptually the logos for psychic images (with the self as the logocentric God-author), all psychic images are condemned to figuring the impossibility of their own logocentrism since they can never comprehend more than a fraction of the possibilities for meaning that Jung theorises for them. By positing logos as multiple archetypes situated in the unconscious, Jung denies logocentric fulfilment to his 'writing' of archetypal images. Psychic images possess *différance* both in their difference and, importantly, in their infinite deferral of a full and sufficient signified to enforce closure. Jungian psychic imagery is 'writing' because it is a system of signs whose structure 'is determined by the trace or track of that other which is forever absent'.[38] For Derrida, 'writing' is the name of the structure already inhabited by the 'trace', which means that signs must be studied 'under erasure' as 'always already inhabited by the trace of another sign which never appears as such'.[39] Consequently, Derrida detects in Freud the perception that the psyche is a sign structure under erasure since it depends upon the radical alterity of the unconscious. Jungian theory similarly demonstrates psychic images as writing already inhabited by the trace. Of course, this is not to argue that Jung did not desire a logocentric system and did not use terms such as 'the unconscious' and 'the self' in ways that Derrida would call metaphysical. The Jungian self is not usually written about 'under erasure' but the other, more postmodern inclined Jung does stalk the texts in insisting upon the Otherness of the unconscious with regard to possibilities for knowledge.

> [T]he concept of the unconscious posits nothing; it designates only my unknowing.[40]

If Jung remains metaphysical in his desires, then Derrida's Freud does not satisfy him either in the psychoanalytic trace.

> Thus, the Freudian concept of the trace must be radicalised and extracted from the metaphysics of presence which still retains it (particularly in the concepts of consciousness, the unconscious, perception, memory, reality, and several others).[41]

Nevertheless, for Derrida, Freud does not only put the psyche under erasure because of the radical alterity of the unconscious, but also because he questions his own meta-narrative, his own topological theory of mind. It is possible to perceive the 'other Jung' suggesting both the metaphorical nature of psychological theory and a crucial insight into the textuality of his ideas. Despite his oft-repeated claims to be an empirical scientist,[42] the empirical truth of psyche is an infinitely deferred signified. Psychology is a kind of writing, inherently metaphorical.

> We may therefore expect that sometime in the future our attempt at explanation will be felt to be just as 'metaphorical and symbolical' as we have felt the alchemical one to be ... [43]

Similarly, there is an important moment in *Mysterium Conjunctionis* (CW14) when Jung abandons the scientific myth that empirical evidence generates his theories. Jung admits that the chaotic nature of raw data from clinical practice requires an ideal, pre-structured reading. He cannot merely relate or reflect evidence because it is without form or coherence, requiring decoding which can only be done by a reader already in possession of the codes: himself. Theory must come before evidence. Jungian theory itself is a mode of reading.

> Anyone who attempted to describe the individuation process with the help of case material would have to remain content with a mosaic of bits and pieces without beginning or end ... [44]

So, in order to enlarge his readership beyond himself, Jung has to abandon 'evidence' for intertextuality.[45] My argument is that Jung discovered that the mosaic of meaningless signifiers can only be assembled by the structures which he found in writings on alchemy. The texts of alchemy structure individuation theory, not clinical evidence. Jung, in my terms, *archi-textualised* these theories from heterogeneous writings on alchemy. Theory partakes of the nature of fiction in the intertextual organising of signifiers around an endlessly deferred, transcendental signified, archetypal psychic reality. There is implicit recognition in Jung's writings for the intertextuality of his theory when he explains how only alchemy has 'made it possible' to describe the individuation process in its basic aspects.[46]

Additionally, Derrida famously asserts that there is nothing outside the text since no significance escapes writing under erasure.[47] While obviously intending a more logocentric and metaphysical construction of the notion, Jungian theory also suggests the textual nature of reality in Jung's suppositions about the ultimate identity of psyche and matter.[48]

To return to logocentrism's structuralist product of hierarchised oppositions, it is worth considering Jungian individuation as an essentially deconstructive process. Like Derrida, Jung comments on the violence of oppositional thinking,[49] and where Derrida recommends inversion as a first step, Jung stresses the reversibility of his oppositional system.[50] Jungian oppositions are not logically exclusive contradictions but function as a deconstructive web where pairs of terms are antagonistic *and* complementary. Opposition in Jung's work is a tension between things alike and interchangeable: individuation deconstructs such logical hierarchies as the opposition of conscious and unconscious into a non-hierarchical relationship. Psychic sickness occurs when hierarchies and oppositions are rigidly maintained. Such neurotic inflexibility denies the healing deconstructive forces of individuation. Jung's system of archetypes which are multiple, androgynous and capable of manifesting themselves in non-human representations also suggests that Jung's theories operate in plural modes in tension with their foundational dualism. Individuation is a deconstructive narrative within Jungian theory's binary codes. It also describes experience in deconstructive terms as under erasure because it depends upon the supplement of the unconscious where presence is both essential and impossible.

Modern literary practices such as feminism, queer theory, postcolonialism and new historicism often employ deconstructive tactics for ethical purposes: to undo the mastering codes that subordinate the Other. Even more overtly than Freud, Jungian theory challenges the supremacy of the heroic ego, founded upon the binary suppression of the Other. Individuation means developing a narrative of becoming not I.[51] The Other must be wooed as Other not possessed or suppressed. It predicates a non-appropriative economy of desire. Jung argues that the Other as unconscious is a source of meaning and value so that the heroic conquering ego is dangerously sick and inauthentic. Deconstructive Jung challenges the founding dualism of ego and unconscious by reversing hierarchies and subjecting the ego to the multiple predations of the unconscious in individuation. The fact that a neurotic and excluding discourse of the feminine as anima is also contained in Jungian writings is a testimony to the way even partly deconstructive master narratives need to be challenged from outside (such as by feminist critique) as well as by inside (by fraying their empirical claims and certainties). My second chapter will explore some ethical implications of Jungian discourse as an historical writing, but I would like to relinquish the topic of Jung and deconstruction by stressing the untapped potential of Jungian ideas for modern literary theories. Freudian discourse has been absorbed into literary theory in ways that have surpassed and challenged the founding father. Certainly, an intentionalist reading of Jung would tend to supply him with the identity of a humanist attempting to reconfigure religion for modernity, but in the age of the death of the author, it is time for readers of Jung to be liberated. The 'other Jung' was capable of examining his logocentric self with a sceptical eye. What is productive for contemporary literary theory in Jungian writings is an awareness of an Otherness to theory embedded in the textuality. Of course, it is Jung's affinities, not identity with, deconstruction which bring the discourse into a relationship with contemporary theory. Jung's ability to contest the borders between theory and fiction opens up a creative space for more modern encounters between Jungian ideas, literary theory and fiction. In writing about women, of course, Jung's texts betray all the limitations of humanism with its construction of the Other as inferiority. If a liberating discourse for the contemporary is to be possible from Jung's work, then it will have to dis-member as well as re-member this both shadowed and open textual body.

ARCHETYPAL PSYCHOLOGY: ONE FORM OF POST-JUNGIAN PSYCHOLOGY ALLIED WITH POSTSTRUCTURALISM

The term 'Archetypal Psychology' was coined to define a distinctive post-Jungian movement in the United States in 1970 by James Hillman, its most prominent exponent.[52] Hillman has become an eminent cultural theorist and is the most well known among a group of analysts and writers who include Paul Kugler, Patricia Berry, David L. Miller and Edward S. Casey. These Archetypal Psychologists have their own publishing house, Spring Publications, Dallas, and their own Journal: *Spring: A Journal of Archetype and Culture*.[53] The movement combines analytical practice with cultural theory, and explicitly allies itself with poststructuralism and postmodernism.[54]

Two departures from Jung propel these Archetypal Psychologists into poststructuralism. First, they abandon the theory of archetypes as such, and thereby refuse to posit a logocentric theory of psyche; and second, they explicitly reconsider the concept of fiction in relation to theory. The archetype can only ever be manifested in its derived image, so Archetypal Psychology refuses to speculate about any prior archetype, any transcendental signified for the image. This is a rejection of the authority of Jung's theory of archetypes with its crystalline metaphors. Archetypal Psychologists claim that the provisional image can always be considered as archetypal and refuse to posit anterior transcendent archetypes as an 'author' for them. They delight in psychic imagery as writing under erasure. The AP version of archetypal theory stresses multiplicity and difference, trying to discard more than defer any transcendental signified.

> From Jung comes the idea that the basic and universal structures of the psyche, the formal patterns of its relational modes, are archetypal patterns ... For Jung, they are anthropological and cultural, and also spiritual in that they transcend the empirical world of time and place and, in themselves, are not phenomenal. Archetypal Psychology, in distinction to Jungian, considers the archetypal to be always phenomenal, thus avoiding the Kantian idealism implied in Jung.[55]

Hillman argues that not only does the unconscious image refer to psychic reality (the Jungian position), but crucially to itself as psychic reality and not to any prior formation process. It does not have any meaning or logos, separate from itself, that can be captured by consciousness. For therapy, this involves a methodology, not of determining significance for the image but a purpose.

> Our way, moreover, does not interpret the image but talks with it. It does not ask what the image means but what it wants.[56]

This refusal of interpretations, going beyond the refusal of concepts hinted at by Jung, is substantiated in the other distinctive break with Jungian practice: the refusal to use Jung's writings as unquestionable theory, as master narratives to structure clinical practice and by extension, case history. Paul Kugler makes explicit this post-Jungian deconstructionist approach in a post-Derridean context. Both Freudian and Jungian analysis tends to seek meaningful results in terms of ego consciousness, though of different kinds. Much Jungian analysis desires an outcome which privileges the genres of individuation found in Jung's texts; mostly his own. The quest for the 'real' sexual trauma or this 'archetype' derived from a textbook becomes a quest for the transcendental signifieds of depth psychology which must operate as absolutes grounding interpretation by transcending the clinical phenomenon of dream image, physical symptom, fantasy, and so on. Problems occur when the signified being sought is never sufficiently detached from the interpretative field because the field provides the frame of reference, the text for the analyst to operate under. The 'outcome' is determined by the language, the tropes the analyst is using to define experience. The Freudian or Jungian text 'frames' the analytic dialogue as a master narrative reproducing itself in the clinical territory. Nor can the symptom be said to choose the analytic frame, be attached to a particular signified, because 'interpretation' places the signified either in the past (for example, childhood sexual trauma) or the future (formation of an archetype). In this way analysis seems to be constructed, a mutual fiction, but one in which only one side has access to the determining master narratives. This is the 'side' of the analyst who will become the 'author' of the fiction of case history.[57] Archetypal Psychology is perceptive of the cultural power functioning in the use of Jung as a master-narrative and firmly rejects it. It eschews the meta-narratives of individuation theory while retaining in the basic trope of the spontaneity and autonomy of the psyche.

So how does Archetypal Psychology differ in clinical practice from traditional Jungian analysis? Hillman stresses the desire to escape from the ego's concerns. Unlike Jung's formations, the dream does not have a message for conscious life: its aim is to ditch the ego, to allow it to 'die' into a multifarious psyche of autonomous images. Consequently, Jung's technique of amplification (where the dreamer's conscious associations to a dream image are explored), is modified to amplifying the image alone. The dreamer's personal, everyday associations are redundant.

> And to take another example, 'black snake' can state both that your snake is black and also that your black is snakey: creepy, hidden, reptilian, ancestral ...[58]

This attempt to assert the ultimate arbitrariness of the image in relation to any meaning-concept accessible to the ego, to elevate image over concept absolutely, cannot, of course, be completely successful. Just as the signifier can never be purified of all significance, Hillman's sliding signifier technique with dream images does not escape resonance and effect. What is distinctive about this method is that by transferring the interrogation of the image from meaning to purpose, he leaves meaning plural while investing the image with a shaping rhetorical power.[59]

Archetypal Psychology joins the project of deconstruction in order to challenge the binary oppositions that try to promulgate the structural inferiorities of the Other and which are grounded by transcendental signifieds that make up phallogocentrism. To further the aim of substituting multiplicity for dualisms and hierarchy, Hillman suggests a polytheistic psyche as a method of discounting Jung's monotheistic archetype of the self and even the attendant quest for 'wholeness'. Hillman characterises ego domination as one more product of western oppositional logic that in turn reproduces power relations such as the privileging of the masculine. This is most obvious in ego psychology's most characteristic genre: the monotheistic hero myth. Polytheism here is a taking further of multiplicity, a necessary step to enable coherent differentiation or to take multiplicity *seriously*.[60] This 'polytheism' is not intended to be a reappearance of transcendentalism. Hillman's 'gods' do not demand worship but are to be apprehended only at the level of unconscious image or symptom, as phenomena in the immanent region of psyche or soul. They are archetypes in an ontological mode. Concentrating on this immanent realm of psychic reality provides a third region to break up the opposition of body and spirit, to deconstruct it. To the body/spirit dualism is added Jung's psyche or soul.

Reservations need to be expressed on the topic of Archetypal Psychology and feminism. On the one hand, the project is explicitly against masculine dominance, seeing it as the most prominent cultural expression of ego psychology with its desire to suppress the (m)Other.[61] On the other hand, James Hillman has aligned himself in recent years with Robert Bly and his anti-feminist mythopoetic men's movement. In fact, Hillman seems to think that there can be a 'feminism that is not ideological',[62] by which he presumably means not engaged in a struggle with discourses of power. He has failed to notice that ideology will infuse his archetypal images since the psyche does not transmit images from another non-cultural place but makes them from the subject's own witnessing and bodily integration into culture. I would compare the creative work of Jung's psyche to the potter moulding a vase. The ultimate *idea* of the vase is archetypal, but both its material (the clay) and the final fixed *form* (linked to a social purpose) is derived from the individual's relationship with her culture.

To be an Archetypal Psychologist is not necessarily to be a feminist, but there are some feminists who use the deconstructive potentials of Archetypal Psychology as part of a feminist and political project. Carol Schreier Rupprecht, who with Estella Lauter has edited *Feminist Archetypal Theory: Interdisciplinary Re-Visions of Jungian Thought*,[63] argues that feminists can use Archetypal Psychology to 'break open the prison house of language that Jungian psychology has constructed for women through terms like "animus"',[64] and can unite with feminist literary theorists (who are well aware of 'ideology') to collaborate in exploring 'the female imaginary'.[65] It is time to consider the vexed issue of whether Jung has any value in contemporary feminism's theoretical debates.

JUNG AND FEMINIST THEORY

Jung's misogyny could not go unchallenged by any contemporary feminist discourse, but it could also be argued that some of his theoretical principles have a distinctive usefulness in re-visioning ideas about gender and the unconscious.

First, Jung's reversal of the conscious/unconscious hierarchy, suggesting that the unconscious is the source of, and a major creative force upon, the ego means that the Other is to be valued above the Same. This has an ethical suggestiveness and might be used to promote the feminine, structurally designated as Other by western thought. However, this is a very limited proposition because it leaves the feminine in the unconscious; it is autonomous, creative and meaningful, but by definition excluded from conscious action. In effect, it seems to repeat the patriarchal move of placing the feminine above, in bodiless spirituality (the Virgin Mary), or below, as sinful body without mind, whorish and evil (Eve) but both in the margins of the Symbolic that excludes the feminine from agency and culture.

'Individuation' as a theory is more promising since its teleological drive and 'self' healing nature of the psyche means that it is an intrinsic possibility that any cultural damage to feminine identity can be restored. Individuation means that Jung's construction of identity is of a subject always 'in process', of making and remaking. Any subject whose identity is marginal in social prescriptions may have the harm recompensed by the powerful actions of the unconscious because of its autonomous nature (so not under the governance of cultural values) and compensatory relation to the ego's trials. In addition, the Jungian individuation psyche 'in process' distinctly resembles Julia Kristeva's subject-in-process in her post-Freudian dissection of gender formation. The work of Kristeva is a large and complex subject, but the following points are germane to my argument. To Kristeva, semiotics reveals 'the speaking subject as subject of heterogeneous process'.[66] A perpetual reconstitution of subjectivity, individuation suggests that the subject is continually deconstructed by the heterogeneous processes of the psyche. Patriarchy may colour psyche but it does not determine its archetypal structures so that individuation has the capacity to heal cultural gender oppression.

As a further argument, the deconstructive aspects of Jung's theories can be used like other deconstructive formulations to challenge hierarchies and rigid dualisms. Jung was well aware of the fallacy of absolutist oppositional thinking but certainly never suggested its 'phallusy'. A typical example of his use of gender oppositions can be found in his writings on Mercurius, a figure from alchemy whom Jung defined as a major archetypal image of the unconscious. Almost all Jung's explorations of this trickster-like 'character' are in a male guise, but if he is archetypal then he cannot be exclusively masculine; he is as much feminine.[67] Much as Jung clearly prefers to describe masculine examples of the bold and original exploits of Mercurius the trickster, archetypal theory means that they cannot be denied to the feminine.

As well as the androgyny of archetypes which makes it impossible to exclude the feminine from the Symbolic, Jung's monotheistic 'self' archetype is interesting in connection with the later work of Kristeva on the pre-Oedipal mother.[68] Before the Oedipal splitting and formation of subjectivity when a third term or 'imaginary father' intervenes and starts the process which results in the subject being inscribed in the Symbolic order, the infant exists in a dyad, in fusion with the pre-Oedipal mother. 'Abjection' is Kristeva's term for the stage of dividing from the pre-Oedipal mother when this figure is not yet a distinct object but still a fusionary abject. Thus the abject threatens the ego and to some extent will always remain abjected as unconscious powers. Clearly there is a potential for psychic disturbance, even horror, because the source of the ego's being could become its annihilation. Kristeva locates the sacred in the site (and sight) of abjection as a supplement to Freud's discussion of religion and the ritualised atonement of the murder of the primal father.[69]

> Could the sacred be, whatever its variants, a two sided formation? One aspect founded by murder and the social bond made up of murder's guilt-ridden atonement ... and another aspect ... oriented towards those uncertain spaces of unstable identity, toward the fragility – both threatening and fusional – of the archaic dyad, toward the non-separation of subject/object, on which language has no hold but one woven of fright and repulsion?[70]

The pre-Oedipal mother is also a pre-Oedipal (m)Other because it is a being prior to the psychic splittings of gender formation. It is crucial to the formation of subjectivity and then leaves traces of abjection in the unconscious. Jung's 'self' archetype is different from Kristeva's formulation in that it is teleological, a drive forwards in time or a goal of subjectivity, not the uncovering of its origins. However, it is a goal never reached and an unconscious being that encompasses all varieties of oppositions including gender and to which the ego must develop an abject relationship. Jung does not use the word 'abject', of course, but describes a position whereby the ego is not fully differentiated from the self which is greater, creative and will remain largely unconscious so without perceptible boundaries. He even writes of the unconscious as a whole giving birth to consciousness, an unconscious prior to gender formation.[71] If subjectivity for Jung is the deconstruction of the ego into his (m)Other, the 'self', then Kristeva provides a similar narrative in her depiction of psychoanalysis. Her pre-Oedipal (m)Other remains abjected, a potential disturbance to the ego but in analysis the (m)Other is constellated by the analyst, by transference, so permitting an initiation of a 'rebirth' into subjectivity.

> [A]nalytic speech is one that becomes 'incarnate' in the full sense of the term. On that condition only it is 'cathartic' – ... for the analyst as well as the analysand, not of purification but of rebirth with and against abjection.[72]

One major difference in these two theories is that for Jung the 'self' is *located* principally in an autonomous unconscious. Although he did not deny transference, his self has more agency than Kristeva's abjected (m)Other.

What this might mean positively for feminist theory is hinted at by an early female Jungian, Linda Fierz-David, when she describes in *Women's Dionysian Initiation* a female subjectivity reformulated in its own terms, not structured in relation to male norms. She makes a radical departure from Jung in insisting that the animus cannot be limited to masculinity and articulates signs of a female's unconscious in ways that anticipate the abjecting pre-Oedipal (m)Other. Her text describes the images on particular Roman frescoes as depicting an initiation rite (which she re-interprets as individuation) for women. The figure of Silenus is first the animus and then the self or goal.

> The archetypal image of the animus as leader of souls is freed also from its previous cloak ... as the Orphic Silenus, a mother-father and wise teacher, such as never exists in reality.[73]

This individuation series culminates in Fierz-David's portrayal of a 'Kristevan' subject-in-process with the abjected Other but it is significantly a feminine-oriented subjectivity in process with the fictionally gendered unconscious, not dependent upon anything phallic. It is the feminine in the Symbolic as feminine. Fierz-David distinguishes her text from that of Toni Wolff, another contemporary female Jungian, who theorised about feminine 'types' but all in relation to the masculine.[74] The work of Toni Wolff will be considered elsewhere in this volume. Fierz-David distinguishes her work from that of Wolff:

> None of these types can give us an impression of how it looks when a woman rests purely and solidly upon her femininity ... In our Pompeiian mystery cult, however, we have an archetypal image of the deepest significance for just this femininity resting entirely upon itself.[75]

By 'femininity' here, Fierz-David means female subjectivity in process with the unconscious and not some simpering relation to the masculine. *Women's Dionysian Initiation* is not an unambiguously feminist text: it has its own 'abject' relation to Jung's own misogynistically gendered concept of Eros/Logos as previously described. However Jung's masculinist constructions cannot be used to sustain a rigid patriarchal hierarchy because the body cannot govern meaning. In addition, individuation is teleological and compensatory and so will balance any female 'lack' that patriarchy has instituted.

I want now to take a two-stage approach to compare Jung's ideas to the theories of Lacan. First, I will use Jung to combat Lacan's contention of female 'lack' in relation to the Symbolic. Then, I will double back to employ Lacan in a critique of Jung's discourse of the anima from a feminist theoretical perspective.

If the unconscious is structured like a language, then this is very suggestive of Jungian archetypes. Lacan's three 'orders' consist of the Symbolic which structures the unconscious by a fundamental set of laws, the Imaginary which pertains to inner world, psychological processes and the Real. Andrew Samuels argues that these three divisions could be said to correspond to Jung's theories of psyche: the archetypal equates to the 'Symbolic', the personal unconscious is coherent with the Imaginary and Jung's elaboration of a psychoid unconscious, which may be seen as 'true' but not directly known finds an echo in the Real.[76] To Lacan, the phallus is not corporeal but a signifier: the father's function is strictly metaphorical in the role of the Name of the Father assigning a child a place in the social world, which is a sexed place through the phallus being a sign of sexual difference. My suggestion is to take a Jungian gloss on this famous phallogocentrism. We might argue that Jung's autonomous unconscious, his Symbolic from which the feminine cannot be excluded because it is already there in the androgyny of archetypes, empties out Lacan's phallus-as-signifier of everything but a provisional cultural meaning. If Lacan sees a female 'lack' built into the system of gender formation, then Jungian theory could suggest that the cultural Symbolic is distorted by patriarchal discourses of which the phallus-as-signifier is a key ingredient. Instead of Lacan's phallus being Symbolic, so generating phallogocentrism and female exclusion, Jung's active Symbolic psyche can put Lacan into reverse: phallogocentrism exists as a cultural distortion of a Symbolic equally capable of manifesting feminine as masculine powers. This enables Lacan to be characterised as a product and producer of patriarchy as transcendence – patriarchy not only naturalised but divinised as worship of the Father.

THE RETURN OF THE ANIMA (AS PHALLUS): FURTHER THOUGHTS ON FEMINIST THEORY AND JUNG

My argument that Jungian concepts can be structured as a positive re-vision for feminist theory in relation to Lacan's Symbolic needs to double back on itself to reconsider the 'anima'. Earlier, I suggested that Jungian writings tend to collapse women into animas despite Jung's dissociation from this strategy on the philosophical grounds that a male theorist's anima will distort any so-called objective claims about women. Here, I want to go further to argue that the anima takes on much of the role of the Lacanian phallus with respect to the feminine.[77] Lacan's descriptions of phallic functions offer a history of the evolution of subjectivity and sexual difference. By conflating Freud's Oedipus and castration complexes, Lacan narrates a drama of a nascent intimation of structure. Whereas Freud tended to employ 'penis' and 'phallus' as synonyms, Lacan stressed the Imaginary and Symbolic roles of the phallus as an often neutral signifier. While the boy-child still languishes in pre-Oedipal bonding to the mother, Lacan's phallus remains Imaginary as a proto-signifier of the mother's desire with which the child seeks to identify. The Oedipus and castration complexes involve the renunciation of the child's attempt to become the Imaginary phallus. Initiation into the Symbolic order involves both the splitting of the subject with the accession of language and the inauguration of sexual difference operating around the Symbolic phallus. Lacan's use of the Symbolic phallus as a privileged signifier of entry into language results in charges of phallogocentrism. Despite there being no corresponding female signifier, the Symbolic nature of the phallus means that it can not simply be equated with the penis: the sexual dissymetry is not one of mere biological possession and absence. Women may lack the Symbolic phallus in one respect, but in another can be said to possess it since, in the Symbolic, not having is a form of having. Similarly, male assumption of the Symbolic phallus is based on a prior notion of his own castration.

Nevertheless, Lacan's theories of sexual difference become ripe for feminist critique when different relationships to the Symbolic phallus become the masculine 'having' the phallus and the feminine 'being' the phallus in a specular economy which splices her into the masculine. In *This Sex Which Is Not One*, Luce Irigaray argues that the feminine is both not *one* because her sexuality is multiple and so cannot be contained in a binary logic of symmetry with the masculine, and also is *not* one because 'woman does not exist' in the limitations of Lacanian thought.[78]

To bring Jungian theory into a relationship with Lacan's phallus, we need to turn to Jung's reservations about Freudian Oedipality. Although Jung wrote little about early childhood, he later clarified his views with regard to Freud by minimising the sexual interpretations of infantile relations. Oedipal narratives represented one of several possible definitions of early intense bondings between children and parents. Jung denied that the Freudian Oedipal scenario was universal; it was merely true of Freud and quite a number of patients.[79] He was particularly scathing of the 'rampant terminology of sex', which he felt threatened to swamp all possible investigations of psychic causation.[80] What Jung offered instead was that the mother was the bearer of the first anima image for the male child. Separation from the mother would be a difficult process, but it would be propelled and energised by the active archetypal unconscious.[81] If at this point we bring in Lacan, we can see that Jung's unenthusiastic refusal to deny relevance to Oedipality means that Lacan's phallus-as-signifier is permitted within a Jungian framework. But my previous discussion of Lacan has gone further in arguing that the autonomous gender-fluid unconscious empties the phallus of all but a cultural significance if we give Jung's definition of the unconscious *priority* over Oedipal machinations. Preferring Jung's definition of the unconscious over Freud–Lacan's enables phallogocentrism to be characterised as a cultural discourse of patriarchy not an inescapable condition of psyche. It is at this point in Jungian theory that we see the anima take on the role of Lacan's phallus in Imaginary and Symbolic modes. Jung's active archetypal unconscious initiates the birth of consciousness in the splitting of the subject, the acquisition of language as signs, and the formation of sexual difference. The anima acts like a Lacanian phallus because it is the structure of the unconscious which is pro-active in propelling the boy-child away from the psychic womb of unconscious bonding with the mother. Constellated by its own causation of the splitting of the subject, the anima is the autonomous agent in the process, not a consequence of repression. Once it is formed by psychic splitting, the anima provides the regulation of sexual difference by gendering the unconscious in a binary relationship with the ego. Jung is quick to condemn the 'rampant terminology of sex' in Freudian theory, but he provides a rampant terminology of his own in the proliferating anima.

Once the male child separates from the mother, then his anima image is borne by the females who attract his erotic attentions. In effect, women act as mirrors for the distortions of his anima. If Jung's writings betray an irrational drive to collapse women into animas, then we may discern a second comparison to Lacan's phallus. As well as taking on the phallic functions of psychic splitting and sexual differentiation, the anima is also the phallus which the masculine has, and which the feminine must become for the masculine. The duty (and destiny) of women is to become the embodiment of the unconscious anima for masculine subjectivity. Jung's depiction of women as irrational escaped animas is the textual re-membering of the anima ('as phallus' in Lacanian language). We might here recall Irigaray's famous retort to Lacan: that in the mirror of masculine discourse woman can only be realised as the inverted other of the masculine subject, 'or as the place of emergence and veiling of the cause of his [phallic] desire, or again as lack, since her sex ... is not subject to specularisation'.[82] My point is that the anima concept flourishes as Jung's femininity as a masquerade, as the phallus that women must assume (in both senses). Woman similarly does not exist in Jungian thought because the anima is the fantasy feminine which acts to veil women in a masquerade.

One might ask what is gained beyond academic speculation by colliding Lacan (and Irigaray's challenges to Lacan) with Jungian theory to characterise the anima-as-phallus. I would like to suggest three justifications for the foregoing argument. In the first place, the broad purpose of this book is to bring Jungian ideas into a dialogue with modern literary theories, including post-Freudian and post-Lacanian feminism. More pertinently, I want to expose what I would term a masculine anima-economy at work in Jungian theory to account for some of the misogynistic drives in the writings. Furthermore, I would like to end this section with my third justification, which is that the anima-as-phallus analysis need not forever (de)form Jungian ideas for feminist theory. Because the Jungian unconscious is both gender-fluid and a superior psychic force to bodily influences on psychic development, the anima may stalk Jung's writings as an anti-feminist trope but is insufficiently theorised to perpetually exclude feminine difference. A female child in Jungian theory cannot be excluded from full participation in the signifying powers that the texts assign to the anima because the archetypal unconscious must compensate for any cultural lack in constructing feminine identity. What follows is that women themselves cannot be denied animas in Jungian discourse in the sense of phallus-like intimations of full subjectivity, forever deferred. This might suggest the elimination of difference with the feminine theorised on an identical model to the masculine. Yet again occurs the eclipse of femininity under an all-engulfing masculinity: women are really men in possessing animas so that the feminine is excluded forever from Jungian constructions. Yet, the fundamental flexibility of Jungian theory founded upon the autonomous androgynous unconscious allows for another perspective on feminine subjectivity. This unconscious utilises principles of difference, compensation and complementarity to gender in the ego. Therefore a female's (phallic) anima will be as powerfully creative but differently modelled to that of masculine subjectivity. We remember that for Jung the body intervenes in, but does not govern or determine, psychic identity. A different body will contribute a far from insignificant 'difference' without confining the feminine to 'lack'. I am avoiding reintroducing the term 'animus' because of the misogynistic textuality surrounding this epithet in Jungian writings. It is Jungian textuality (not fully supported by Jungian theories of the unconscious) which exhibits the anima-as-phallus as a masculinist construction of femininity as a masquerade. Feminist deconstruction of Jungian texts is facilitated by the affinities of Jungian discourse with deconstruction as argued earlier in this chapter. Consequently, the anima-as-phallus is open to challenge. It may not demand as a tribute that feminists ditch all of Jungian thought. Feminist theory can still make use of Jung's gender-fluid archetypal unconscious and Symbolic, so potentially productive for theorising feminine identity. Later chapters of this book will show how pro-feminist literary texts negotiate the treacherous anima while seeking positive functions for Jungian ideas in representations of female subjectivity.

JUNG FOR FEMINISM?

What seems to me to be of final value in Jung's works for feminist theory is the way Jungian ideas open up a space to interrogate patriarchal imagery; a space that is not outside in emptiness but inside at the point of formation, where psyche meets culture. Jungian theory could provide grounds (in both senses) for resistance in the struggle for female identity. Despite a patriarchal culture, the feminine is not empty or 'lack', for archetypes are not 'empty' but just without form, before culture. Consequently, patriarchal formulations can be challenged on a *creative* basis, the possibility of creating another kind of image or discourse. Jungian theory, used deconstructively, provides some possibilities for imagining challenges to patriarchy from the inside, to criticise culturally coloured images that are not wholly constituted by culture, and to imagine a female subjectivity that is autonomous, healing. The key concept is that of an autonomous psyche creatively interacting with cultural processes in the ego: it means that there is a *site* for feminist theory in the place of the creation of culture. It is with the imaginative possibilities of Jungian theory rather than its empirical claims that a feminist writer such as Michèle Roberts becomes engaged. If phallogocentrism can be regarded as a cultural fiction, then bodily difference is also deconstructed, though not negated by Jungian theory. This undoes any claim to a privileged male access to writing and to the sacred, and indeed also suggests that divinity, since it is encountered in the androgynous archetypal unconscious, cannot be of fixed gender. With little encouragement from Jung himself, his still misogynist discourse could be dismembered and re-membered to contribute to a feminist theology and perhaps a feminist textuality.

JUNG AND TEXTUALITY

Chapter 3 will describe in detail my ideas about a Jungian textuality of writing and reader-response theory more fully. As an introduction to this area of literary theory, I would suggest that, given the primacy of the autonomous psyche in Jungian theory, unconscious processes cannot be excluded from reading and writing. Since meaning is located in the unconscious and is inherently plural, this requires that a Jungian paradigm would privilege a play of signifiers over any concept of an imprisoning signifier/signified bond. Both Jungian theory, and the alchemy which Jung uses, combat the ego's claim to complete control over signifying, a complete control that sacrifices the Other. In addition, the Jungian motif of romance with the Other and of shadow, the negative, undoing, unmeaning side are suggestive of a more 'postmodern' approach to writing. In *Women's Dionysian Initiation,* Linda Fierz-David at one point describes her text as a 'dismemberment', implicitly recognising that to write may be to enact a (w)rite, not only to describe one, when the text is aware of the sacrifice of unconscious possibilities.[83]

If writing dismembers, then it also re-members, puts together but as a fiction, one version of the many possible versions needed to exhaust unconscious significance. Additionally, if the writer must sacrifice such ego claims as complete mastery of a text and its signifying, then so must the reader renounce similar fantasies of control. It will be the task of this book to explore how contemporary fictions (where Jung is a source) may stage new encounters between Jungian ideas and modern literary theories in practice. It will consider whether individuation could also be regarded as a description of the processes of reading and writing. If there is a Jungian textuality, and the reader re-members the text, does the text re-member the reader? My aim will be to describe the potentials for Jungian theory to enter the literary field after poststructuralism. This chapter has discerned a neo-postmodern and a deconstructive Jung despite his logocentrism as well as staging a productive exchange between feminist theory and Jungian ideas. Such an encounter may lead to new Jungian feminist theories in addition to a feminist critique of Jung. The site for these theoretical developments is the challenge embodied in contemporary Jungian fiction.

Throughout this chapter I have explicitly and implicitly stressed the need to take a post-Jungian and not a Jungian position, where post-Jungian implies a critical distance from, a challenging and rewriting of Jung, rather than absorption into his system. Chapter 2 will suggest further reasons why this stance is desirable.

2

Jung: Political, Cultural and Historical Context

The long-foreshadowed, traumatic breakdown of the close relations between Sigmund Freud and C.G. Jung was the inevitable result of a struggle for power. This struggle, recorded for succeeding generations in The *Freud/Jung Letters*,[1] ranged over theory and language, and was particularly concerned with the infringement of psychoanalysis on religious and occult territory. It enacted a personal combat for dominance over an emerging cultural movement. The correspondence of Freud and Jung delineates a relationship in which it is now impossible to separate passion, ambition, warring ideas and antagonistic cultures. Indeed, *The Freud/Jung Letters* serve as a reminder of how a personal drama can be written through ideological conflict and how a discourse such as Jungian theory is saturated with history. This chapter will consider some of Jung's sources, to look at his relation to esotericism and to a contemporary Germanic culture which was breeding nationalism, anti-Semitism and Nazism. It will further consider Jung's historical role in his dealings with Nazi Germany before the Second World War. I will draw on recent research, particularly by Richard Noll in *The Jung Cult: Origins of a Charismatic Movement* (1994), F.X. Charet in *Spiritualism and the Foundations of C.G. Jung's Psychology* (1991) and two articles by Andrew Samuels on 'National Psychology, National Socialism, and Analytical Psychology' in the *Journal of Analytical Psychology* (1992).[2] My purpose is to show some of the historical weight of Jungian discourse, partly so that this work does not reproduce a subservient relation to Jungian ideas that might occlude any oppressive or anti-Semitic, proto-Nazi areas, and partly to provide a further perspective on the way contemporary novelists have treated Jungian theory as a fictional resource. My aim is to provide grounds for a new historicist approach to Jungian theory in relation to literary works: in Chapter

5, when dealing with fictions of spiritualism and feminism and in Chapter 6, for a novel dealing with Jungian ideas and the emergence of the Nazis.

The historical or cultural substance of Jungian discourse affects its fictional realisation particularly if Jungian ideas operate as a form of authority in the fictional text. Most of the novels considered later use Jungian theory to support and structure the representation of what is marginalised or hidden in traditional narrative realism. This inevitably draws in the dynamics of authority even if it is the fictive pole of Jungian ideas that the text desires. In contrast to this implicit tension in the writings of Lindsay Clarke and Michèle Roberts, Nicholas Mosley's *Hopeful Monsters* is an exceptional case where the explicit deference to Jungian theory as authoritative becomes a readable flaw in the text's desires to reform ideas about power and dominance. This book goes on to consider Doris Lessing's far more sophisticated treatment of the problem of textual and theoretical authority.

This second chapter's treatment of the cultural Jung is designed to give his discourse an historically and culturally located body, in addition to the challenges alluded to in Chapter 1. It does not aim to offer a detailed account of Jung's intellectual, scientific and cultural sources and influences since the genesis of Jung is not the subject of this work. The chapter merely seeks to identify some problematic areas in order to situate Jung as an historical product and agent, and to provide some context to his role in contemporary culture.

The narrative of the internecine battle with Freud is patterned by conflicts over theory which centre on the tensions between psychoanalysis and religious experience. Is it to be a romance between analysis and religion (not a complete bonding, a 'marriage') as Jung finally formulated, or an attempt to draw rigid, defensive borders as Freud insisted? In 1910, Jung suggested to Freud that psychoanalysis might be the basis of a new Dionysiac Christianity.[3] To Jung's neo-pagan outpourings which link him to much contemporary esotericism, Freud unenthusiatically replied: 'you mustn't regard me as the founder of a religion'.[4] Freud's greater status in this dialogue is signalled by the more persistent use of his theories to structure the encounters. Freud's 'family romance' operates in Jung's admission of a father complex[5] in relation to the senior man, the paternal role that Freud often cites and his 'anointing' of Jung as 'my successor and crown prince'.[6] However in the midst of this translation of the family romance into the language of power and dominion, are the anxieties perhaps signalled by the hint of a religious metaphor?

> It is strange that on the very same evening when I formally adopted you as eldest son and anointed you – *in partibus infidelium* – as my successor and crown prince, you should have divested me of my paternal dignity, which divesting seems to have given you as much pleasure as I, on the contrary, derived from the investiture of your person.[7]

Just as Jung's religious fascinations are recognised by Freud as partly questions of power and leadership ('*me* as the founder of a religion'), so here the family romance seems to exploit the regality of Oedipus, a king who is both a killer of a king and father. To Freud and Jung their theoretical differences are inevitably expressed in the language of power-seeking and defending so that it is impossible to say whether theory, power or desire is paramount in this battle: they are inseparable. That such a struggle cannot be isolated from contemporary culture and history is evident in the way both theorists can characterise psychoanalysis in imperialist metaphors.

> Occultism is another field we shall have to conquer ... There are strange and wondrous things in these lands of darkness ... I shall return laden with rich booty for our knowledge of the human psyche.[8] Jung, 1911

> Just don't stay in the tropical colonies too long; you must reign at home.[9] Freud, 1911

Jung is, of course, happier about psychoanalysis plundering other discourses: Freud seems to fear contamination from those who stray from the 'motherland' of neuroses.[10] Whether Jung did ever conquer occultism, or whether he produced a creative form of the significant nineteenth-century form of occultism, Spiritualism, now needs consideration.

NINETEENTH-CENTURY SPIRITUALISM AND TWENTIETH CENTURY JUNGIAN PSYCHOLOGY

Jung claimed throughout his career to have a philosophical basis for his psychology in the work of Immanuel Kant (1724–1804).[11]

F. X. Charet gives the essential principle that Jung gleaned from Kant as the distinction between noumena and phenomena. Whereas noumena are objects of belief in that they are the result of intellectual intuition, phenomena are the world of appearances apprehended by the senses.[12] What Jung does not mention is that as his earliest writings, the *Zofingia Lectures,* show,[13] he came to Kant's theories of knowledge via his works on spiritualism,[14] concerns which Jung, unlike Kant, never relinquished. In his autobiography, *Memories, Dreams, Reflections,*[15] Jung describes his early sense of himself as split with a mysterious 'No. 2' personality. This irrational side is strongly associated with spiritualist phenomena and the philosophies of Kant and of his follower Schopenhauer (1788–1860).[16] In his *Zofingia Lectures,* Jung wrote: 'if Kant were alive today, he would undoubtedly be a spiritualist.'[17]

Possible reasons for Jung's apparent 'split' and his lifelong fascination with spiritualism can be found in his family and early life. The second marriage of his maternal grandfather, Samuel Preiswerk (1799–1871) was enlivened by his habit of spending one day every week communicating with the spirit of his first wife in his study.[18] Not to be outdone, the second wife, Jung's grandmother, was reputed to see spirits, a gift Jung believed she passed on to his daughter, Agathe.[19] Jung's mother, Emilie Preiswerk, left a diary in which she recorded spiritualist phenomena, and Jung attributes two personalities to her in *Memories, Dreams, Reflections.*[20] The autobiography describes the pressure of Jung's two inheritances: the maternal spiritualist medium side and the paternal one of orthodox religion and medicine. Jungian psychology provides a creative synthesis of the medical and the esoteric in a way that was foreshadowed in some aspects of nineteenth-century spiritualism. This was a movement that was religious in implications but that nevertheless sought to bond with science. 'Spirits' could be regarded as affording 'empirical evidence' of post-death existence. If spiritualism can be seen to be an attempt to maintain a religious dimension to science, thereby making visible what nineteenth-century science aimed to marginalise in a post-Darwinian age, its attitude to Christianity ranged from orthodox harmony to a near-science fictional radicalism. Some spiritualists rejected notions of heaven and hell for an afterlife as a continuation of embodied existence and recast Jesus as a highly evolved being moving onto another plane.[21] Spiritualists continued to describe themselves as empiricists because their beliefs were based upon direct experience in the form of communication with the dead by means of a medium.[22]

This is precisely the line Jung took in the lectures he gave as member of the Zofingia fraternity at the University of Basel in 1895–9. Spiritualism, supported in the philosophies of Kant and Schopenhauer in Jung's view, provides empirical data for metaphysical speculation and is a means of positing the immortality of the soul.[23] There is a shift in the final lecture where Jung gives great prominence to sexuality, a notion probably derived at this point from his extensive reading of Schopenhauer, who stressed a fundamental role for sexuality in human motivation.[24]

This is the beginning of an intriguing spiritualist narrative in Jung's career and writings. His own account of his family and early life and his earliest compositions indicate a credence in spiritualism situated within a struggle for a comprehensive world-view, to reconcile religion, spiritualism and science. Then Jung employs theory, first Freudian sexuality and dream theory, and second his own archetypal theory to submerge spiritualism in psychology. Later, there appear works that indicate more than a residual belief in spirits and not just a 'scientific' or sceptical explanation for Jung's habitual attendance at seances in the 1920s and 1930s.[25]

Jung's *Collected Works* open with his doctoral dissertation, 'On the Psychology and Pathology of So-Called Occult Phenomena' published in 1902,[26] an analysis of the seances he attended featuring his medium cousin, Hélène Preiswerk. Here, Jung explicitly parallels investigations of the medium's manifestations of different spirit personalities with Freud's theories of dreams as the transformation of repressed material.[27] Therefore it is unsurprising that Jung is able to diagnose the spirits' complex trans-generational narratives as 'romances'[28] attributing the fundamental drive to 'her budding sexuality'.[29] However, Jung also asserts the teleological nature of unconscious processes when he describes the main spiritual personality, Ivenes, as what the medium not only desires but *anticipates* for herself. Ivenes is a creative realisation of a superior being. In effect, Preiswerk 'dreams' a fantastic and idealised future personality for herself.[30]

In Jung's own 'characterisation' of Ivenes can be discerned the prototype of the higher 'self' archetype and the teleological individuation process of his later theories. It is interesting that recent research has suggested that this dissertation itself is a suppressed romance, re-formed into a medical document which seems to embrace Freud as a displacement for possible erotic tensions between medium and author.[31] Jung provides a pseudonym for Hélène Preiswerk in 'Miss S.W.', but hints at his relationship to the medium, a revelation that was said to have cost Preiswerk a marriage proposal.[32] Jung also claimed that the medium died mentally defective when in fact Preiswerk died at the age of 30 from tuberculosis.[33] Her family, worried about Jung's undue influence over her, had finally sent her to France in order to stop the seances which his enthusiasm was prolonging.[34] If, for Jung, an entanglement of eroticism and attraction to spiritualism is a subtext of his dissertation, it is interesting that his later letters to Freud also speak of a 'religious crush … [with] … undeniable erotic undertone'[35] in his adherence to the older theorist. Charet argues that Preiswerk was the first (after Jung's mother) in a series of erotically charged relationships with 'medium' women: she is succeeded by Sabina Spielrein and Toni Wolff, who all have a psychic referent in Jung's characterisation of his anima figure, Salome,[36] in *Memories, Dreams, Reflections*. In this text, when Jung describes his confrontation with his unconscious after the break with Freud, he uses some of the techniques and characterisations of the spiritualist seance.

> I reflected that the 'woman within me' did not have the speech centres I had. And so I suggested that she used mine. She did so and came through with a long statement.[37]

Toni Wolff herself identified the female medium as a psychological type and, like all her types, delineated it in relation to the male, remaining firmly within Jungian binary structures. Interestingly, she mentions contemporary feminists as diverging from the medium type, a point to which I shall return.

> The Suffragettes were identified with the intellect and the mediumistic types with the unconscious psyche. This identification took concrete form as the former tended to play the part of men and the latter that of spirits. The differentiated mediumistic type … is manifested in the woman who assists a man to realize his unconscious ideas …[38]

So women become men or spirits in two of Wolff's types, a succinct demonstration of the way the female body and female difference can be written out of Jungian psychology. It is also very suggestive of the way a male-authored psychology might be employed to contain some of the subversions of spiritualism, such as the pre-eminence of female mediums and the possibilities for female leadership. Another way might be for men to enter spiritualist practice and writing itself, which Jung does by composing *Septem Sermones ad Mortuos*,[39] *Seven Sermons for the Dead*, in 1916 after his traumatic break with Freud. Inspired by a Spiritualist experience, this text casts in gnostic language virtually all Jung's later developed ideas. In *Memories, Dreams, Reflections*, he describes his composition as spirit-possessed automatic writing, a typical spiritualist phenomena.[40] Where Jung differs from the usual (female) medium is in the demonstration of who is in charge. He does not offer the lore of the dead to a wider public but is himself a teacher of the dead, conducting a lofty dialogue with the spirits in which the writer also claims to be the *authority*.[41] Jung admitted that such 'dialogues' with spirits became the pre-text for his theories.[42]

In *Septem Sermones*, he introduces several key theories in embryonic form. Among these are 'individuation' as *Principium Individuationis*, a striving of the living towards distinctiveness or the phenomenal,[43] every human possessing a single star or 'god'[44] which seems to anticipate the self archetype and a dualistic concept of god who is called Abraxas. Charet discerns a link between Abraxas and the unconscious which is neither good nor evil but the source of all values.[45]

By 1919, Jung was still reflecting his split nature as described in *Memories, Dreams, Reflections*, in his attitude to spirits. Psychologically speaking he was defining them as demonstrable evidence of the autonomy of the unconscious complexes while drawing on Kantian philosophy to assert that they may also be objects of belief. In the same year Jung wrote that 'the universal belief in spirits is a direct expression of the complex structure of the unconscious'.[46] 'Complexes' are Jung's prototypes for archetypes. Originally there were two types of complexes: those split off by repression, in a fashion similar to Freudian theory (for which Jung retained the term complex) and those other complexes which he characterised as autonomous psychical energies. In 1912, the latter were 'primordial images', then in 1917 'dominants of the collective unconscious', and by 1919 they were called archetypes,[47] at the time defined as, 'a priori, inborn forms of "intuition" ... the ... determinants of all psychic processes'.[48] The later distinction between archetypes and archetypal images allowed Jung to approach a synthesis of his psychological and spiritualist perspectives. The archetypal image is conditioned by its medium, the psyche, and so is psychic; but archetypes themselves can be theorised as spiritual and possibly transcendent realities because of Jung's claim that the psyche is rooted in matter, instinct and spirit.[49]

So even in his theoretical works, Jung leaves a conceptual gap for archetypes to *be* spirits and not only act like them in manifesting themselves in conscious existence. Jung's behaviour in attending seances in the 1920s and 1930s as well as his final work, the autobiography, in which he mentions his own dreams of communications with the dead, suggest his credence in his continuing Spiritualist experiences.[50] As well as Salome, *Memories, Dreams, Reflections* records his encounters with a psychic figure called Philemon. Jung hints that Philemon may have been an historical figure by calling him a 'guru' and linking him to the historical spirit guru of an Indian friend.

> 'Then you are referring to a spirit?' I asked.
> 'Of course it was his spirit', he agreed.
> At that moment I thought of Philemon.[51]

Interestingly, Philemon, who, Jung said, 'taught me psychic objectivity, the reality of the psyche',[52] may be connected to both Jung's own father and Freud. Jung states in both *The Freud/Jung Letters* and *Memories, Dreams, Reflections*[53] that he projected his feelings towards his father onto Freud, and Charet points out that Philemon's kingfisher wings are a verbal echo of Jung's description of his father as a wounded fisher king in the same text.[54] If Jung's theories and writings are infused with the popular nineteenth-century esotericism of spiritualism to which he had lifelong personal connections, then his most spiritualist statements often betray an erotic subtext which can be patterned as a family romance (particularly if all the medium women can be projected back onto his mother) or an Oedipal contest with Freud. This is not to argue that Freudian psychoanalysis is the 'right' theory and Jung's works mere esoteric mystifying, but instead to suggest a web of connections between Freud's innovations, Jungian ideas, nineteenth-century spiritualism and the related areas of mesmerism and hysteria. The two psychologies are distinct but related discourses arising from the interactive field of nineteenth-century occultism and sicknesses particularly associated with women. The spiritualist ideas inhabiting Jungian discourse may well surface in practice in the therapeutic technique of active imagination whereby conscious control is relaxed to allow the unconscious (or spirits in a medium's trance) to operate through words and images.

Spiritualism in the nineteenth century was overwhelmingly associated with female mediums, as Diana Basham demonstrates.[55] Paradoxically it can be seen as offering women a powerful cultural role at the price of alienating them from their 'speech'. The medium in a trance, speaking a voice not her 'own' but of the dead, is enacting, to a fascinated public, her exclusion from cultural meaningfulness. The medium demonstrates processes of the erasure of the female voice and body from public utterance. In effect, the voices of the dead seem to express the deadness of the woman medium, to cultural signifying, while simultaneously disrupting (even if spiritualists saw it as extending) powerful discourses of science and religion that themselves marginalised (sometimes by demonising) the female. Basham argues that the occult popularities of mesmerism and spiritualism served as stages where the anxieties about Woman, could be enacted. They were arenas where what has been excluded or defined as evil in dominant discourses such as theology and medicine, the female body and its troubling differences, could be performed and viewed.[56]

Here, Basham would appear to agree with Wolff on the divergent paths of the medium and the feminist (New Woman or Suffragette), but she also argues that spiritualism in particular was a near-relation of the succeeding Women's Movement because it enacted and confronted many of the prejudices surrounding the Woman Question. Such activity prised open an ideological crack in the patriarchal edifice of ideas which could be exploited by succeeding activists.[57] Like Toni Wolff, Basham links 'women' to 'spirits', but in a more coherent attempt to explain why women were so essential to spiritualism, its 'essence'.

> The centrality of women to the Spiritualist Movement is perhaps explicable by the fact that they too, like the spirits, existed within an uncertain medium whose dimensions were simultaneously literal and metaphoric. Without legal rights or representation, they had their own metaphoric power in the vague but pervasive concept of 'female influence', an influence that the spirits themselves seemed eager to enhance or promote.[58]

Similarly, Basham argues that spiritualism 'existed in a dramatic tension between two evaluative modes'.[59] On the one hand, it was held to be revelation of 'higher laws', and on the other, it proliferated 'irresponsible writing' both in the sensationalist popular press and in automatic writing where the medium claimed no responsibility for the productions. Not only do concepts of and attractions to spirits pervade Jung's writings, but so does this dynamic since much of his work seems to be an attempt to theorise in this field. In his doctoral dissertation he tries to generate universal psychic laws from the midst of 'irresponsible' psychic narratives such as Hélène Preiswerk's 'romances'. Indeed, it could be argued that Jungian theory is forced to reproduce this dialectic in the concept of the transpersonal, archetypal collective unconscious and the contingent archetypal image with only a metaphoric or fictive relation to higher laws or realities.

Spiritualism seems to have been a shaping force on Jungian psychology in many respects including: Jung's personal experience and family background, the philosophical grounds he chose, the methods he used both in writing (his *Septem Sermones* 'automatic' writing) and therapy, and as key structures within the theories and dynamics of his works. I would also argue that Jungian psychology could be seen as a medicalised attempt to appropriate spiritualism, part of the drive of science to assert dominance over esoteric discourses. Such a move was facilitated and anticipated by spiritualists themselves when they tried to align spiritualism with empiricism. By further extension, it could be argued that Jungian psychology is an attempt by a male-authored patriarchal discourse to submerge and rewrite a multifarious female movement with dangerous potential political energies. Jung replaces the woman medium with the 'anima', a masculinist discourse of 'the feminine'. The male subject assumes the medium position while the feminine becomes displaced into the unconscious anima. Jungian psychology through Toni Wolff redefines the woman medium as 'the woman who assists the man to realize his unconscious ideas'.[60] However, as I showed in Chapter 1, Jungian discourse is not impenetrable to feminist unravelling and rewriting.

Additionally, this second chapter seeks to demonstrate the spiritualist narratives still occupying Jungian texts in ways redolent of the fictive pole of both Jungian theory and spiritualism. Jung wrote to Freud that he set out to *conquer* the occult,[61] but I would argue that he colonised it in such a way that it infiltrated and organised his writings profoundly. His language to Freud exhibits a lust for power over occult discourse which was simultaneously a symptom of submission: he was always one of its own.

JUNG AND CONTEMPORARY GERMANIC *VOLKISCH* CULTURE

The term *volkisch* as used in this work is taken from Richard Noll's *The Jung Cult* where he explains the epithet as follows:

> Nineteenth-century Europe witnessed a revival of what has been termed volkisch ('folkish') movements, nationalistic groups bonded together by a common ethnic and cultural identity ... Many volkisch groups – especially Pan-German and Pan-Slavic groups – elevated notions of racial purity to a quasi-scientific, quasi-mystical ideal ... [I]t is primarily the Pan-Germanic movement of the nineteenth-century that is meant by the term *volkisch*.[62]

Noll argues that nineteenth-century pan-Germanism became anti-Semitic by the end of that century and that there was a significant overlap between esoteric movements like spiritualism and Theosophy and *volkisch* culture, although the two areas are by no means identical, with some esoteric groups being transnational in ideology.[63] Furthermore, *volkisch* cultural groupings do not necessarily imply explicit political aims and programmes. Noll's position is that Jung is essentially a *volkisch* thinker and his psychology at least in part a *volkisch* product, but that Jung and his writings are not part of political *volkisch* movements which were the antecedents of the Nazis: '... Jung's volkisch interests were not political ones.'[64]

The rest of this chapter will evaluate some aspects of the alleged *volkisch* nature of Jungian ideas and theories and Jung's historical role in Nazi Germany to examine further the weight of history within his discourse.

Jung was undoubtedly a reader and collector of many contemporary esoteric works such as the eighteen studies in his library by G.R.S. Mead (1863–1933) on Gnosticism, Hermeticism and Mithraic Liturgy, all published by the Theosophical Publishing Society.[65] Theosophy was developed by Madame Blavatsky from her spiritualist practice and included the teachings of divine beings on reincarnation and a cosmic memory bank called the 'Akashic records' which could be consulted by those trained and initiated by the Theosophical Society.[66] Noll argues for a structural similarity between Jung's confessed origins for his theories and Blavatsky's legend of her own initiations. Jung, like Blavatsky, would undergo 'visionary' time travel and be assisted by a series of imaginal figures, most notably his spiritual guru, Philemon.[67] Noll seems less secure in identifying the subsequent results, the secret and hierarchical Theosophical Society, with Jung's more permeable clinical practice connected to wider psychiatric movements. Of course, Theosophy itself is not a *volkisch* phenomenon nor limited to Germanic culture in operation.

As well as Theosophy, Jung's work refers to openly *volkisch* neopagan texts which were influenced by the interpretation of a solar root of all myths, especially hero myths from ancient Aryan sources, by Friedrich Max Muller (1823–1900).[68] Muller used the widely accepted nineteenth-century categories of Aryan and Semitic as divisions of the original Indo-European root. The *volkisch* mysticism that drew on Muller strove for a 'grounding of mythological, religious, and linguistic differences in biology ...'[69] and thus could claim that any anti-Semitism had a 'scientific' basis. *Volkisch* neo-pagan cults might openly adopt sun worship or some form of ancient Teutonic (so defined as 'Aryan') religion or argue for a Hellenic Christ from the common story of Mary's seduction by a Roman officer introduced by the overtly anti-Semitic Ernest Haeckel.[70] Other common features linking *volkisch* mystical groups and sometimes suggesting political energies are detailed by Noll below.

> [A] rejection of Christianity in favour of a mystical Volk connection with the ancient Aryan peoples (especially the Teutons); nature worship; hiking; nudism; neo-pagan rituals ... the study of the Aryan roots of occult symbolism (such as the swastika ...); the idealisation of the ancient Teutonic warrior (such as Siegfried) ... the preference of intuition over rational judgement; techniques for the direct experience of God without Christian intercessors; a fascination with the medieval Grail legends and Wagner's *Parsifal*, with the purity of Aryan blood depicted as the Grail ... and of course, anti-Semitism.[71]

The best documented contemporary neo-pagan cult of sun worship is that inspired by the work of Eugen Diederichs

(1867–1930), who called for a spiritual aristocracy to lead the state or people to redemption. Jung's library contains many works from his publishing house.[72] As well as Jung's extensive *volkisch* mystical reading, Noll argues that his patients at the Burgholzli clinic were likely to contain a high proportion of *volkisch* mystics who would not supply unbiased empirical evidence for Jung's evolving theories of the collective unconscious.[73] He also identifies Jung's long mythological work of 1912, *Wandlungen und Symbole der Libido*, as a text of *volkisch* sun worship since its attempt to blend psychoanalysis, comparative philology, mythology, evolutionary biology and philosophies of personal religions operates within a general solar and Aryan frame. That psychoanalysis is not going to control and organise this esoteric material is evident from Jung's famous redefinition of the libido as a term for general psychic energy, not sexuality, a move which propelled the deterioration of his relationship with Freud.[74] Sun worship was a key element in *volkisch* neopaganism and remained important to the Nazis, who made the summer solstice a national holiday.[75] Not only does Jung offer experience of God as a blazing sun or star within *Wandlungen*,[76] but solar theology may have found a home in his theories in his extensive adoption of the mandala, originally a sun symbol in Sanskrit, to represent the goal of individuation, the self or god-image in the psyche. Jung wrote that the mandala 'represents an inner sun'.[77]

However, Jungian psychology is not in an overtly subservient relation to sun worship, and Jung's lifelong fascination with Christianity[78] suggests that Noll's thesis that Jung was 'virulently anti-Christian'[79] is an exaggeration. Nevertheless, *The Jung Cult* seems justified in indicating that Jung's early approach to Christianity was shaped within *volkisch* esoteric narratives just as in later years he adopted alchemical tools. For the same reasons that Jungian psychology needs to be considered in relation to its spiritualist antecedents so Noll convincingly describes how it also evolved in similar ways to contemporary mystery cults where initiates were encouraged to follow the descents of a charismatic leader.

Jung's confrontation with his unconscious in the years 1912–14, which like the spiritualist *Septem Sermones* inaugurated his later theories, is partly given in *Memories, Dreams, Reflections*, but the full text of what he confessed orally in his 1925 *Seminar in Analytical Psychology* was not published until 1989.[80] What Jung did not reveal in print earlier about his encounters with Salome is what he here calls a mystery of deification which he links to Mithraic liturgies, newly popular with *volkisch* groups. Salome openly worships Jung as he finds himself transformed into the figure of a lion-headed god.[81]

According to contemporary scholars, Mithraism was said to be a survival of ancient Zoroastrianism and thus such visionary initiations were a direct link to the earliest Aryan peoples, associating Jung with *volkisch* initiations into Teutonic mysteries.[82] Jung identifies the lion-headed god as *'Aion,* the eternal being'[83] from Mithraic symbolism, and this becomes the title of his book, *Aion: Researches into the Phenomenology of the Self* (1951; now CW9 II). There is also a strong suggestion of Jung's assumption, if only momentarily, of the Aryan Christ motif and we might return to his earlier enthusiasm for a Dionysiac (so non-Semitic) Christ in his letter to Freud, cited earlier in this chapter, and see it as a *volkisch* remark. The fact that *Aion* becomes a major 'self' image and the title of one of the *Collected Works* indicates how far this *volkisch* mystery of deification penetrated into the shaping structures of Jung's theories about archetypes as inherited meaning potentials with transcendent and numinous attributes. The *volkisch* interpretation of Mithraism as a survival of ancient Aryan creeds has been discounted by later scholars.[84]

Another pagan figure inspiring *volkisch* culture was Wotan.[85] There is no evidence to link Jung with any active Mithraic or Wotanist groups but the resemblance between the practice of active imagination (particularly using mythological material) giving access to the self or god within and active cults offering initiations to the divine and ancient gods within, is significant. Wotan is no stranger to Jung's writings. In a letter of 1923, Jung explicitly aligns himself with those in the 'Germanic tribes' for whom Christianity was a foreign imposition on Wotanism and barbarism.[86]

Through Wotan Jung appears to reject Christianity as unsuitable for the Germanic soul and places himself within its *volkisch* culture. However, a total rejection of Christianity is not a stable position in Jung's works. I would argue that these inconsistencies show that despite the attraction to esotericism and *volkisch* mysticism (which form significant sources and contexts for Jung's ideas), he was never completely absorbed into any particular creed and was able to move on to other cultural resources later in his career. Certainly Jung's most sustained writing on Wotan, his 1936 essay of that title,[87] reframes the *volkisch* myth as a warning about the Nazis, and Hitler in particular. Significantly, Jung could be said to be participating in Wotanism in this essay in suggesting that Wotan is a true god, or character of the Germanic peoples, linked with Christ and Dionysus.[88] Yet, if *volkisch*, this essay does not confine its criticism of the Nazis to associating them with the 'Middle Ages' and opposing them to 'civilised' behaviour. Wotan, a 'fundamental attribute of the German psyche',[89] has given rise to 'anti-Semitism'[90] and may be leading the nation to 'perdition' through its 'possessed' leader.[91] With historical hindsight, this criticism, given in 1936, seems wholly inadequate, but perhaps it is significant that Jung felt he could articulate criticism from *within* a *volkisch* discourse, that he felt (and Noll's research agrees), that there is no necessary identity of *volkisch* mystical interests with proto-Nazi ideas, although there is a cultural continuum.[92]

What can also be elided with Jung's *volkisch* interests are his often implicit suggestions that individuation in its higher forms is not open to all but will constitute a spiritual elite to guide mankind. 'Only a few are capable of individuating',[93] he wrote in 1916, and in 1928 Jung emphasised the need for an enlightened elite of individuated persons in order to 'guide' the majority.[94] Jung develops or clarifies his position in a talk broadcast in 1946 and published in *Essays on Contemporary Events*.[95] Proper individuation can still be fully achieved by only a few who will be moral, not political leaders.[96] This clearly does not exonerate Jung from the charge of advocating spiritual elites and suggests that his preoccupation with power and leadership continues late into his career, even if modified by his experiences in relation to Nazi Germany.

An additional aspect of Jung's *volkisch* explorations is that whatever the paucity of evidence for accusations of active anti-Semitism, he was certainly in contact with, and sometimes made use of, explicitly anti-Semitic material beyond the connotations of *volkisch* evocations of sun worship, Mithras and Wotan. As well as citing recognisably anti-Semitic works (without commenting on the racist contents) in *Wandlungen*,[97] there is also the testimony of Sabina Spielrein who conceived Wagnerian fantasies during an erotically charged analysis with Jung.[98] Wagner's essays testify to his pan-Germanism and anti-Semitism,[99] and although Spielrein records only *her* fantasies and does not attribute their origin directly to Jung, the context is suggestive. It is time to discuss Jung's historical activities in detail, some of which show a dangerous presence in Nazi Germany in more than common *volkisch* influences.

JUNG'S HISTORICAL ROLE IN ANTI-SEMITISM AND NAZI GERMANY

Evidence for Jung as actively anti-Semitic in word, action and theory is not substantial as opposed to his passive complicity in a pervasively anti-Semitic *volkisch* culture. As Andrew Samuels, a contemporary Jungian theorist, points out, when Jung asserts his belief in Aryan and Jewish differences, he is engaging with a contemporary mind-set that included Sigmund Freud.[100] However, most of Jung's contentious remarks about Jews not only go further than mere difference in implying inferiority and incompatibility between Jewish and Germanic attitudes, their context is crucial since most appear in an article, 'The State of Psychotherapy Today', published in the *Zentralblatt für Psychotherapie* in Nazi Germany in 1934.[101] Remarks about racial differences include the following:

> The Aryan unconscious has a higher potential than the Jewish.[102]

> The Jew, who is something of a nomad, has never yet created a cultural form of his own ... since all his instincts and talents require a more or less civilised nation to act as host for their development ...[103]

> The Jews have this peculiarity with women; being physically weaker, they have to aim at the chinks in the armour of their adversary.[104]

Samuels offers further instances of Jung's obsession with difference which must be seen as active interventions in the current anti-Semitic and politically violent culture. Unfortunately and culpably, Jung chose to play out old battles with Freud in Nazi territory. Jung warns against regarding 'Jewish psychology' (by which he means Freudian psychoanalysis) as equally applicable to Germanic Christendom.[105]

What compounds Jung's guilt in this instance is that he is in fact editor of the *Zentralblatt für Psychotherapie*, having acquired the position in 1933 when he took over the Presidency of the *General Medical Society for Psychotherapy*, based in Germany already under Nazi dominion. Jung later claimed that he accepted this position in order to try to protect the Jewish membership of the *General Medical Society* and that, as an absentee editor in Zurich, he was unaware of the pro-Nazi content of the *Zentralblatt* nominally under his control.[106] In fact, Jung did create a special category of individual membership which allowed Jews to remain participants for a time, but Samuels argues convincingly that not only was some editorial work on the *Zentralblatt* carried out in Zurich (though not personally by Jung),[107] he also had at least a moral responsibility for the Nazi pseudo-psychology that the Journal began to proliferate.[108]

Jung threatened to resign from the General Medical Society in 1935 over Nazi anti-Semitism, but did not do so until the outbreak of war when his psychology simultaneously lost official approval in Germany.[109] It is, however, worth remembering that Jung's Wotan essay of 1936 is explicitly critical of Nazi policy and of Hitler in particular, however inadequate it may be as a moral response to Nazi violence and policies.

If Jung appears to engage in anti-Semitic practice in this context, he must also be called a voluntary participant in Nazi cultural politics, although his own actions and words are not identical with an endorsement of anti-Semitic violence and systematic oppression. It is worth considering whether this Nazi stratum to Jung's career has any theoretical areas. Is there anything beyond opportunism and the common *volkisch* discursive field of Nazism and German esotericism to position Jung in his official roles in the *General Medical Society* and *Zentralblatt*?

There is no space here to consider the whole range of racial narratives inhabiting Jung's *Collected Works*, but it is worth noting that beyond the impersonal and transcultural collective unconscious, Jungian theory does posit a racial layer in the collective psyche. This is detailed in the Jung-approved volume by Jolande Jacobi, *The Psychology of C.G. Jung* (1942),[110] but is fully expounded in his 1925 *Seminar on Analytical Psychology* with a very similar geological diagram of the psyche.[111] Samuels points out that this controversial aspect of Jung's theory is not what we would today consider racist when it causes Jung to warn against Eurocentric judgements on other cultures,[112] but it does become offensive when it becomes literal, when the imaginal African or Jew becomes a reductive stereotype that omits any consideration of historical forces, and is implicitly or explicitly in a hierarchical relation to the European 'norm'.[113] Yet it is not specifically the racial node of Jungian theory that draws him close to National Socialism but his ideas of a psychology of nations. In a *volkisch* essay in 1918, Jung argued for a mystical bond between land and psychology using the example of America and arguing that succeeding generations of white Americans would take on the physical and psychological characteristics of the Native Americans,[114] a nationalistic move perfectly congruent with his contemporary attitude to Jews. In the same essay he described Jews as lacking the rooted quality gained from a 'chthonic' connection to ancestral soil.[115] This is not conventional racism because it suggests that all peoples living long enough in one particular place acquire distinctive national characteristics. It is not nationalism in an aggressive sense as it provides no rationale for expansionism. However it is a theory that significantly excludes Jews, whose homelessness becomes a basis for their 'difference'. Just as National Socialism and all forms of virulent nationalism will desire to absorb and shape a psychology of nations which can become part of a web of its violent ideology, so Jung may have been attracted to Hitler in a way that harnessed his own power drives and those of his discourse. As Samuels most evocatively puts it, 'we have been discussing the hypertrophy of psychology, *its* expansionism, *its* search for *Lebensraum,* "living space"'.[116]

This, together with Jung's persistent espousal of *volkisch* theories of racial difference and national psychology, could be the nexus of narratives that constitute the dynamic between Jung and pre-World War II Nazi Germany. The elitism and related concerns for power, for different forms of authority in Jungian writings, moral, spiritual, cultural, find political expression in his voluntary participation in 1930s Nazi Germany. Such participation makes visible the political shadow of Jungian discourse, what is unspoken and unacknowledged in the writings. In taking on an historical and political role in Nazi Germany, Jung made visible the gaps in his textuality, embodying the not simple but real connections between his esoteric, occult and philosophical sources and contemporary politics. Jung himself wrote that Hitler incarnated the shadow, and in that he was irresistible.[117]

It would be crude to argue that for Jung, Hitler was his shadow but perhaps more apt to suggest that if Jung's 1930s career embodies a shadow to his discourse, then it could also be seen as a visible aspect of the political impacts of psychologies in general, how they are structured through and by contemporary ideologies of racial, gender and sexual identities. However, this is not to argue that there is not an historical specificity to Jungian discourse, constituted by the writings and the intertextuality of those writings, and their embodiment in the cultural practice of analysis. Noll's *The Jung Cult* reveals the secret rules of Jung's Analytical Psychology Club of Zurich, formed in 1916, which limits Jewish membership to 10 per cent of the total and Jewish guest membership to 25 per cent. This quota was removed in 1950, but only became generally known in 1989.[118] The most benign interpretation of this anti-Semitic move would align this quota with Jung's belief in the different racial psychologies of Jews and Aryans and a desire to keep the club 'Jungian'. This is not a complete identification of 'Jungian' and 'Aryan' since Jung had many Jewish friends and patients.[119] I would suggest that this evidence for active anti-Semitism could also be part of the narrative of the battle between Freudian psychoanalysis and Jung's analytical psychology, which is clearly signalled by Jung's remarks about the inapplicability of 'Jewish psychology' to Germanic peoples in the 1920s and 1930s. Andrew Samuels argues that Jung's voluntary participation in pre-war Nazi Germany is also part of the same drive for power, the search for breathing space for this new body of knowledge.[120]

Jung is not innocent with regard to the charges of anti-Semitism. He was a passive consumer of *volkisch* and anti-Semitic material and actively anti-Semitic in voluntarily imposing a quota and participating in psychological politics in pre-war Nazi Germany. To this extent he was a willing participant in Nazism, although he did make increasingly critical statements about Hitler and Nazi policy from 1936. I would argue that it is incorrect to call Jung a Nazi because that implies unequivocal support for Nazi policies which never seems to have been Jung's position. Even at his most contaminated in 1933, he did create a form of membership for the German *General Medical Society* which aided Jewish practitioners. Jung's most anti-Semitic remarks do not straightforwardly allege Jewish inferiority and he never advocated any political actions or repressions. Samuels points out that even what appears to be an assertion of racial supremacy has an ambiguous context.

> The Aryan unconscious has a higher potential than the Jewish; this is the advantage and disadvantage of a youthfulness not fully escaped from barbarism.[121]

Written in 1934 in *Zentralblatt*, this could be read as suggesting the greater civilisation of Jews and a coded warning to the Nazis. The question is the extent to which Jung is valuing the 'primitive power' he ascribes volkischly to the Germanic psyche. It is difficult to be unequivocal about Jung's anti-Semitic guilt from his published writings: the anti-Semitism rests in covert actions (the quota) and the public association with Nazi Germany. Similarly, Jung never repented personally in print, but in 1945 he does name concentration camps as part of a general European shame.[122] It is therefore regrettable that Jung provides a final qualification which demonstrates his moral inadequacy: 'despite our good conscience'.[123] Published in *Essays on Contemporary Events* in 1946, the essay shares space with Jung's argument for individuation to develop, 'not the political but the moral leaders of mankind'.[124] Jung's career demonstrates both the connections between these two forms of leadership and how, by engaging in politics in pursuit of cultural supremacy for his own psychology, Jung failed to provide any kind of moral leadership, incarnating an anti-Semitic shadow.

Chapter 1 considered how the fictive and the feminine are both incorporated yet also remain marginal challenges to Jungian ideas. Chapter 2 has attempted to provide some historical and cultural grounding for Jungian theory; to locate it in a particular cultural site and indicate the importance of struggles over race, nation, gender, as well as issues of power and leadership. Jung's writings are continuous with philosophical and esoteric traditions and are deeply marked by the struggle to exist independently within a field of medical, scientific, psychoanalytic, esoteric and gender discourses. Jungian theory is a record of both its author's drive for power and of privileged male-centred discourses to appropriate and control marginalised, gender-oriented discourses such as spiritualism. The collision of the nakedly personal and theoretical is visible in the web of psychoanalytic, occult, cultural narratives pervading *The Freud/Jung Letters*. Similarly, Jung's writings are transparently intertextual, transmitting esotericism and spiritualism into a theoretical field which privileges fictionality and creativity. However, they do so weighted by historical matter, demonstrating that even a fictional text is governed by authoritative mechanisms which penetrate beyond isolated textual pleasures. Perhaps one attraction of Jung for contemporary novelists is precisely the desire to operate beyond literary play, to change the contemporary by reconstructing it. Although all four novelists whose works will be considered in later chapters aim for a liberalising discourse in opposition to traditional restrictive codes (particularly of gender), perhaps a consideration of the historically and culturally written power drives of C.G. Jung reveals a trace of the risk taken by such fictions. Such a trace might be constellated in ideas and structures of power and authority between author, reader, text. It is not a coincidence that another similar triad is formulated in the analytic frame by analyst, patient, psychic or dream text. Any new Jungian literary theory in these contexts must show awareness of structures of power, politics and gender. So far I have introduced Jungian theory for literary studies and placed his writings in poststructuralist, feminist, political, historical and esoteric contexts. The next task is to look at Jungian theory as manifest in contemporary writing. The following chapters will explore the challenge from fiction in articulating a new relationship between Jungian discourse and the theories of modern literary criticism.

It remains to consider Jung's later adopted mode of alchemy, partly as another esoteric narrative and partly because to Lindsay Clarke in *The Chymical Wedding*, it defines a royal road to Jungian theory.

3

A Jungian Reader Theory: Alchemy and *The Chymical Wedding* by Lindsay Clarke

> As is shown by the texts and their symbolism, the alchemist projected what I have called the process of individuation into the phenomena of chemical change ...
>
> Jung, CW12[1]

In this chapter I want to propose a Jungian reader theory which works by splicing Jungian definitions of the unconscious into traditional theories of reader-response. Such a Jungian reader theory draws upon Jung's reinterpretation of alchemy as an essentially psychological process. The result is an 'alchemical literary theory' in Jungian terms. In turn, this theory can be employed in the feminist critiques of Jungian ideas by exploring Lindsay Clarke's profoundly Jungian novel, *The Chymical Wedding*.

Chapter 1 argued that Jung *archi-textualised* some of his theories from the intertextuality native to alchemy. Chapter 3 will examine the romance of Jungian ideas and alchemy further in order to describe a mode of reading which could itself be called 'alchemical' when applied to fictional texts. This form of 'reading alchemy' corresponds closely to the reader-response theories of Wolfgang Iser, but is not identical to them, mainly because it is dependent upon a Jungian construction of the unconscious. *The Chymical Wedding* by Lindsay Clarke needs to be considered, first, as an example of reading alchemy, demonstrating how the text's structures themselves offer an alchemical mode of reading concentrated in narratives of romance and sacrifice. Second, the text requires a critical evaluation of how far its liberal agenda is achieved through its Jungian frame. Therefore this chapter also continues the critique of Jungian ideas in relation to feminist theory which will be developed further in

Chapters 4 and 5. By 'romance' here, I do not refer, in the first instance, to the genre, but to an erotic principle that takes on some of Jung's definitions of Eros as a principle of connectedness or relationship. 'Romance' in these Jungian terms means love and desire, the urge to connect. It is structured upon the model of the ego's ideal relationship with the unconscious which is one of connections without the drive to dominate. If the ego should claim to exhaust or comprehend fully unconscious powers, then this is an inauthentic romance since it betrays the essential independence and fundamental unknowability of the unconscious Other.

Jung's distinctive conception of alchemy is that metallurgical attempts to turn lead into gold were projections of the ego's constant interactions with the unconscious, which he called individuation. Alchemists were not primarily prototype chemists: they were practising Jungian analysis upon themselves, facilitating their own individuation. It is worth noting that this is by no means the only twentieth-century definition of the art. Alchemy runs counter to Cartesian dualism, arguing that matter, body, mind and spirit are not separable and that transformations in one area will affect those in another. It was believed that transmutations of metals occur naturally over long periods of time but could be induced by the arts of alchemy which sought for spiritual gold as well as its material correlative.[2]

> It is thus not quite right to say that gold represents the sun, and silver the moon; rather it is the case that the two noble metals and the two luminaries are both symbols of the same cosmic or divine realities.
>
> Titus Burckhardt, *Alchemy*[3]

Since the sacred, the psychological and the metallurgical modes merge in alchemy texts, modern writers can choose to stress one element or value all equally. Jung's conception of alchemy as primarily a psychological operation is disputed by Titus Burckhardt[4] but has become influential[5] as *The Chymical Wedding* itself demonstrates.

READING ALCHEMY

All hermetic theorists agree that alchemy requires the training of an adept. It is time to consider the reader as an adept, although not engaged in mystical training, according to the reader-response theories of Wolfgang Iser in *The Act of Reading* (1978).[6] Iser argues that literary texts provoke performances of signification in the interaction between text and reader. It follows that any aesthetic quality resides in the text's performing structure (the text in itself), but that aesthetic pleasure and 'meaning' can only be formulated by the reader within the act of reading.[7] Reading words as meaningful, as more than mere signifiers, causes the reader to project mental images from the signifieds and this Iser calls 'ideation' and 'image building', a process to which the reader brings her own 'repertoire' of literary and social competencies.[8] The reader's individual experience as a reader and as a social being crucially intervenes in building a mental understanding of the literary text. The reader's sense of gaining meaning from a text is therefore of a temporal character because the act of reading forces the reader to relate individual elements together, to construct parallels, links and correspondences within the time-frame of the reading process.

> It is therefore difficult, if not impossible, to isolate individual phases of this process and call them the meaning of the text, because the meaning in fact stretches out over the whole course of ideation. Meaning itself, then, has a temporal character, the peculiarity of which is revealed by the fact that the articulation of the text into past, present, and future by the wandering viewpoint does not result in fading memories and arbitrary expectations, but in an uninterrupted synthesis of all the time phases.[9]

However, the mental operation of the 'synthesising' processes which the reader performs upon the ideational record of the text are not just those of consciousness. Iser admits that the time structure of reading allows the unconscious to offer what he calls 'passive syntheses' (as opposed to the 'active' syntheses of consciousness) to in-form the reader's constructions of meanings. The structure of reading literary texts is a mode permeable to unconscious forces. This has implications for subjectivity itself: reading is an ontological mode; it reformulates the subject.

> The temporal character of the reading process acts as a kind of catalyst for the passive syntheses through which the meaning of the text forms itself in the reader's mind ...
>
> Thus the meaning of the literary text can only be fulfilled in the reading subject and does not exist independently of him; just as

> important, though, is that the reader himself, in constituting the meaning, is also constituted.[10]

Iser's definition of ideation as the construction of mental images provoked by the signifieds of the text's signifiers has already dissolved boundaries between the reader and aesthetic object 'because it has no existence of its own [that is outside the mind of the reader] and because we are imagining and producing it, we are actually in its presence and it is in ours'.[11] Now he argues that reading is a form of enlarging of subjectivity by providing structures by which the unconscious can influence ideation, provoke and shape images, so constructing the subjectivity of the reader anew.

> The significance of the work, then, does not lie in the meaning sealed within the text, but in the fact that the meaning brings out what had previously been sealed within us. When the subject is separated from himself, the resultant spontaneity is guided and shaped by the text in such a way that it is transformed into a new and real consciousness. Thus each text constitutes its own reader.[12]

Iser quotes Freud to support his view that reading liberates some unconscious forces from repression to become ingredients of an evolving consciousness in the act of reading.[13] Yet if we substitute a Jungian definition of the archetypal unconscious (as inherently meaningful) for Freud's, Iser could be said to have described reading fiction as a form of 'active imagination' whereby reading provokes the unconscious shaping of subjectivity which Jung called 'individuation'. 'Active imagination' is Jung's therapeutic method of using an image as a stimulus for the patient to fantasise upon. If mental control is sufficiently relaxed, the autonomous unconscious will be able to release its spontaneity upon the unsuspecting ego, so permitting unconscious material to 'surface' within analysis.[14] The image, for active imagination, could be personal and psychic, as in a dream image, or it could be drawn from culture by being taken from an external text. A 'reading active imagination' is an intriguing mix of the cultural and psychic. Self-evidently, the literary text is a cultural product and available to others, but the ideation, the actual images coursing through the reading subject, will be psychically coloured and one person's ideation will not be identical to that of any other reader. What is different in kind in these various forms of active imagination is their different relations to authority. A subject meditating alone upon her dream image is autonomous, but the same activity with an analyst incarnates an authority 'outside' the patient's psyche. That authority is different in kind again if it is the analyst suggesting the image from a myth or cultural source. 'Reading active imagination' dethrones an embodied authority for a textual one. Such a textual authority still remains an issue of power but that does not perturb Iser. He suggests that the text 'guides'[15] and 'regulates the interaction between text and reader ... through a history which is actually produced in the act of reading',[16] and his aim is clearly to head off the horrors of deconstruction by arguing for a consistency in the meanings which the texts initiate. If a text 'regulates' it cannot signify absolutely anything or nothing at all. By such means the cause of aesthetic 'value' is not lost. Iser does not explore what the text's 'regulations' mean for subjectivity, but I will consider further the implications of a text's more powerful position in reading as active imagination in a later chapter on *Hopeful Monsters*.

The pathway back to alchemy is apparent in the connections made between Iser's reader-response theory and Jungian active imagination. If the reader-response structure can be rewritten as active imagination, then in *Jungian* terms it is also a form of alchemy. Reading alchemy occurs by adopting Jung's conception of alchemy as a psychological projection of active imagination within individuation. When reading fiction which allows unconscious forces to participate in ideation or image formation, the reader is engaged in alchemy, whereby reading becomes a kind of rite since the Jungian unconscious is intrinsically religious in nature. This can also be extended to fiction writing. If the unconscious is allowed to operate by the ego sacrificing the claim to control all signifieds, all possible constructions of meaning, then active imagination (as alchemy) becomes a part of writing as well. In such a case, the infusion of unconscious potential in the writing of fiction becomes a (w)rite. This form of alchemy or active imagination in (w)riteing is more autonomous than the reading rite of an-Other's text.

Before looking at examples of these ideas in *The Chymical Wedding*, it is worth considering some of what Jung gained by his tenet that '[i]n short, the alchemical operation seems to us the equivalent of the psychological process of active imagination'.[17] To start with he gained so-called 'evidence' in the form of a large body of texts from a range of cultures and periods containing similar symbols which by definition possessed no fixed or singular meanings. These he regarded as an historical validation of his theories of the collective nature of the unconscious.[18] Importantly, the multicultural nature of alchemy also enabled Jung to break out of *volkisch* mysticism for examples of myths and sources of images. It is suggestive that although Jung becomes interested in alchemy as early as 1928,[19] his first major writings on the subject occur in the late 1930s when political tensions provide reasons to detach himself from *volkisch* topics.[20] Alchemy's span of cultures begins in Ancient Egypt where the legendary Hermes Trismegistos, identified with the Egyptian god Thoth, allegedly left a text on the mythical 'emerald tablet' which survives only in much later translations.[21] The flexibility of alchemical narratives and crucial indeterminacy of its symbols meant that it could be absorbed into Christian and Islamic cultures.[22]

The fact that Jung first became enthused by alchemy from a Chinese text[23] perhaps indicates that he devoted his later works to the elucidation of alchemical sources as a means of release from the dark specificities of his native *volkisch* mysticism. Nevertheless, alchemy does not escape culture even if it is an esoteric system with transcultural modes. Alchemy's alleged sources are mythical: there is no original body of work as a standard by which to judge later derivations, and alchemy is avowedly intertextual. Therefore, although alchemy's parallelisms in the forms of female and male in the crucial narrative of 'sacred marriage' or 'chymical wedding' suggest a native gender parity, it is unsurprising that alchemy texts and practices can exhibit a gender bias. Alchemists are traditionally male with the only two female names mentioned sounding distinctly legendary: Maria Prophetissa and Kleopatra.[24] In the heyday of English alchemy in the sixteenth and seventeenth centuries, the art records only female assistants in a 'mystic sister' role.[25] Burckhardt, for example, will not allow alchemy's mysterious symbols to be read as gender equality.

> Although ... the two forces or poles of human nature ... lie on the same level, there is nevertheless a difference of rank, similar to that of the right and left hands, so that the masculine pole can be said to be placed above the feminine.[26]

Neither alchemy nor Jungian theory necessarily or intrinsically enfranchises those subordinated under a regime of gender bias. For a literary text that tries to use both alchemy and Jung to defeat male hegemony, we must now turn to *The Chymical Wedding*.[27]

LINDSAY CLARKE'S *THE CHYMICAL WEDDING*

The Chymical Wedding is structured using two related narrative strands. The first is a contemporary account narrated by dried poet and cuckold, Alex Darken, of his lonely exile in Norfolk and his relationships with the much older failed poet, Edward Nesbitt, and Edward's young psychic assistant and lover, Laura. Both Edward and Laura are using psychic and historical methods to investigate the careers of Victorian alchemists and writers, Henry Agnew and his daughter, Louisa. The second of the novel's strands omnisciently relates the Victorian story mostly from Louisa's point of view as she encounters the new parson, Edwin Frere, and his wife, Emilia. Energies generated by these new relationships contribute to Louisa's composition of an alchemical text, called *An Open Invitation To The Chymical Wedding*, so recalling the novel's title. A culmination occurs in a passionate rite between Frere and Louisa, echoed in the twentieth century by Alex and Laura. This initiates a romantic and sacrificial re-formation of the two trios, Alex, Edward, Laura and Louisa, Frere, Emilia. These events precipitate the sacrifice of Louisa's book by burning and of Frere's body by self-castration. The novel ends by attempting an emotional resolution on both narrative temporal levels.

Alchemy in the novel exists in multiple manifestations. It is physical in Laura's pottery and in sexual coupling, psychological-Jungian in Darken's dreams which dismember his own sense of superiority to the feminine, and spiritual in Louisa, Frere and Edward's grappling with metaphysical forces. It is also explicitly an alchemy of reading and writing in this novel of blocked poets and of Louisa's struggle to write, which becomes a (w)rite.

> Completion must be her watchword now ... the chymical wedding ... the meeting of the dark and light in close embrace from which the golden stone was born ... It was more than intellectual comprehension; and to write of it she must strive to become that meeting. She must submit to its ordeals. (pp. 298–9)

There is an unambiguous attempt to challenge any gender bias in alchemy by having the potter, Laura, as the physical practitioner in the contemporary story assisted by two males, and the emphatic identification of Frere as Louisa's 'mystic brother' to reverse the mystic sister's traditionally subordinate position. Perhaps some of the crudity and violence of this reversal is signalled by authoritative Edward's initial refusal to believe in the mystic brother, asserting that the male role is always that of the 'Master' or 'Magister' (p. 237), as well as the fact that Frere has to be castrated into this position.

> Priest to both God and Goddess now, never again to be the lover of Louisa Agnew, he had become, and would forever remain, her mystic brother. (p. 471)

The plot represents a further deployment of alchemy as the major characters experience *nigredo* (death-like depressive states with Edward nearly dying in a heart attack), passionate *conjunctio* in the union of opposites (most often male and female in a chymical wedding), and the *solve et coagula* in the dissolution and solidifying during the reorganisation of relationships. The story is alchemically structured. In addition to the narrative of relationships, alchemical stages occur in the psyches of the protagonists and in their (w)riteing and reading. *The Chymical Wedding* organises its reading and writing alchemy around narratives of romance and sacrifice that constitute both plot and a mode of linguistic operation. What is meant by an alchemy of writing occurs within a romance with the Other where that Other can be both an-Other person and the Other within, the unconscious. It is a romance which must sacrifice all claim to control the Other, either by a possessive relationship or by a claim to fix or exhaust all possible meanings of the Other in composing the text. Such (w)riteing is a rite that is alchemical in Jung's conception of alchemy and a form of Jungian active imagination initiating individuation. In the stories of how the blocked writers, Alex, Edward, Louisa, learn to read alchemically both the symbols of alchemy texts and their own psyches (using dreams or tarot cards), *The Chymical Wedding* is a commentary on the implications of Jungian alchemy for reading and writing. Once reading becomes alchemical, a paradigm of active imagination initiating individuation, then the (w)rite can begin.

> Day by day the stack of written pages mounted higher ... They came as dreams still, or as waking dreams ... so little did they

> have to do with time, and interpenetrating through the states of wakefulness and sleep. (pp. 306–7)

Narratives of romance and sacrifice dominate all the textual levels, not only as structures of a Jungian reading and writing alchemy. The novel tries to use these narratives to critique gender relations. A successful romance in all forms in this text is a romance with the Other that sacrifices ego control lest a romance become a prison like the very Victorian marriage of Frere and Emilia and the claustrophobic relationship of Edward and Laura. In effect, the novel structures successful romance as Jungian romance: failure is the failure to respect the Jungian Other as an autonomous, never completely knowable entity. Even Alex, a rather crass reader-representative who doubtfully imbibes alchemy in a way intended to divest the external reader of some disbelief, even Alex comes to realise that he has imprisoned his wife by making her into his anima, his feminine self. This anima rebels because male possessiveness only allows her to signify more of his ego, not true Otherness (p. 122).

The realisation that to indulge in a possessive romance can be a man's way of trying to confine a woman into an anima precipitates Darken's individuation through dreams. It leads eventually to a reading alchemy of alchemy texts and so finally to the moment of his (w)rite.

> I had invented the dream; now it was re-inventing me. (p. 158)

> Yet in that fantastic cavalcade of monsters, freaks and angels, there were two moments in which I recognized something of myself … (p. 220)

> And then … a line of verse came … They were to become, much later, the closing verses of *The Green Man's Dream*. (p. 329)

Not all achieve the alchemical (w)rite of romancing the Other and sacrificing the ego. Emilia and Henry fail out of fear, and Edward's possessive desires over Laura almost confine the signifieds of his signifier 'heart' to the literal. His breaking heart becomes a heart attack: his possessive urges become enacted on a linguistic level allowing no Otherness beyond the one bodily signified. The drive to possess or restrict is wedded to fear of the Other as female, which is Edward's own *nigredo*.

'Those particular lips can't talk ... the only sound they make is a sort of munching ... I think it is the black hole ...' (p. 455)

In criticising as a patriarchal flaw a male tendency to confine women by perceiving them as animas, *The Chymical Wedding* both implicitly criticises Jung whose works contain just this dynamic and remain true to Jungian theory's awareness of the spurious nature of this projection. The novel tries to offer additional perspectives to Jung's idiosyncratic conception of alchemy and indeed the *Acknowledgements* (pp. 541–2) cites Titus Burckhardt's *Alchemy* as 'a provocative corrective to the Jungians' (p. 541). Alex Darken offers summaries of some of alchemy's non-Jungian positions (p. 223). Yet the reader, through Darken's narration, is not asked to accept all the arcane metaphysics, only the patterns of change in the major characters and the imaginative modes of reading and (w)riteing alchemy, none of which strays from the Jungian field. The novel offers reading fiction as a form of active imagination promoting individuation: the readers become alchemists according to the paradigms of this Jungian text. Alex, somewhat patronisingly, condenses his lessons for Bob, the sympathetic Marxist materialist, by explaining that both alchemy and dreams are important for 'personal evolution' (p. 500).

The Chymical Wedding uses Jung as a resource, both in adopting Jungian psychology as a Jungian perspective on alchemy, and in celebrating the fictional imagination as a privileged site of subjectivity. It uncritically adopts Jungian theory as authoritative and unproblematical and does not treat Jungian ideas as themselves forms of fiction. Jungian theory forms an intact authoritative ideological layer in the text's narrative strategies. In this way, the novel leaves dualism unchallenged except in deconstructive reversals, which leave binary structures in place. A prime example of this is the use of the words 'symbolic' and 'diabolic' as diametrical opposites. 'Symbolic' signals the uniting discourse of alchemy in the text, the true romance that sacrifices possessive control while 'diabolic' means splitting, which includes the splitting of the atom in the novel's depiction of the fear of nuclear war (as Alex goes to a CND meeting), and the splitting of minds or marriages within the story.

Gradually, the novel seems to suggest that the symbolic, that which unites dualisms of female/male, spirit/matter, body/psyche, can supersede the diabolic, the power that splits apart binary oppositions. The *nigredo* or deathly tone of the diabolic can become alchemically wedded to the symbolic and a peace achieved after the mutilation of Frere, the burning of Louisa's book and the near-death of Edward. How successful a romance this is will be explored below. The rest of this chapter will consider if the novel, while remaining within Jungian dualism, can surmount the tendency to erect a hierarchy of gender. Can *The Chymical Wedding* harness the Jungian frame to a liberatory cause?

Here it is important to look at the two points of excess to both Jung's writings and the other textual sources cited in the Acknowledgements: these are Frere's castration and the direct attempts at gender reversal concerning Laura and Louisa's alchemy, aimed at promoting female equality within a Jungian field. Why does the castration occur, and does the gender reversal succeed in its intentions?

Frere's castration is not germane to alchemy. In none of the cited alchemical works, nor in Jung's texts, does bodily mutilation feature in the art. Yet Frere insists on sacrificing the literal body and real blood (p. 468). Principally, Frere is aiming to unite two religious discourses: his patriarchal Christianity and worship of a Mother goddess associated with Louisa, which the text assimilates to alchemy. He claims 'that there was a rite in which a man might make his sacrifice to God and Goddess in a single act' (p. 470). Frere is presented as one who is 'crucified' or 'the hanged man' of both a tarot card and a chapter title, repressed by patriarchal Christianity prior to this act. In this sense, dismemberment brings him some peace. Nevertheless, his mutilation remains a violent supplement (in addition to the distinctive gender reversals), in a novel which has an intimate relationship with its source matter.

GENDER AND HIERARCHY: A CONSIDERATION OF SOURCES

In the first instance the title, *The Chymical Wedding*, is derived from a seventeenth-century alchemy romance called *The Chymical Wedding of Christian Rosenkreutz* by Johann Valentin Andreae. This earlier title, together with a riddle from the same text, is quoted in the contemporary novel (p. 160), but it does not appear in the Acknowledgements. The only English translation available before the composition of *The Chymical Wedding* is a rare volume by E. Foxcroft, Fellow of King's College Cambridge (dated 1690). Clarke may have consulted it in Cambridge University

Library.[28] Interestingly, Clarke may have come across '*Christian Rosenkreutz*' in Jung's writings, where he cites both text and author repeatedly. Numerous references occur in CW14, *Mysterium Conjunctionis*[29] where Jung remarks parenthetically of Andreae: 'his *Chymical Wedding* is so rich in content that I could touch on it only lightly here'.[30]

The second major source is mentioned in the Acknowledgements. The story of Louisa Agnew and her alchemist father who had her alchemical work burned, closely resembles the career of an actual Victorian, Mary Anne Atwood (*née* South), who, unlike her fictional descendant, contracted a happy marriage to a clergyman. Mary Anne Atwood's text, *A Suggestive Enquiry into the Hermetic Mystery* (1850), does survive in a few rare copies and has recently been reprinted.[31] The Acknowledgements offers the information that this history was provided to the author by a friend (p. 541), but Jung is also a possible source since all the details that *The Chymical Wedding* employs can be found in CW16, *The Practice of Psychotherapy*, together with a mention of the renowned alchemical text, the *Mutus Liber* which Clarke uses as Louisa's resonant epitaph (p. 25).[32]

Another source reference in the Acknowledgements is to *Psychic Energy* by Jung's follower, Esther Harding, for providing 'the seed of what was to become Darken's dream in Chapter 5' (p. 541).[33] Darken dreams himself into alchemy, envisaging what is later confirmed as correct alchemical apparatus, fuelled by the delicate energy of the sexual *conjunctio* of two lovers who turn out to be his wife and her lover. Harding's dream belongs to a woman and it provides the frame of Darken's dream. However, the novel caps the episode by inserting a quotation from Jung's *Mysterium Conjunctionis* as a final pronouncement of the dream's value; itself a citation from a male alchemy text.[34] It is interesting that *The Chymical Wedding* not only frames a female Jungian source with a quotation from the 'magister' himself, but it transforms a dream by a woman in the text of a woman to a dream of a man in a novel by a man. Somehow this source in both female psyche and female author becomes marginalised into a 'mystic sister' or even 'anima' role in its reconstruction in *The Chymical Wedding*. It is the creative and vital ingredient of representation, but remains marginalised as 'Other'.

The novel ends with an illustration from an old alchemy text depicting 'the gesture of the secret', the need for silence after engaging in alchemy that afflicts the major characters at the novel's conclusion (p. 539). The illustration is almost certainly taken from Jung's CW12, *Psychology and Alchemy*,[35] where it accompanies the text quoted at the head of this chapter. Jung includes an injunction to tear up alchemy books, which is perhaps alluded to in novel's endorsement of book destruction (p. 529). The last view we have of Louisa and Henry Agnew is of their peaceful contemplation of the golden fire consuming their alchemical writings.

Despite some references to original alchemy texts and earlier, non-fictional alchemists (pp. 233–4), the reader is not asked to move far from Jungian conceptions of alchemy as active imagination, and from a Jungian alchemical model of reading and (w)riteing fiction. Even acknowledged sources seem to be constructed in relation to Jung's *Collected Works*. In effect, the novel seems to make an effort to go back to Jung's sources in its employment of *Christian Rosenkreutz*, the Atwood frame, and by largely staying within a Jungian perspective on the whole field of alchemy. The novel operates at the interface of Jungian theory and some of Jung's own cited 'evidence'. In *The Chymical Wedding*, references such as *Psychic Energy*'s input into Darken's dream, the Atwood story, Andreae's romance, are shown to generate, or at least sustain, the overall Jungian frame, whereas in Jung's texts such elements are referred to in ways that underpin his theories. What some examination of *The Chymical Wedding*'s cited and uncited sources seems to reveal is the text's close identity with Jungian writings which makes the two points of excess – Frere's castration and the alchemic gender reversals – all the more remarkable and worthy of further consideration. The fiction would indeed appear to challenge the wholehearted adoption of Jungian theory throughout this literary text.

GENDER REVERSALS

The novel's gender reversals are designed to promote the female from the subordinate 'mystic sister' role to that of independent and equal alchemical artists. Laura, the medium-potter, takes the role of the physical alchemist and at the end of the novel is described as 'virgin' or separate in her independence (pp. 512–13). It is suggestive that it is Edward who names and defines Laura's condition, while she herself seems to have achieved 'sibylline' (p. 519) silence.

Significantly, Edward explicitly dissociates himself from 'feminists' (p. 513). Although Laura is said to have achieved independence from Edward, she seems to have done so at the cost of escaping textual sacrifices into silence: she is still named and defined by the masculine. A similar dynamic seems to inhibit the impressive female alchemical writer, Louisa Agnew, who becomes golden and 'bright-eyed' in the destructive fires of her own text (p. 525). Like Laura, Louisa is presented as successful in Jungian alchemy in so far as she escapes representation. Her text is sacrificed in its material form so that it can become spiritually infused within her (p. 529). The novel is unambiguous about presenting Louisa, not her father, as the more successful, but the gold of her writing alchemy is the flame that extinguishes her textuality, her participation in representation.

> And so, hands tightly clasped, father and daughter stood for a long time, golden together in the light of the flame, while there, in the embers of the blaze that burned their secret, the secret thrived. (p. 530)

It is worth emphasising that a clear distinction made in the text between the murderous sacrifice of the Other and the alchemical sacrifice of the ego. For example, in this scene we have a nuanced presentation of the alchemists sacrificing only their *own* texts. Nevertheless, the very act of book burning remains a violent image in a novel aware of historical precedents. Perhaps the violence is acknowledged by the paralleling of Louisa's sacrifice of her writing with Frere's sacrifice of his flesh. Attempts to enact gender reversals in *The Chymical Wedding* are pervaded with violent images (the book burning) and violent acts (Frere's castration into 'mystic brother'), and seem to evacuate females from textuality into silence. The successful female Jungian alchemist is found to be unrepresentable in the Jungian frame pervading the fiction. 'Louisa' is a demonstration of the sacrifice of representability required to evoke female autonomy both in her incendiary fate as female writer, and in her relation to her historical analogue, Mary Anne Atwood. Louisa's text is named *'An Open Invitation to the Chymical Wedding ...'* (p. 152) and so is the female Other, the 'anima' to Clarke's novel, *The Chymical Wedding*. The book burning of this textual anima's sacrifice is presented as Louisa's alchemical sacrifice of her own textual body but it is also an enactment of the novel's sacrifice of the Other. It records some of the violence inherent in representation whereby even a text which aims at alchemical receptivity to the Other will restrict and organise meanings. That the sacrifice of the Other is often identified with the sacrifice of the feminine even in this ostensibly pro-feminist text is apparent in the construction of Louisa Agnew's role as writer of the novel's Other, *An Open Invitation to the Chymical Wedding*, taken from the real Victorian alchemist. In effect a textual anima is made from a real female alchemist with a genuine female text, *A Suggestive Enquiry into the Hermetic Mystery*. Clarke's *The Chymical Wedding* constructs itself as within a masculine tradition by suppressing a female text in favour of Andreae's *Chymical Wedding* by appropriating the feminine text. In a similar move, the Jungian Esther Harding's material is subordinated to Jung's magisterial note from his *Collected Works*.

By turning a female artist into an anima of a male-authored novel that recognises only 'fathers', male sources as authoritative, *The Chymical Wedding* betrays its Jungian frame. Atwood's history has been appropriated to construct a male tradition which, despite benign intentions on the surface of the text towards female autonomy, sexualises representation so that it is the feminine which is sacrificed in the struggle to organise meanings. In terms of the novel's sources, the Jungian frame converts feminine artistry into the novel's anima and acts out the violence of its suppression in the burning of Louisa's text. The gender reversals stamped into the careers of Laura and Louisa seem to propel them into extra-textuality, beyond the novel's symbolic into a sealing silence. At the level of realistic plot, the two women resist the role of anima and assert autonomy (p. 177). However, at the textual level, the impulse to liberate the feminine from male imprisonment seems to drive it into unrepresentability and into the role of animas to textuality itself. Louisa becomes author of the novel's anima, the Other *Chymical Wedding*, entitled from the male tradition's text (Andreae) not Atwood's, and Laura's 'sibylline' completeness is Other to Alex's narration of the closing pages. Such a tendency for the females to escape the anima role in plot terms only to fall into it in textual terms not only reproduces the biases of Jungian writings but perhaps explains why Louisa cannot be the narrator of the nineteenth-century story focused upon her while the contemporary tale is narrated by the incompetent but securely male, Alex Darken. *The Chymical Wedding* prefers textual fathers and no authoritative mothers, and so reproduces its most powerful father.

The novel replicates Jung's habit of asserting the importance of the feminine and even his noting of a theoretical independence from the male view, but it also reproduces his tendency to reconceptualise the feminine as the Other to male signifying, the anima. Again, as in some of Jung's texts, the feminine is represented through masquerade as the anima. Indeed, *The Chymical Wedding* provides an apt illustration of my argument that the anima supplies Jung's feminine as masquerade. Chapter 6 will return to the issue of 'fathering' in a Jungian context.

'JUNGIAN SPIRITUALISM' AND *THE CHYMICAL WEDDING*

What is fascinating about *The Chymical Wedding*'s equivocations over the feminine within its Jungian frame is its mimicking of Jungian theory's intimate yet ambiguous relation with nineteenth-century spiritualism with its characteristic female mediums. Within Jungian writings, structures of gender tend to convert female mediums into animas. This operates first by displacing the position of the medium onto Jung himself or the male subject; and second, contrary to dictums that men can never pronounce objectively about women, the theory generalises about women from anima figures. It must be stressed that the medium position is not inherently liberatory for women; nineteenth-century female mediums are simultaneously an assertion of female voices speaking in public and a demonstration of the alienation of women from their own agency. Mediums can never simply equal feminists. Yet, if the female medium can be seen as both symptom and protest at nineteenth-century gender paradigms, she is nevertheless a figure not obviously in the control of a superior male such as a doctor or analyst. By taking the medium position for himself and relegating women to metaphor or anima, Jung's theory seems to suppress any autonomous potential in the medium figure as female in favour of a male-centred psychology that offers no established position for a feminine subject nor grounds to posit feminine 'difference'. Indeed, Jungian theory offers only a theoretical 'mirror' in the damaging 'animus' concept.[36] At least women as mediums could express their own alienation while women as animas are Jungian theory's alienation of women into Otherness, to be represented as mere metaphorical ingredients of male subjectivity.

Jung's textual progeny, *The Chymical Wedding*, aims to reverse Jung's tactic of translating women from mediums to animas by making both Laura and Louisa figures who ostensibly resist the anima position and assert themselves as mediums. The novel fails in its genuine aim to reverse this aspect of Jungian discourse in the cause of female emancipation both because it remains within the Jungian paternal authority and because it fails to dissect the medium position's limitations as a mode of feminine enfranchisement. The medium/anima oscillation in *The Chymical Wedding* is most clearly apparent in Laura who claims to 'see' Louisa using details that subtly echo Louisa's first appearance in the text (p. 170). The novel offers some substance to her role as medium despite Alex's narrative scepticism. More profoundly, mediumship is used as the connecting thread between the two temporal narratives when the passionate chymical wedding of Louisa and Frere is penetrated by Laura and Alex through Laura's psychic perceptions.

However, in spite of Edward claiming that he values and employs the medium quality in Laura, he persists in a drive to collapse her back into an anima, as she puts it, 'the way he cast me as a member of his dream' (p. 256). Although we are told that he learns better, *The Chymical Wedding* concludes with Laura confined in the textual anima's 'sibylline' position as previously described. Bob, the novel's sympathetically but condescendingly presented Marxist materialist, most clearly identifies Laura as medium in the nineteenth-century spiritualist tradition. Significantly, he speaks in a tone of concern for her welfare.

> 'The gossip is she's some sort of medium. Table rapping ... stuff like that ...' (p. 322)

Bob's is a choral voice, concerned about Laura's position as a medium precisely *because* he discerns her vulnerability to being compressed into an anima.

> 'I came across a man once who'd set himself up as a "perfect master" ... He came unstuck when it turned out he'd been having it away with all the women – secretly, conning each of them into thinking she was the chosen handmaid.' (p. 120)

Bob is a retired psychiatric nurse but not of any analytic or depth-psychological provenance. Not only is his 'nurse' role another attempt at reversing traditional gender categories, but his distrust of charismatic male esotericists' treatment of their female followers grazes Edward in the text as well as standing as an implicit challenge to Jung's complex career with his female assistants. Another point of excess to the Jungian and neo-Jungian sources, Bob is a marginalised yet critical voice, significantly perceptive of the dangerous contingency of the medium/anima roles for women.

Like Laura, Louisa is also a kind of medium. When she summons the spirit of her grandfather, Ralph Agnew, from her unconscious and/or the land of the dead, she takes on a medium role. Subsequently she is able to embark on her alchemical (w)rite which resembles spiritualist automatic writing (pp. 306–7). However, Louisa also acts as her father's muse, thereby demonstrating the instability of the medium role for women in a Jungian frame. Louisa appears to surmount her patriarchal anima-muse position by becoming a full medium and author almost simultaneously. Unfortunately we last see her subsiding into the anima role as her psychic gains become excess to representation: her alchemical opus is burnt. It is an interesting reprise of Jung's own appropriation of the medium's position for male subjectivity, displacing the female into the metaphorical anima. This medium/anima oscillation in Louisa is a parallel to her textual role as author of the novel's anima, the Other *Chymical Wedding*.

At this point it is worth referring again to Diana Basham's construction of the crucial position of women with reference to nineteenth-century spiritualism explored in Chapter 2.

> The centrality of women to the Spiritualist Movement is perhaps explicable by the fact that they too, like the spirits, existed within an uncertain medium whose dimensions were simultaneously literal and metaphoric. Without legal rights and representation, they had their own metaphoric power in the vague but pervasive concept of 'female influence', an influence that the spirits themselves seemed eager to enhance or promote.[37]

Chapter 2 argued that this literal/metaphoric dialectic became a key organising principle in Jung's writings and is clearly reproduced in Jungian theory's pressure to convert female mediums into animas. It is unsurprising that a novel so dependent upon Jungian authority, even as it tries to reverse the slide of mediums into animas on a narrative level, shows traces of the return of the repressed Jungian drive on a textual level. The literal/metaphoric dialectic is so unstable in both Jungian theory and *The Chymical Wedding*, that it forms itself into a continuum, defining itself as a key alchemical structure for allowing the unconscious and Otherness into understanding. This continuum between literal and metaphoric is a mode of being for the feminine in the text. The feminine shifts between incarnation as literal medium and de-substantiation into anima (acting as a metaphor for masculine subjectivity).

JUNGIAN ALCHEMY AND TWO ONTOLOGIES

The literal/metaphoric continuum is not the only ontological mode structuring *The Chymical Wedding*. It is the dynamic that inhabits the representation of female characters as they struggle between mediums and animas, and through this struggle are assimilated to the Jungian alchemical frame in the text. In fact, the novel stages its attempt to promote the feminine by offering two ontological modes: the literal metaphorical continuum and another distinguished by a literal metaphoric opposition or disjunction. The literal metaphorical continuum is the simplest form of the Jungian alchemical discourse (the literal Other without can also signify the metaphorical Other within), signalled by the sliding positions between medium and animas, and is assimilated into a feminine alignment by the roles of Louisa and Laura. Both female characters struggle to become literal mediums, thereby acquiring identity in their own right in their various connections to their unconscious Others. Unfortunately, they are subject to dispossession of their literal selves in representation and they lapse into becoming subordinated animas or metaphors for the masculine psyche.

The Chymical Wedding tries to promote the feminine by aligning it with its authoritative frames of Jungian alchemy. In doing so it fails to promote women (or feminism) because the novel remains enraptured by Jung's masculinist appropriation of spiritualism which tries to suppress the literal female or medium into a metaphor of the male subject, the anima. The novel fails to realise that this literal metaphorical continuum enhances the feminine as metaphor at the expense of representing feminine autonomy or difference. Feminine difference is eroded as the feminine becomes a metaphoric fantasy of masculine identity. Nevertheless, *The Chymical Wedding* does oppose its feminine alchemical mode of literal metaphorical continuum to one assigned a masculine position in the sexualising of the novel's structures: that of the literal and metaphorical in opposition. This 'masculine' mode is the ontology of diabolism or splitting, opposed to the ontology of symbolism or uniting, as the text defines them. Such an opposition offers at last some explanation for Frere's non-alchemical castration. The masculine ontology cannot tolerate a literal metaphorical continuum so Frere cannot allow himself the *metaphorical* blood of alchemy. He tragically assimilates the *literal*, the letter, to the bodily, as he pores over the references to blood in his patriarchal Christian texts. The signifier 'blood' must be restricted to one signified and have no Otherness. Frere's linguistic instinct is an oppressive, imprisoning bond between signifier and signified, a version of his marriage to Emilia. He sacrifices without romance as this text defines romance: a desire for the Other that does not restrict or try to control the Other or meanings. Consequently, his masculine ontology is opposed to the alchemical Jungian literal metaphorical continuum and so must be 'outside' the novel's adherence to its Jungian sources. His sacrifice *must* be of the literal body (p. 468). Frere's sacrifice without romance is literal because it is opposed to a metaphorical mode and therefore results in imprisoning the signifier to one signified. It wants to fuse body and letter, introduce the body into the linguistic process. So Frere sacrifices in a way that is intended to unite the rites of the Mother goddess (associated by the novel with alchemy), with Christianity at the level of the letter because he finds references to castration written into both religions. It is also intended to unite him to Louisa as 'mystic brother'. Despite the attempt to 'unite' in Frere's act, it remains opposed to the alchemical mode in its insistence on the literal at the expense of the metaphorical. On a narrative level, the castration serves as a commentary on Victorian social conditions that would not facilitate a subsequent marriage between an alchemist and a wedded clergyman. On a textual level, it illustrates both the novel's difficulty in evading Jungian alchemical and textual paternity, and the somewhat frustrated attempts to reverse gender bias within Jungian concepts.

Edward is another sufferer from the masculine ontological mode of literal metaphorical antagonism. He is pained by Laura's adultery but finds intolerable her attempt to allow in 'Other' explanations, to make it both literal unfaithfulness and a means of literal-metaphorical psychic communication with both Frere and Louisa. He insists on divorcing the literal from the metaphorical by permitting no Otherness to Laura's explanations (p. 424). Edward's version of the masculine mode of literal metaphorical splitting makes it clear that if the feminine continuum is ultimately of dubious value in the cause of feminine autonomy, this masculine mode is an imprisoning discourse that inevitably becomes substantiated as the male subject's urge to control and restrict Otherness, structured as the feminine.

Translation between what I have termed the masculine and feminine modes is indicated by the two ontologies being categories of gender rather than of sex, although it is suggestive that both Emilia and Henry, in opposite gender camps, are presented as unhappy failures. Despite all the pain and violence, the novel does try to reconcile the two ontological modes, or perhaps it would be more accurate to argue that it expands conceptions of alchemy to include deathly splitting, and the inability to hold together literal and metaphorical forms of meaning. It does this by deploying alchemy's concept of *nigredo,* or the deadly depressed state that precedes higher transmutations. Edward dies both literally and metaphorically: he is considered dead but returns bearing a narrative of a near-death experience of a chymical wedding. He tells Alex that he can now hold together the two ontological modes: the alchemical literal metaphorical continuum and his previously agonised pursuit of literal metaphorical exclusions.

> 'It's just that if the art is to hold two absolutely contradictory truths inside you at the same time, then that may have been one of them.' (p. 536)

Similarly, Alex Darken has his *nigredo* of feeling trapped in the literal that is also the possibility of endless violence when he goes to a CND meeting and learns about what splitting can mean on the atomic level (p. 354). Alex sees that it is the unwillingness to explore Otherness, to understand metaphorically as well as literally that has formed this particular 'diabolic' discourse. Petrified into possessiveness by the horrors of nuclear splitting which the novel marks as the extreme pole of the masculine mode of resisting Otherness, Alex diagnoses a solution. His idea 'solves' by dissolving literal horror into Other modes of understanding, establishing an alchemical continuum that can hold the horrors of splitting as *nigredo,* as one stage in a process of transmutation. The novel dramatises this process of uniting these two ontological modes in the alchemical relationships and romances of the central characters. Narrative itself partakes of the novel's alchemical and Jungian dialectics.

THE CHYMICAL WEDDING: SOME CONCLUSIONS

The irreparable violence of Frere's castration signals that *The Chymical Wedding* fails to unite completely its two ontological discourses; it merely succeeds in suggesting that they shadow and infiltrate each other. The novel remains wedded to dualism, and its binary structures provide a shifting hierarchy rather than the equality it apparently seeks. The alchemical feminine looms larger because it is the progeny of the sources that the novel ranks as authoritative, Jung and Jung's own alchemical texts. This feminine colonises opposing ideologies just as the Jungian alchemical source material colonises Other sources, notably the historical Mary Anne Atwood. However, the colonising triumph of this Jungian feminine is no victory for feminism. *The Chymical Wedding*'s adherence to Jung as authoritative 'father' replicates Jungian theory's double-edged move of promoting 'the feminine' in culture but simultaneously suppressing any gender difference into animas, the feminine as metaphorical ingredient of male subjectivity. On a textual level, independent female sources become textual animas as the feminine is designated as that which is sacrificed in representation. On a narrative level, *The Chymical Wedding* tries to reverse the Jungian drive to convert female spiritualist mediums into animas but merely produces an uneasy oscillation. It fails to use Jung as effectively liberating because it fails to liberate Jungian theory from its cultural prejudice on gender and from the weight of its authority which operates as a kind of lead in a text that is ambitious to be inspired into gold. If Jungian alchemy colonises the text, then it does so as an uncanny repetition of Jungian theory's previous appropriation of spiritualism. Bob's comment on Edward and Laura is revealing.

> '[O]ld men ... needing disciples ... and sex. Young sex ... It's a way of colonizing – deceptive and self-deceptive. Sad really.' (p. 119)

Bob thinks Laura and Edward are both deceived but that Edward is still exploiting Laura, the medium. Later, Bob is entangled in the novel's dominant field of Jungian alchemy and Alex's last word on his attitude seems to suggest a future conversion (p. 501). Bob's 'progress' records the advance of Jungian alchemy's colonisation of the text which echoes the novel's absorption of women into the medium/anima continuum. Of course, the medium/anima discourse about women is a product of the limited friction between *The Chymical Wedding* and its Jungian frame in attempting to reverse the Jungian drive, but ultimately allowing the magister's authority to occupy the text.

In the last analysis, the novel fails to use Jung as a mode of social and psychic liberation for women because it tries to construct itself in a male tradition, to reproduce textually without authoritative mothers so subordinating Atwood to Andreae and Jung. The major departures from the sources; the gender reversals over alchemy and Frere's castration, demonstrate a genuine desire to disrupt the smooth transmission of masculinist narratives, but the text fails to distinguish promotion of the feminine (which too easily slides into metaphorical celebrations of male subjectivity and female 'sibylline' silence), from representations of feminine autonomy and difference.

The difficult negotiations of Jung's authority and different writers' varying needs to absorb or challenge this authority will be explored throughout this book. The question of authority in literary texts' absorption of Jungian writings has profound consequences for Jung and literary theory in a poststructuralist era. Particular attention will be paid to the 'colonising' attributes of Jungian ideas in Chapter 7 on Doris Lessing, where the novels offer a postcolonial critique. Chapter 6 will develop the theme of a male writer adopting Jung as a textual 'father' and the implications for structures of authority in the text. Theories of Jungian psychology in relation to literary constructions of history and culture, textual gender and colonial politics will be explored here. The following two chapters explore in depth the theoretical implications of Jung in feminist writing by considering Michèle Roberts' growth as a writer always concerned with the issues of feminist representation. Chapter 4 looks at how Jungian theory can respond to a profound artistic need and be a way of structuring feminist responses to cultural myths. The subsequent chapter using Michèle Roberts' work will show how some of her later novels explore further the problems inherent in a feminist use of Jungian ideas with particular focus on Roberts' revisiting of Jungian theory's primal scene; the nineteenth-century female medium. The final Roberts' novel considered, *In the Red Kitchen*, responds to Jung's seminal writings on spiritualism in a way that develops concerns first made visible in this chapter about *The Chymical Wedding*, therefore completing a detailed study of Jung in relation to feminist literary practice. These chapters will substantiate the productive encounter between Jung and feminist literary theory suggested in Chapter 1.

Clarke's novel may be fatally flawed by its uncritical loyalty to Jung, but it does show that Jungian alchemical theory can formulate reading and writing fiction as a kind of alchemy to offer a distinctly Jungian reader theory. Such a new form of reader-response theory may have applications beyond 'Jungian novels' to the wider arena of literary studies. Jungian fiction is not only a challenge, it is also a textual embodiment of new Jungian literary theories. In exposing the reader to an 'alchymical' marriage with the text, *The Chymical Wedding* offers considerations of romance and sacrifice as fundamental modes of experiencing language. 'Romance' can be the desire for Otherness or the selfish bond to one signifier. 'Sacrifice' can mean the murder of the Other by imprisonment in the literal or a romantic alchemical ego sacrifice of the drive to control or exhaust all signification. Such a sacrifice desires the Other as Other and does not seek to colonise it. 'Active imagination' as reading alchemy may be a fictional derivation from the intertextuality of Jungian writings and *The Chymical Wedding*. Yet it remains a structure through which we may speculate on the unconscious dancing in our textual pleasures.

4

Jung and Feminist Narrative: Romantic Virgins in the Early Novels of Michèle Roberts

In keeping with this book's task of examining Jung in relation to modern literary theory, Chapter 4 will look at the use of Jungian ideas in response to artistic and feminist needs in the early novels of Michèle Roberts. In Chapter 1 some suggestions were made about the value of Jungian theory for feminist ideas. Consideration of Roberts' texts will demonstrate the utility of Jung for the evolution of feminist narrative forms. As stages upon the journey to a feminist narratology, Jungian concepts are used in the representation of an autonomous female identity, the female artist and female art, and are constellated in the figure of the 'virgin'. A fictional motif pre-dating Roberts' discovery of Jung, the virgin becomes incorporated into Jungian theory as a vehicle for expressing Jung's structure of individuation and in *The Wild Girl*[1] for the articulation of narrative form. What immediately distinguishes Roberts' novels from *The Chymical Wedding* is the determination not to use Jung as a textual master. To this end, the early novels construct a female transmission of ideas through 'Jungian feminism'[2] and formulate Jungian theory in its most deconstructive mode. These novels do not respond to specific texts by Jung and evade the vexed question of animas. Nevertheless, the anima will return, as an object of the text's critique, in Roberts' later work.

Chapter 5 will trace the critical interrogation of Jungian ideas in Michèle Roberts' fiction through two later works. By her fifth novel, the treatment of Jung culminates in the artistic deployment of Jungian structures in narrative form while critically dissecting a seminal Jungian text: the doctoral thesis with its pertinent portrayal of a female medium. Chapter 5 will show how Jungian feminist narrative succeeds in challenging Jungian discourse at the point of its veiling of the feminine in the anima, while at the same time deconstructing productively the potentials of Jungian theory for feminist writing. In Roberts' work we not only have the establishment of a feminist Jungian narrative art but also a cogent challenge to the biases and meta-narratives of Jungian theory.

JUNGIAN THEORY AND THE EARLY NOVELS

Michèle Roberts' first novel, *A Piece of the Night*,[3] was written before her reading of Jung and a brief consideration of it demonstrates the inherent difficulties for feminist art within the traditional novel genre. What is distinctive about subsequent novels is the way the texts start to explore Jungian theory, in order to transform the novel genre for feminist practice. *A Piece of the Night* identifies a difficulty that traditional novels have in the presentation of autonomous and secure feminine identity while simultaneously criticising the patriarchal forces which have shaped it. Roberts' second novel, *The Visitation*,[4] records the discovery of Jungian ideas, bearing traces of an essentialist approach to female Jungian texts and their 'feminine archetypes' as a means of representing a female identity not wholly subjected to external coercive patriarchal myths. By *The Wild Girl*, the fictional text is able to make full use of the deconstructive properties of Jungian theory. These 'postmodern' powers native to individuation are explored in a feminist text which has absorbed Jungian concepts into its narrative form in order to re-present feminine desire, autonomy, creativity and art. This novel refines Roberts' use of Jungian ideas to undo the exclusion of the female body and sexuality from patriarchal Christianity. *The Wild Girl* also investigates the artistic problems implicit in the binary form of Jungian romance which seems to reproduce a form of romance shadowed by tragedy; a structure tackled further by the novels considered in Chapter 5.

The Jungian essentialist trajectory exists in the novels as focus of desire only or as an archetypal stratum in the genuine Jungian sense of archetypes that are unreachable and unknowable except through a multiplicity of competing and conflicting fictional images and structures. In 'The Woman Who Wanted To Be a Hero',[5] Roberts first appears to see 'female archetypes' as a solution to a woman's desire for wholeness under patriarchy but even here she defines them as intertwined, plural, finding the solution in the *solution*, the fluidity of the archetypal unconscious.

> [T]he ideas of Jungian feminists ... were helpful. I discovered four archetypes which exist within the female psyche: the virgin, the mother, the companion to men, the sibyl ... None is totally separate from the others; they interconnect. For a long while I thought they were all at war in me ... This system of imagery helped me to see that sexuality and spirituality can be connected, need not be at war.[6]

Roberts' evident desire for personal wholeness is articulated in terms of ending a needless war between sexuality and spirituality. We need now to look at the first, pre-Jungian novel, *A Piece of the Night*, in order to explore this psychic conflict formulated within patriarchal society. Such a search will allow us to trace her need for Jungian theory if feminist narrative is to be manifested within the arts of representation.

THE ROMANTIC SPLIT VIRGIN OF *A PIECE OF THE NIGHT*

Tracing the Limitations of Lacan

A Piece of the Night is a lesbian 'coming out' novel. It both employs and experiments with traditional realism in its attempts to diagnose society's structural oppressions of feminine subjectivity. By interweaving the stories of the lesbian mother Julie, her mother Claire, and Julie's husband's relative Amy, the text traces the limits of Freudian and Lacanian psychoanalysis as well as that of traditional realist narrative in the figuring of feminist identity as not only oppressed but potentially whole and satisfying. Roberts' motif for the desire for feminine psychic wholeness in her early novels is romance, and romance as the object of a quest. In the main, *A Piece of the Night* exposes the problematics of feminist narrative both by its successes and its failures. Its success in analysing modes of patriarchal oppression penetrates the realist genre of the novel itself and critiques its reliance upon forms of representation that exclude or subordinate the feminine. Whereas the novel's failure convincingly to provide the consolations of *novel* forms of feminist identity as romantic wholeness similarly uncovers the difficulties of feminist art seeking direct expression in patriarchal society. If the novel reveals patriarchal drives inhabiting traditional realism and Lacan, both of which are shown as capable only of signifying the feminine as 'lack' or monstrous Other, then textuality awaits Jungian theory in a feminist practice.

To illustrate my argument let us consider the motif of the romantic yet fatally split virgin of *A Piece of the Night*. Roberts has stated, in a revealing phrase, that her aim in the novel was to 'look at' the construction of the feminine in a patriarchal society.[7] Consequently, the text is rooted in omnisciently narrated traditional realism describing ('looking at') the characters from an external viewpoint. However, such traditional realism is troubled by the eruption of another narrative voice: angry, first person and feminine.

> Don't let me want. If I wanted who knows what I might do? Get angry, start shouting ... (p. 155)

Similarly, the narrative intercuts historical and contemporary tales and disrupts linear chronology in ways that question conventional causation. For example, childhood traumas are revealed late in the text, so offering the reader additional possible reasons for Julie's insecurities of gender. Realism is also fractured by the intervention of Lacanian theory in the form of the mirror stage and Freud's family romance, inverted in the mother's too soon abandonment of her daughter in patriarchy.[8] The mirror stage occurs as an era of primordial splitting when the infant sees herself as if in a mirror, as dual, and starts to condense a sense of subject and object. The text also employs Lacan's ideas of the phallic signifier of the Symbolic and female 'lack' in relation to it. Lacan himself described the mirror stage as a metaphor for an infant's nascent sense of identity reflected in the body of an Other or (m)Other. Roberts' novel uses Lacan's mirror both as explanation for psychic pain and as metaphor for how the dominant male gaze splits women in patriarchy as either virgin or whore. True to theory, Julie, aged ten, sees a stranger in the mirror after mourning her separation from her mother (p. 35) but is more perilously splintered in Ben's eyes, leading to her mental breakdown in Oxford.

> Julie continues to sleep with Ben to discover herself ... at the final moment with her lover and her mirror, vision distorts: she is

> presented with a fractured picture of herself. Because she perceives this in wordless ways, in her feelings, in her gut, she does not know which to trust: the splintered yet separately concrete vision of herself Ben offers, or the hidden whole self that struggles to say that his vision of her is distorted and moves in fantasy. (p. 67)

Such an encoding of theory as this is an 'explanation' for Other parts of the text where Roberts dramatises Julie's fragmentation or the recovery of Jenny as a 'good' mirror giving herself back to herself, or her feelings of 'lack' in the Symbolic because still partly stuck in the imaginary with her (m)Other. Lacan, in most of the novel, has sunk to the level of a signifying system capable of organising the portrayal of women split in patriarchy. When used as explanation as above, the text becomes rather bloodless as though a man has been smuggled in but can only make it through female transmission as a corpse. Victim of the Freudian subordination of the feminine in Oedipality, Julie's gender identity is unstably structured and is then insufficiently mirrored by her husband, Ben, who denies her sexual expression. Because the daughter in patriarchy is denied a satisfying (romantic) mirror stage with the mother who abandons her, Julie seeks fulfilment of her unstable identity in the mirroring of Others in sexuality. The 'virgin' is the novel's image for the plight of feminine identity in patriarchy with its compulsory heterosexuality. Julie is virgin not because she never has sex but because she is denied her sexuality which might allow her a satisfactory mirror stage. In turn this would allow her to assemble a more feminist identity of autonomy in the form of romance with the Other. Julie is a 'split virgin' because she is also whorish in Ben's male gaze. Female sexuality is unrepresentable 'lack' as cold virgin or monstrous excess to a patriarchal society organised around phallic sexuality.

> I am harpy, vampire, monster and whore. I am pure, silent, ice-cold and virginal. (p. 83)

Lacan's 'phallic' Symbolic is explicitly deployed as a patriarchal base substance of society of which the traditional realist novel is a superstructural expression. Only when Julie takes a lesbian lover can she approach a healing identity: lesbian romance appeases the mirror stage and starts to conjoin the split virgin.

Nevertheless, there remains an artistic problem in the lack of means to represent this healing feminist romance, a problem which focuses on the use of religious imagery. Most of the religious motifs in *A Piece of the Night* are firmly defined as patriarchal manifestations exterior to feminine consciousness which therefore operate to 'empty out' and negate the possibilities for representing autonomous feminine identity. Religious motifs serve to indict the feminine as 'other', in the sense of marking her as 'lacking' or deviant, not the Jungian Other as autonomous and creative. This structure is embedded in the use of the exterior omniscient narrator. However, Roberts is trying to move towards a feminist narrative which will enact a romance between sexuality and spirituality in order to offer a feminist form of art in which spirituality can be a positive expression of the feminine, not oppressive to it. Even in *A Piece of the Night*, this drive is detectable in the unacknowledged echo of Genesis when Julie's daughter, Bertha, explores gender in the making of clay figures and in the Mass symbolism of Julie's semiotic soup when she is described as 'feeding herself' (p. 101) to her lesbian friends. Jungian theory will enable Roberts to articulate feminist identity in a romance of sexuality and spirituality *openly* in later works. The virgin will return as a positive feminist form of art in new Jungian narrative garb.

I want to end my discussion of *A Piece* by returning to the challenges to traditional realism. The use of Freud and Lacan substantiates the textual insight of *A Piece of the Night:* that the omniscient narrator operates in patriarchy as a male gaze which can only serve to represent the feminine as lack or monstrous Other. Turning to Roberts' own comment on the text, the novel confuses 'looking at' in the sense of a critical examination with the 'gaze' of omniscient narration in traditional realist form. The gaze becomes a male gaze because it structures textuality by means of a patriarchal Symbolic. The novel's demonstration that the Symbolic or traditional means of literary representation is saturated with patriarchy is its use of Freud and Lacan to depict phallogocentrism. By using an external narrative perspective to Julie, the narrator is inevitably a collaborator in the patriarchal Symbolic since representation in phallogocentrism is dependent upon the suppression of the feminine. In fact it is the achievement of the novel to identify the omniscient narrator with the suppression of the feminine since we end with Julie's emergence as a writer, in effect, *the* writer of this text. We remember the infrequent eruptions of the second narrative voice:

the angry 'whorish' 'I'. *A Piece of the Night* proves that traditional narrative realism needs to be disrupted in order to expose its reliance upon a Symbolic which excludes the feminine. *The Chymical Wedding* has already shown us that a simple importation of Jungian theory (as an 'authority') does not automatically provide the means of feminist representation, but the rest of this chapter and the next will explore Roberts' evolution of a feminist narratives using Jungian ideas to structure a romance of sexuality and spirituality. Roberts' later works increasingly reveal the need for a feminism to deconstruct and combat misogynistic aspects of Jungian writings, including the anima as masquerade, in the development of Jungian feminist narrative forms.

THE VISITATION

Roberts' Jungian Feminism

Between 1978, date of publication of *A Piece of the Night* and 1983, when *The Visitation* appeared, what Roberts calls 'Jungian feminism' becomes a conscious influence on her writing. Jungian ideas in this later novel provide overt access to religious images. In addition, individuation structures a myth for the heroine to enact but not yet the text's narrator: Jung provides a personal not a narrative myth until *The Wild Girl* absorbs Jungian ideas as a narrative meta-myth. By the composition of *The Visitation*, Roberts' 'discovers' the four female archetypes (see earlier quotation) first propounded by Toni Wolff in 1934,[9] and elaborated upon by Nor Hall's self-help therapy work, *The Moon and the Virgin* (1980). In 'Outside My Father's House' (1983),[10] Roberts describes a personal commitment to the *hetaira* archetype, a recuperation of the split virgin/whore of *A Piece of the Night* into an image of feminine completeness.

> One book ... Nor Hall's *The Moon and the Virgin*, helped me particularly: it proposes that women can be seen in the light of at least four aspects: mother, sibyl, amazon and hetaira ... The image of the hetaira erupted for me with peculiar force, offered me a way of validating my life as a single working woman who is not a spinster, not a virgin, not a whore. Patriarchy offers, of course only corrupt versions of these archetypes ... To escape

> from the double bind of mother-whore provided by patriarchy, I put up the flag of hetaira.[11]

The desire, even the belief, that these Jungian 'archetypes' (the term used by Roberts in 'The Woman Who Wanted to be a Hero') offer access to a full satisfying identity to women clearly marks this passage, a solution to feminist 'romance'. It is, of course, an essentialist reading of Jung that is in danger of distorting his theory since he never offers concrete portrayals of archetypes; they are essentially unknowable and content-free with the resulting archetypal images as variable. Nor Hall herself uses 'types' not archetypes, after Wolff, and asserts that Wolff's four images are more ambiguously interconnected.

> The remaining chapters ... were inspired by an article on feminine psychology written in 1934 by the Jungian analyst Toni Wolff, who described the feminine psyche as embracing four complex types: Mother, Amazon, Hetaira (or companion), and Medium (or mediator) ... In the course of eliciting images ... I have found that they do not stick to Wolff's structure, but rather that each of the four 'poles' constellates a core of related images, symbols, and goddesses that seemingly belong to each type, but are none the less autonomous.[12]

Jung, in turn, is clear about 'types': they are not the potentials for the meaning of archetypes but are ideal models of the human psyche; they are fictional and textual, rather than empirical and clinical.

> Types are not individual cases, neither are they freely invented schemata into which all individual cases have to be fitted. 'Types' are ideal instances ... with which no single individual can be identified.[13]

'Types' are *fictionally* whole, complete models and thus do not fit 'people'. Roberts is beginning to articulate this in the above quotation by noting that she finds her four 'aspects' as debased images in patriarchal culture and that they are interconnected. What Roberts seems to grasp here is that Hall's 'types' represent a desired end, not an achievable one, a form of closure that Roberts' texts never endorse. There are two aspects here in Roberts' treatment of Jungian ideas: first, that the fiction's artistic use of Jungian theory resists unambiguous essentialism from the start, and second, Roberts' always considers Jung from a political, feminist point of view. There is no subservient assumption of Jungian theory as a transcendent force in any of her texts. The essays record a provisional and transitional reactions to 'Jungian feminism' in an essentialist manner at first as a *strategic* staking out of a means to a secure feminine identity in patriarchy. *The Visitation* and *The Wild Girl* bear traces of this reading in their use of 'archetypes' of the virgin, hetaira, from *The Moon and the Virgin*, but build up deconstructive challenges to it. Later novels pursue a feminist path by challenging aspects of Jung's writings themselves: the founding dualism and the anima in relation to the female medium.

The Visitation represents a move from the 'manifesto' elements of *A Piece of the Night* to a more overt female *bildungsroman* through interrogating religious myth and, simultaneously, its own narrative processes. The faltering omniscient narrator is still with us, but since Jungian ideas allow the novel to construct myths positively for women, the narrator can construct its own myth, its Other, in the depiction of the processes of integrating 'male' and 'female' aspects of Helen, the blocked writer. The narrator thus examines its own en*gender*ing, and the relationship of gender to writing itself. If Helen is able to renounce her pretence of a gender-less, unbodied, authorial self she may be able to write. Such an argument objectifies the desire of the omniscient narrator to banish the male gaze from textuality: it is perhaps an advance suicide note.

Also, by using the flexibility of Jungian images, Roberts is able to explore and challenge such female desire from within the religious myths which once limited and merely repressed. Jungian ideas are used to provide a Symbolic for the feminine in textuality. The consequence of employing Jungian imagery to deconstruct religious patriarchy is to inscribe a Jungian myth of feminine desire in the processes of psyche and writing. By using the theory of individuation to chart a character's psychic process and one who happens to be a female writer, the feminine gains some autonomy and substance to her desire. The feminine is more able to be portrayed as 'artist' in touch with a creative unconscious not structured around phallic sexuality. However, the persistence of omniscient narration fatally weakens the representation of the female artist as truly independent of the male gaze which is embedded in realistic narrative.

Despite the incorporation of greater narrative consciousness into the structures of the novel, *The Visitation* retains some of the problems of the previous text. Neither Helen, Beth nor Felix especially, achieves full realisation as a 'character' of the omniscient narrator because they are all Other to the textual processes, in effect Other narrators. The novel is formed around 'twin' groupings, the narrator and Helen; Felix and Helen as actual twins (but Felix is barely embodied in the text, operating mostly as Helen's Other or unconscious), and Helen and Beth. The weakest part of the novel occurs when Helen and Beth sit down to discuss their political and feminist 'differences'. Much more effective are the aspects of the novel that allow a Jungian conjunction of these narrative selves (on an individuation model), which facilitates an analysis of the processes by which the narrative is constructed, principally by way of religious myth.

Jungian Ideas and Religious Myth

Crucial to *The Visitation* is Jung's theory of the androgyny of archetypes, which means that religious images refer to an energy that cannot be appropriated exclusively by patriarchy. Such images can be rewritten to support an autonomous feminine identity. Part One of the novel is titled *Genesis* and details the Fall from the integration of the twins in the mother's womb to the splittings and separations of birth, childhood and adolescence. Felix, more male Other than inhabitant of this family, enacts the Fall through sexuality in his passionate embraces after a Youth Club disco and Helen's Fall is the discovery of death and menstruation when visiting a dying family friend, Felicity. It is thus a fall into sexuality and death from joy, from felicity, figured by the twins as one, before difference.

> The first thing that she sees is an enormous pale face, close to her own. Not having seen her own face yet, she sees the other's. It swims, flat and round, like a mirror with fins. Like a moon at the bottom of the sea. Blank, white, shimmering. (p. 3)

Rewritten religious myth structures experiences of love and loss but the myth is no longer identical to its cultural manifestation, the Catholic Church which divides and separates. Helen's access to myth through cultural forms and practices is cut off by the patriarchal Church in the form of a priest denouncing sexuality (p. 34). Exiled from cultural access to religious myth as a means of structuring identity and desire, Helen requires the unconscious and 'Jungian feminism' to save her:

> There can be no consolation for the like of her, cutting herself off from the sacraments, their saving grace, fleeing into the outer darkness where there is weeping and gnashing of teeth and no God. She will die there ... unless some saviour comes. (p. 34)

This shows Roberts no longer trying to elide Church and religious myth into pure external oppression; she is now able to use the language and narratives to articulate desire, here for a saviour, a virgin birth into the Symbolic that is ultimately an individuating engendering of the novel itself. The novel enables the Symbolic to evolve into a Jungian Symbolic; one that cannot exclude the feminine from representation since the feminine is always inherent in the androgyny of archetypes. This Symbolic evolution plus the compensatory and autonomous role of the Jungian unconscious permits religious discourse to be re-appropriated by the text as positively potent for feminist identity.

Part Two, *The Visitation,* divided into four visits in four seasons, is built around visits of Beth to Helen, the blocked writer in London, living in Felix's flat. It charts a progress through the angel's fertilising descent upon Mary and her subsequent visits to the also miraculously pregnant Eliza-Beth. Beth becomes pregnant, gives birth and seems to suffer loss in Helen's dream, while Helen is reborn into the Symbolic, giving birth to her-*self* in an explicitly Jungian conjunction with her unconscious-male side and also to the Word, *The Visitation* itself.

Jungian imagery and 'marriages' with the unconscious deconstruct mythic structures as purely 'outer' and reinscribe a Jungian myth, not in absolute opposition to cultural and religious myths but in process with them. It is in the myth-in-process in the novel's own spinning that solutions can be formulated within the means of representation usually appropriated by patriarchy. The 'solutions' can, of course, only be temporary, even in this novel where Jungian images bear traces of an essentialist desire for wholeness. The myth deconstruction must begin again in a post-modern–Jungian alliance.

Consequently, we find that *The Visitation*'s dominant image systems enact a process with Jungian ideas. The twins, who begin in the Lacanian mode as splitting and loss at the acquisition of consciousness and to represent women in patriarchy, then go on to acquire a primordial Jungian structure as Helen undergoes a conjunction with her unconscious as male twin. This employment of individuation in the relationship between characters serves to underline Felix's disembodied presence in the novel. He is in effect always a fantasy of Helen, her Other, which the omniscient narrator has substantiated as 'real'.

'A Piece of the Night'?

Labouring under her burden of being Other to the narrator, Helen's story makes a spirited attempt at challenging phallogocentrism. Lacanian theory of the phallic signifier encodes the 'homelessness' of women in the Symbolic, grafting patriarchy onto the deep structures of ego formation. Helen's family or patriarchal name is 'Home' and she is still living in male structures, her brother's flat, just as her mother has no room to herself in her 'home'. However, feminist images using Jungian ideas of a productive unconscious contain authentic religious experience which can begin to figure a new kind of (Jungian) Symbolic where the feminine need not be assigned to 'lack' or inferiority. One such image is the virgin as huntress in association with other females. It is far from an image of emptiness or otherness in relation to a potent male. The huntress becomes a means to represent the mother giving to her daughter unencumbered by bonds to men. By such methods, feminist use of Jung enables a Symbolic for women to emerge, out of the very processes of acknowledging and reworking male structures of exclusion. Driving between male Homes, male religions, the virgin as container of splits of oppositions, as vehicle for feminine 'wholeness' can be glimpsed, if not captured.

> Her mother is a huntress, Artemis who gives her the grey dawn like a pelt ... (p. 56)

Such imagery is a 'discovery' of a liberatory potential in Jung's theory of the androgyny of archetypes so that the female cannot be automatically excluded from the Symbolic. Phallogocentrism is not the 'whole' story. Jungian theory allows writing to be construed as feminine when born of a virgin (one in touch with her archetypal unconscious) after a (divine) conjunction with her 'male' unconscious.

The Moon and the Virgin is a source for a number of Jungian images which similarly provide material for feminist representation in a Jungian Symbolic. 'Moon' and 'virgin' themselves are cited as containers of differentiations and unconscious Otherness, ways of figuring female 'completion', but the most sustained use comes with the mermaid image of Beth and Helen together.

> They are twin mermaids, the sea slapping at their tails which dangle into the water. Only now, when they are together again after such a long separation, when they hold up their mirrors to one another and gaze therein, they have to recognize their differences. (p. 91)

So, at this point, the mermaid is another myth of union-separation, twins, oneness that develops 'difference' and splits. Nor Hall mentions the mermaid's mirror as the property of the hetaira/virgin (the image that Roberts claims for herself) reflecting masculine desire and going on to describe how she can 'either play the role of awakening psychic life in a friend or companion or play the role of temptress and lure the other away from realistic adaptation to the world'.[14] Is this the hidden structure of Beth's visitations? Helen clearly aims to awaken psychic life in Beth, or herself (the boundaries are blurred), but at the end, Beth seems to have suffered loss, if only in Helen's vision, possibly of lover and baby. The mermaid here may point to a repressed narrative of damage, running counter to the apparent healing nature of these exchanges; that Beth is not only the Other who heals Helen but is also the Other who is Helen's damaged self. In the person of Beth the *shadow* of Helen is concealed, in the Jungian sense of the negative, destructive side. It also demonstrates that Jungian images themselves have a shadow, a destructive as well as constructive aspect: the mermaid deconstructs Helen/Beth in relationship. Some of this is realised in the text at the end of the 'conversation' episode when Helen recognises herself as mermaid, as half 'cold and seductive' fish.

> Helen goes on sitting on the rock ... She is weary of mirror-gazing, of hair combing. On a sudden impulse, she reaches down and hauls her tail, slippery and shining, out of the sea. Fish-woman. Fish-woman from the waist down. Seductive and cold. (p. 92)

This seems to be directly alluding to Nor Hall's elaboration of the mermaid as a psychic stage in the hetaira, not yet mature, integrated, complete.

> The mermaid ... is either sad because she knows that the source of her allure will keep her from being truly recognized or she is frightened because she feels deeply resistant to looking into her own nature. It takes great courage for a woman to begin to pull her 'fish nature' up into the air where it can be seen. This would mean revealing the coldness concealed beneath her charm. Or the selfishness behind her apparent ability to please everybody. When a woman can too easily change her hue, her costume, her face value to suit the desires of an onlooker, she come to experience herself as 'slippery' and ultimately unembraceable ... The hetairic aspect of the feminine principle remains immature until surrender becomes possible: not the surrender of the first stage to an intruding masculine principle, but a surrender to the full image of unrealized self.[15]

Hall's text itself, and not only the images it spins but how it spins them, seems to become one of the underlying myths of *The Visitation,* since it here offers hints for Helen's progress. Present in *The Visitation* as an importation of a myth of female desire for completion, Hall provides some of the Jungian imagery of the text's desire for a *romance.* However, both Hall's myths and the novel's use of Jungian images are also opaque, marked by failure, destructiveness, shadow. Even the freedom of the huntress cannot be sustained within the patriarchal family. Such a use of Jungian ideas as both constructive and fragmenting inculcates Jungian motifs of desire in a more deconstructive sense, refusing to use his theory to impersonate a master narrative in the text. The danger of a master narrative is also avoided by the lack of Jungian ideas in the narrative form. *The Visitation* uses these Hall images of mermaid and so on as part of the processes of 'looking at' Helen, so confining the Jungian myth itself which is not able to be 'looked through' by the limitations of the omniscient narration in this 'realistic' novel.

Jungian Ideas and Narrative Form

The Visitation has difficulties in structuring its fictional energies because of the split between Jungian religious images and the narrative structure's adherence to omniscient narration. The novel's use of Jungian religious images involves making psychic connections between events, objects and characters whereas the weakened omniscient narrator has to try to be a hermetically separate 'voice' from the characters 'he' is describing. The examination of religious myths bearing patriarchal cultural weight from the inside is frustrated by the division between narrator and protagonist which appears increasingly artificial. *The Visitation* offers a spectacle of a heroine questing for a romantic whole identity by Jungian individuation with her Others, Beth and Felix. In acknowledging Helen's Jungian involvement with the Other gender in the unconscious, the omniscient narrator is externalising its own pretensions to be 'hero' by distancing and thus making the text controllable. This leads to a lack of energy in the text and a fatal disjunction between its consciousness (its surface realistic form controlled by the omniscient narrator), and the text's absorption of unconscious processes in the interrogation of mythic structures through Helen's individuation. Because there is an attempt to keep Helen at one remove from the narrator, the narrator is repeating the mistakes of the early Helen in heroically suppressing, and thus distorting, its Other. So Helen is a 'blurred' figure in the text, subjugated to its ideological aims, marginalised from its voice, somewhat enervated. More able to 'signify' than Julie (because she has access to rewriting religious myths and the Symbolic is no longer necessarily male because Jung's theories of a meaningful unconscious do not confine it to the phallic signifier), Helen still lacks full access to signification because she is the denied 'I' in the text. Instead she *acts out* conjunctions according to Jung's theories: of male and female in the unconscious, with male lovers ultimately signified by 'twin' Felix; of psyche and body as a writer, and of psyche with world, dissolving momentarily boundaries of outside and inside with Beth in the garden. Where Jung's work has limited penetration in this text is at the level of narration. We have a feminist *story* but not yet a feminist *narrative*. The omniscient narrator comes between the reader and Helen in a way that frustrates imaginative participation in her evolving feminist identity: the narrative form works against one feminist purpose in the text and one that full absorption of Jungian individuation into the narrative myth of the text would facilitate. Beth is Helen's Other and the text acknowledges this when, on the final page, Helen's completion and meeting Felix and Beth's pain may all be Helen's dream, leaving only the omniscient narrator fighting for externality to the myths-in-process.

> Beth's face is sad. Helen ... takes her in her arms. She lays her own cold cheek against her friend's, and feels wetness between them, whose tears, Beth's or her own, she cannot tell. (p. 177)

The Visitation is full of such encoding of its own provisional status as writing desiring wholeness, stasis, truth but not able to figure more than fleeting traces of such *presence* in the conjunctions of its myths. Helen's diaries, which she regarded as 'history', she now sees as 'lies' to conceal conflict (here with Felix). The lying diaries encode divisions in a writing that betrays the Other and her Other is also Felix (pp. 100–1). The myth of Helen as a writer is not only the need to discover her own psychic Other and shadow, but to realise the shadow of writing itself: the gaps, the incoherences, the unrepresentability of full presence, full meaning. The continued use of the omniscient narrator in realism's mode, disguises Helen's discovery of writing and its shadow, undoing, with a thin illusion of control. It is also not *Jungian* to have a textual consciousness pretending to be separate, repressing unconscious voices such as Helen as Other narrator-writer.

Despite Helen's exploration of her monstrosity, her shadow, negative side is not fully brought to consciousness in the text and is in part displaced onto Beth. The omniscient narrator similarly cannot really cope with Helen's approaches to the shadow of writing, its 'postmodern' undoing of itself, so the novel stops when these disjunctions erupt into the text. Helen comes to a moment of fulfilled desire, of wholeness in explicitly Jungian terms: the Jungian individuation myth as *romance*:

> She is whole ... and she can see all the different sides of herself: the masculine and the feminine; the productive and the reproductive; the receiving and the creative; the light and the dark; the rational and the irrational ... Here are the twins after all ... not, as she once thought, warring archetypes exhausting her energy. The twins lodge simply, deep inside her, as images of different parts of herself, as needs for different sorts of activity ... Out of the tension, the meeting between the two, she forms the synthesis of who she is today. (p. 175)

But her final dream reacts violently to this idea of a completed identity of a fulfilled feminine desire. The novel's realism literally cracks, effecting a splitting of consciousness not only in Beth's loss but in the most extreme metaphor of nuclear fission, war.

> Aeroplane smoke tears the sky in two, grey cartridge paper. The precursor of nuclear bombs ... Felix's front door is made of grey glass ... she sees her own face hanging there as he steps through it, down the corridor. (p. 177)

Nuclear fears do permeate the text as part of its realism (teachers Robert and Anna are active in CND) and as part of its anxieties over splitting, but this final metaphor is unbalanced. It doesn't work because it works too much, is too evocative of real fear to be contained in the text's Symbolic system at this point. Since the terrors of nuclear fission try to be mainly metaphorical here, they betray rather than portray. Feminist narrative form is not yet fully realised. Yet, like Clarke, Roberts comprehends nuclear war as a real social issue which can be structured within Jungian paradigms. It will return, considerably less repressed, in the more adventurous *The Wild Girl.*

Becoming Virgin: *The Wild Girl*

In this third novel, written in the form of the lost fifth gospel narrated by its protagonist, Mary Magdalen, Jungian ideas can be traced not only in imagery and myth but also in its narrative processes. The novel interrogates its own version of Jungian 'deconstruction' in investigating the problem of dualism within individuation. In effect, the Jungian individuation of 'I' *is* the structure of the novel and the means of testing individuation's deconstructive properties. Additionally, Roberts' uses Jungian theory to reposition the female body and sexuality as meaningful and not excluded from religious significance. We have an embodying of feminist narrative which goes on to explore its own limitations in the use of binary forms. *The Wild Girl* both constructs Jungian theory as valuable for feminist narrative and stages its own challenge to Jungian theory's feminist theoretical claims.

Like *The Visitation,* this novel's Christian myth is in dialogue with an-other substantiated in writing in the traditional Gospels. *The Wild Girl* is the product of that dialogue with the 'outer' patriarchal myth of male religious traditions that only include women as secondary, as 'other', which operate on the basis of bodily difference. Roberts uses Jungian theory here as later (in *The Book of Mrs Noah*) to argue that the Jungian association of bodily experience and unconscious potentialities means that bodily difference cannot exclude women from religious authority and art. Whereas Jung argued that religious experiences of transcendence could not be distinguished from psychological experiences of the God-image within (the self), so that transcendence does form part of his ideas,[16] Roberts stresses the Jungian motif of sacred marriage (the interaction of gender in the unconscious inscribing sexual and religious experience together), and then associates the notion of transcendence with denial of the body. Consequently, she figures religious experience as immanent and bodily, and tends to link transcendent forms with patriarchal dominance.

By integrating the idea of the body offering access to unconscious powers in a far more emphatic way than Jung (although it is strongly present in the idea of sacred marriage), Roberts makes it a feminist thrust her work, countering misogynistic exclusion of women from religion and art by bestowing on the body positive meanings as a way of articulating gender difference. Such a difference is not an essentialist separation of powers, claiming the body as absolute and fundamental, because Otherness encountered in the unconscious can be the Other gender and because the body cannot govern meaning in Jungian theory, it merely intervenes in it. Consequently, Roberts' reconceptualising of Jungian ideas (as opposed to Jung's flawed obsession with his anima figure) articulates gender difference in a theoretical way, leaving no justification for a gender hierarchy.

The Wild Girl more fully explores the potentiality of Jungian ideas for feminist narrative in its use of Jungian individuation as the career of the narrative 'I'. According to the individuation narrative, such conjunctions as persona encountering shadow, male and female in a 'sacred' marriage, psyche and 'outer' world, can result in images of birth, a 'child',[17] representing the self archetype in all its potentiality for psychic completion. *The Wild Girl* brings to textuality the virgin birth motif concealed in *The Visitation*, divided between Beth and Helen. Mary Magdalen, or 'I' the narrator, gives birth to a daughter after her Jungian 'sacred marriage' with Christ, and to her text. So by using Jung to interrogate a patriarchal religious myth, the text re-creates a Jungian myth permeated with romantic, quest desires for narrative completion in such satisfying images of 'sacred marriage' or birth of a child. However, the Jungian myth is also explored more unflinchingly in this novel: it demands the shadow, the opposition, the undoing destructive side to archetypal configurations, the enactment of partiality, of limited access to 'truth' (in the unconscious). Jungian myth becomes the myth of its own writing, challenging its own ability to produce or to reproduce meaning. *The Wild Girl* represents the culmination of Roberts' use of Jungian ideas to formulate a romantic feminist identity, to figure the female artist (including valuing her body) and female art in the Jungian virgin image. The 'marriage' with Jesus is both sexual and psychic, both a physical bond with a man and an interior conjunction with Mary's Other, 'male' unconscious: Jesus and Mary become differentiated, not wholly different to each other. Thus *authorship* of the resulting gospel is a Jungian process between male and female, Jesus and Mary, rather than ostensibly an objective record of what Jesus said. It is impossible to confine the teaching to one, to secure *authority* to the male, thereby demonstrating the artistic value of Jungian individuation for feminist purposes in this novel. By adapting Jungian ideas about gender and the body and by exploring the individuation structure of sacred marriage, Mary has legitimate claim to the sacred words:

> [M]y own voice whispering ... this is the resurrection, and the life. (p. 67)

It is Mary's daughter's daughter, we are told, who digs up, copies and transmits the text. 'I' the narrator gives birth to her-*self* as author, female creativity, text and a line of female transmission. The chapter will conclude by examining this novel's construction of the Jungian reading (w)rite explored in Chapter 3. Mary's 'assumption' (in Catholic doctrine) is the reading of the novel, resurrecting it, not whole but differentiated each time, from the page. Jungian feminist narrative reaches a fulfilment *in the reader* as Jungian reading is represented as a way of 'becoming virgin'.

Patriarchy and First Person Narration: the Uses of Jungian Imagery

A major feature of the novel's first person narration is the ability to present patriarchal myth as directly experienced by the narrator so that the pain of exclusion is immediate to the reader. Women are excluded from the Symbolic in that the words of men are needed to mediate God to them. Simon Peter never moves from this position, calling Mary's speech 'unreliable and wild' (p. 112) when she tries to report Jesus' communication to her after his death. To him, Mary's female body cannot be allowed to be a site for a Jungian conjunction from one state of difference (from the unconscious, or death) to the conscious world. Making the body, the crucial guarantor of presence and meaning, recalls Freudian tropes, in distinction to the Jungian theory that refuses to privilege the body in a hierarchy of meaning formation.

Artistically, the examination of patriarchy is more satisfying (romantic?) in this novel because its presentation does not just empty out women characters, making them other, or shadows of the novel's images in process with 'outer' patriarchal myths. The difference is partly the first person narrator, so we are no longer 'looking at' women's exclusion, reduplicating the male gaze, but it is also the role of pain and negativity in the reception of patriarchy. This novel is a major advance on previous works because pain and shadow have real significance and a role in the processes of representation itself so that Mary's pain becomes the source of her songs, her teaching.

> There is a hurt which women carry inside them from birth, and which I had surrounded with my songs and prayers just as an oyster surrounds the painful grit forced between its lips with layers of mother-of-pearl. (p. 59)

The pearl image represents how the processes of women's pain within patriarchy themselves become meaningful. Pain, here, is a Jungian conjunction between differences, the male excluding gaze and female subjectivity, producing a Jungian image of the pearl, representing the self,[18] the child.[19] The pearl image contains women's pain and exclusion, excision from the Symbolic as controlled by men but is also an image of autonomy. It resists the 'emptying out' of women in patriarchal myths, and allows Mary to 'author' some of Christ's parables.

So, using Jungian images to represent the pain of patriarchy, 'other' to the narrative 'I', allows the novel simultaneously to formulate female desire as transgressive but not wholly separable (differentiated, not different) from dominant cultural myths. It is the narrator's encounter with Jesus that releases the Jungian multiplicity of the images as forerunners of the 'virgin birth' of the text itself. Before Jesus, Mary is pinioned in the virgin/whore patriarchal splitting of her culture. Jesus rewrites images of gender separation as Jungian images of conjunction, of differentiation between male and female. So true marriage is the Jungian 'sacred' marriage of joining male and female in the psyche, achievable through sexuality or abstinence but resulting in 'virginity' as an image of 'wholeness':

> When you make the two one, and when you make the inside like the outside and the above like the below ... so that the male is no longer male and the female is no longer female, then you will enter the kingdom. (p. 61)

> There are those like Mary and me who marry each other in the body and then find the marriage happening in our souls. What matters is the marriage in the soul. And all of us are becoming virgin again, for all of us are becoming whole. (p. 63)

The presence of the unrelentingly patriarchal Simon Peter as addressee shows that this is not the easy assumption of answers in the text. He finds it impossible to accept that sexuality and contact with the feared female body could have a positive religious function. This romantic and sexual Jungian myth is articulated only in opposition to its own deconstructive shadow, here as Simon Peter.

Not only is Jungian romantic 'wholeness' only momentarily achievable in the text (as in Jung's theories of the impossibility of sustained union with the unconscious) but it seems to engender its own 'shadow', as though the imprint of signification casts an instant shadow of non-signification in the unsubtle sunlight of ego perception. Myths are not so much challenged by 'outside' myths as by their own 'Otherness': it is never possible wholly to separate conscious from unconscious contamination, the patriarchal excluding gaze from subjective female desire, and Christianity from its pagan (m)Other, here incarnated in the character of Salome. At first Mary feels Salome to be the 'shadow' of her new faith, fearing her as a negative part of herself. Seeing Salome dance, she shudders at the memory of 'wild frenzy' (p. 55). This is the 'wild' part of the narrator which she fears as split off from the conjunction with Jesus which she desires. But shadow is only purely destructive *when* it is split from the body of the myth. After Jesus' death, Mary needs Salome, as priestess of female divinity, as a route back to a sacred marriage with Jesus as self. Mary's grand vision of sacred union in the unconscious after the bitter separation of the cross is both the 'Other' to Simon Peter's patriarchal bodily resurrection of Jesus (gendering *authority* as male), and the interpenetration of two mythic structures, giving birth to an author as female. Salome is the pagan crone who never quite converts to Christianity (the part of Mary least touched by it) and Queen of Heaven promoting the sacred marriage of Jesus and Mary. She is a Jungian image herself, a Jungian figure, both anterior and opposed to the narrative 'I''s erotic processes and a divine enabling unconscious force in the text.

> I am the Queen of Heaven, she made answer to me ... For I am She who is three in one. For I am Martha the housewife and I am Mary the Mother of the Lord and I am Mary the prostitute. (pp. 124–5)

In this novel, feminism is most developed in the narrative processes, the revolution, turning round, of once fixed images of patriarchal culture. Roberts is no longer afraid to let the narrative voice 'I' structure the text. In fact, the Jungian deconstruction of 'I' is the structure of the novel.

Jungian Narrative Form: Romance

Romance with the Jungian unconscious is the dominant trope of the narrative form of *The Wild Girl*. Mary's telling of her story is principally structured through her Jungian encounters with her Others. Nevertheless, representations in the text of Jungian 'marriages' with the unconscious, providing psychic 'wholeness', also require the ingredient of negation and reversal. In order to inscribe, to write of archetypal multiplicity, the entire Jungian deconstructive myth must be evoked, of 'I' and shadow, dissolution and sacred union. Mary or 'I' becomes aware of this when trying to expound a vision of pre-Symbolic union, pre-temporality, in words that are necessarily saturated with time as loss of paradise, loss of the womb.

> [T]o tell it, with much fumbling and clumsiness with words. As though I possessed a robe of dazzling beauty, woven complete without any seams or joins ... and yet sought to unravel it thread by thread ... (pp. 77–8)

By such metaphors, the myth of writing as a Jungian deconstructive process is instituted in the text.

Mary can resurrect from the pre-Symbolic as well: it is she who heals Lazarus after three days' 'death', returning him to a womb-like state by rejoining words to flesh, signifier to signified.

> My brother is a bee ... We must put him in the hive again to keep him warm. (p. 39)

Jesus actually wakes Lazarus (Lacan's Law of the Father), but Mary tells him that she did not act in his or the Father's name but in the name of divine multiplicity including the female, 'in the name of God who has many names' (p. 42). Just as Mary balances the divine virgin birth of the male by producing her daughter-text, she here takes the role of female divine (unconscious) resurrecting after death – an anticipation of, and contrast to, Jesus' own future. Jesus partakes in her act of resurrection because absolute difference, between male and female, Christian 'male' and pre-Christian 'female' myths, is not achievable. Attempts at such a 'divorce' are described as very dangerous in *The Wild Girl*.

In addition to the evocation of the emerging of the narrative 'I' from the pre-Oedipal unconscious, Mary's romance with Jesus as 'male' Other makes Jesus the Other of the narrative voice. The advantage of this structure is the marriage of male and female authoring of holy texts. Each partaking of the Other's imagery, songs, parables, enacts textually the psychic/sexual marriage described and thereby dissolves the bodily difference which claims to exclude women from the divine and its powers of signification. However, the result is to make Jesus less viable as an independent character: he is so much a focus of 'I''s desire that he seems almost blanked out by it. It is unfair to criticise 'Jesus' for a lack of definition and realism when he is not a realistic character; he is designed specifically as male Other. Yet instead of the emptying out of the heroine (which occurs through the slipping in of patriarchal discourses by way of the omniscient narrator in the earlier novels), Mary's first person narration seems almost *too full*, draining Jesus of substance, thereby making their presentation less erotic. The romance structure within the narrative voice is in danger of an anodyne note, with the tension between male and female displaced onto Mary's relationship with Simon Peter.

However, Jesus' function as male Other is not his only role in relation to the narrative voice. After his death, Mary meets him in the garden and he gives her words to communicate which are not reported in the text. Also, Mary falls into a long spiritual vision culminating in a rite of sacred marriage, aided by Salome. She meets her bridegroom in the dark:

> Every age in history has invented ... copious names for all the forms of the partners in the couple. Body and soul. Woman and man. Darkness and light. Matter and spirit. Nature and culture. Death and life ... Devil and God ... This is where words will not do. (pp. 122–3)

After death, Jesus becomes the Word that ultimately cannot be spoken, cannot be re-presented, the object of desire that the text falls towards in a slide to wordlessness and death. He is the narrator's and the text's *self* archetype, present as a (w)hole in the text, the Other of writing as impossible full presence; holiness is only representable as a (w)hole. Jesus as the self archetype of the narrative voice is thus a 'postmodern' consciousness of the limits of representation within the formulations of belief and desire. He is postmodernism as romance by courtesy of the Jungian myth, and perhaps is more effective erotically than in his previous incarnation as mild archetypal image, Mary's male mirror.

Jungian Narrative Form: the Shadow and Tragedy

The narrative voice's conjunctions are not confined to the romantic: perhaps the most successful artistic aspect of the structuring myth is the narrator's encounters with the Jungian shadow. At one textual level, the idea of the shadow is patriarchy and the pain of women in its discourse. At a deeper level it is the interrogation of writing and myth itself, fracturing and shattering the romantic myth of wholeness also suggested by the Jungian quest. To invoke a myth to heal splits, to make whole, is also to call up its shadow, its own unravelling, unmaking side. The narrator dreams a myth to rewrite Genesis, which involves a criticism of its patriarchy. Sophia, the Mother aspect of God, bears a son who forgets his origins.

> So Sophia named him Ignorance, because he forgot who made him. And his children became the adversaries of the fullness of God and of the full knowledge of God. (pp. 78–9)

Ignorance is not only an enemy, a shadow, an undoing of the myth, 'he' is also an inescapable part of its writing for without acknowledgement of ignorance, some attempt to integrate the shadow, a myth becomes a swollen ego creating an absolute, oppressive system. The shadow must be taken into the writing of the myth itself: it is also the shadow of writing, its opacity. In this novel, when myths become shadows of each other such as Salome and Christ, they undo *and* mutually incarnate in an archetypal process.

> [M]y words are lies if they do not manage to convey how much ignorance I have acquired as well as conviction ... With every mark of ink on the page, I obscure what lies behind it. What my language reveals, it also hides. (p. 162)

This authorial consciousness is part of the shadow's textuality in *The Wild Girl*: the rest is contained in Mary, the narrator's, dramatic encounters with opposition, from Simon Peter, from Ignorance personified as the Master and from her final visions of Apocalypse and nuclear war. These narrative dramas make up much of the energy of the novel and qualify, by seeking to undo, the romantic 'whole' vision of narrative sacred marriage.

Simon Peter is not an unsympathetic figure. Although he articulates his culture's patriarchal discourse, that 'women are the gateway to evil and death' (p. 62), Mary perceives that he is motivated by his own unrealised shadow, fear of his own sexuality. Unlike Jesus, Simon Peter can operate as a character as his dark side gives him weight, a trace of subjectivity not eradicated by the pervasive presence of the narrative voice. Despite constant opposition to Mary and the replacement of her pluralist vision of the future church after Jesus' death by a creation of a hierarchy based upon bodily difference, his final appearance in the text is to give Mary a piece of his fishing net (p. 138). Mary grasps the net, a physical representation of what she simultaneously perceives: 'Simon Peter ... represented the dark side of myself I had to keep searching for and marrying ...' (p. 138).

If the image of writing as a net can help to integrate one shadow, the narrator is far more terrified of her psychic shadow, Ignorance, raised to a God and his patriarchal creature, the Master.

> You will burn, Mary, the Master whispered: that is your curse. Little prostitute ... The Master in the dream had had my face. (pp. 101–2)

This is both a counter-myth to the bright romance of the narrator's sacred marriage with Christ *and* the unperceived darkness within that vision, the anti-Christ.

> I could not believe it possible that this was the other side of Christ, the anti-Christ, for had not the Jesus I knew and loved been wholly good? (p. 169)

What Mary does not yet realise is that the claim to know something as 'wholly good' casts a deep shadow because that *claim* cuts out so much that is Other. It is a claim to authority over a discourse, a text, not within it. It is ignorance of the shadows cast by myths, within writing, so unsurprisingly Mary or 'I' becomes Ignorance in the text. Driven by the Master or patriarchy's cruelty, Mary in her vision joins vengeful women in indicting and punishing a representative male. It is, of course, Jesus, reprising his role as male Other to the narrative voice (pp. 172–3). 'I' becomes Ignorance, anti-Christ, prepared to kill Jesus. The fact that this motif is contained within a series of violent, colourful dream visions enhances the falsity of 'I''s claim to *mastery* over the text. As patriarchal church, the Master burns bodies (mostly female) and books. Only when Mary takes 'ignorance' into her authority as a writer, becomes an author-in-process with authority by deconstructing claims to absolute signifying power via the Jungian shadow myth, only then can she renounce the violence of writing.

Yet the shadow has not quite finished with the narrative 'I'. Mary's last dream vision explores the nuclear war metaphor so uncertainly used in *The Visitation*, but now cloaked in biblical structures of the Apocalypse and St John the Divine's vision of the Whore of Babylon. The portrayal of Ignorance's city is predicated upon absolute difference signified by anatomy in its phallic weapons and is surrounded by women moving in loving circles. Such a scene has a contemporary political dimension within its myth. The triumph of the male signifier becomes the nuclear weapons of destruction, deliberately recalling the women's protest against nuclear weapons at the Greenham Common military base in England in the 1980s (the novel is dedicated to these women). This time the nuclear element works because metaphor and realism, myth and political comment are not working against each other but to one end. Within the Jungian myth, the structures of separation into absolute difference (here of men and women) lead to tremendous shadow inflation and terrible darkness, which is congruous with the evocation of Greenham Common as a concrete instance. And this is not the shadow absorbed into a romantic 'wholeness', the triumph of love. The walls of the city do not fall, and *because* they do not fall and separation continues, the female returns as terrible goddess, full of her denied signifying power engendered by the absolute opposition of the male. The result is a war of terrible destruction. Nuclear war, in this novel, is the representation of the undoing, unravelling of Mary's myth but it is not the end of her vision. Nothing in writing is pure shadow, non-signification, violence. So the myth continues with a final image of peace.

Finally, the shadow encodes the narrator's awareness of the danger of myths demanding their own purity since the demand for purity is the demand for the violent erasure of the Other. Yet ideas, structures, cannot be renounced for they are the only means of countering what is wrong with the world. Also, the human mind cannot evade constructions or myths. It is the achievement of Jungian ideas in this novel that a consciousness of the structuring power of myths can be figured in the narrator's growing self-awareness through individuation. The narrative 'I''s last offering is its own partiality, the need for shadow in the substance of writing, for her to depart with a divided mind. Jungian feminist narrative requires a renunciation of claims to control signifying. Such a narrative is paradoxically a fulfilment of the complex possibilities of Jungian individuation in signifying. It provides a romance with Otherness which also summons up a deconstructive shadow of undoing and a demonstration of the perils of the dualism latent in Jungian theory.

> It seems to me that ideas are dangerous. Have not my visions taught me how we are willing to kill each other for the sake of an idea, for the sake of keeping a dream pure and intact? Yet, too, the force of Ignorance is an equal danger and my mission … is to warn against Ignorance and to preach an idea. In this great … confusion, and with a divided mind, I shall depart with a baggage of doubt. (p. 180)

In order to embody this final position in the text's enactment of its own mythic structures, Mary has to disappear, to leave no body, no grave, no relics that would elevate her into a material fixity in the text. The signifier slides out of the text so that she cannot become its transcendental signified. She herself becomes the immanent myth of her text: she produces it and is produced by it as her only material trace.

Jungian Ideas: Writing and the Reading (W)rite

It is worth reconsidering the three major images used for writing in *The Wild Girl*: the fishing net, the Tree and Flesh, the divine child. Simon Peter's fishing net becomes looped and knotted string or a web in Mary's brooding upon her task of authorship. It is an image of writing from a shared source, of no one secure point of origin. However, it is an intertextuality that does not just link Mary's text to her hierarchical shadow, Simon Peter, but to sources within her psyche bonding with the teachings of Jesus; here the male Other to the narrative voice.

> I was able to join together the teachings of Jesus and the knowledge I had gained from my dreams ... (pp. 146–7)

Writing as sharing, as a dissolution of absolute authority, has its shadow myth of writing as sacrifice. Mary's final visions tell her that myths that claim virginal purity can kill and that, written down, they can be used as authority for violence. To write is to sacrifice the Other by making it the shadow of that writing, but a text is not just a dead body, it resurrects in the reading. And in the differentiations and partialities of each reading, the sacrificed Other is resurrected, just as in this novel Mary tries to re-member Jesus as her, the narrator's, Other. The Christian myth enters the pervasive myth of writing in the novel, as a marriage with death, an-Other of the more romantic marriage motifs. Mary will make her book out of bark and lambskin. It will signify the Tree and the Flesh of Jesus's martyrdom in a second image of writing.

> The Lamb of God hung on the tree. He embraced a wooden bride, he went back to the tree-mother, to the Spirit of life who hid in the bark and the jostling leaves. He was cut down, and laid in the ground to rot, and he sprouts forth and is green again in the words he planted in me. He and I have re-joined them, the tree of life and the tree of death. So I shall marry them again, the flesh and the tree, in making this book, in additional remembrance of him. (p. 154)

In this way the materiality of the book enacts its myths just as the body is not excluded from its discourse, sexuality is not excluded from Mary's Christianity. The body signifies but it does not signify only itself. That myth would lead, on the one hand, merely to textual pleasures and, on the other, to a hierarchy of signification privileging the male signifier. The body in the sacred marriage myth can signify the Other (gender, shadow, spirit, and so on) so the material body of the book in Tree and Flesh can rise from its textual 'death' to live in the Other as the reader. In the Lamb and the Tree textual myth, the literal and metaphorical signify each other in a Jungian marriage of signifying processes. As in *The Chymical Wedding,* we have a Jungian literal-metaphorical continuum but here embodied in a feminist narrative form, not resulting in the silencing of the feminine.

The literal/metaphorical continuum is extended to the third writing motif: the text as divine child of the virgin. Mary gives birth in her body as well as from her pen, Deborah 'issued forth like a strong song' (p. 151). As well as being a Jungian self image, the divine child leads back to the 'marriage with death' motif and even to the fishing net with its insecure and non-patriarchal 'paternity'. In being images of incompleteness, partial darkness or mystery, these myths of writing demonstrate the incapacity of writing to be complete, full of presence, unambiguously meaningful. They have their spots of opacity, prints of shadow, but also, their very mythic power seems to call up a darker shadow, of writing as undoing of signification, meaningless signifiers. *The Wild Girl*'s myths of writing cannot incarnate 'wholeness' and a happy, faithful marriage of signifier and signified, but they represent such a desire, forever shadowed. *The Wild Girl* is writing as a romantic quest for a whole that can only be signified by a hole in the text: the (w)holes of Christ can only be figured by the net of writing.

Romantic desire within the act of writing is also a feminist desire for female presence in the Symbolic (denied by patriarchal culture, theoretically restored by Jungian androgyny of archetypes) inscribed into the text's own myths. On a narrative level, Jungian ideas encourage a rewriting of Christianity to include the feminine, provide a criticism of patriarchy without starving women of the powers of self-representation (by giving images of separation or patriarchy an individuating process with the Other) and allow the narrative voice to examine the dangers and pleasures of myth-making. Roberts' use of the 'sacred marriage' motif provides much of the romantic and quest coding of the novel; use of the shadow and dream, much of its drama and tension. The first person narration encounters some problems in devouring the representative capacities of 'Other' figures in the story. It nevertheless allows a much more radical formation and qualifying of authority which has political, social, psychic and textual resonances for the reader.

This chapter has described the value of Jungian ideas in these early novels in the struggle for feminist narrative, in the quest for feminist identity as romantic myth, and in interrogating the binarism implicit in both Jungian theory and the single narrative voice. These fictions suggest possibilities for a feminist literary theory of spirituality and identity as romance as well as exploring some of the problems with such concepts. So far, consideration of Roberts' fictions have allowed for substantial possibilities for feminist literary theory to be developed from Jungian discourse and for the utility of Jungian structures in a feminist narratology. *The Wild Girl* concludes by demonstrating the tendency of Jungian romance in narrative form to conceptualise itself into another dualistic structure: romance shadowed by tragedy. This is not to negate the considerable artistic and feminist success of the novel. *The Wild Girl* knows it is whore to its readers. It will be read in multiple ways, but in its holding on to its own shadow, bringing it to textuality, it is archetypally virgin. An archetype, to Jung, is numinous, androgynous and cannot be represented except as incomplete, provisional, archetypal images. In a novel sliding towards its own (w)holes, *The Wild Girl* possesses an archetypal form that knows it is a virgin text. This virginity lies in its autonomy that refuses absolute separation, refuses to deny its intertextual relationship to the 'male' Other gospels. The novel offers a reading rite in reading as a kind of resurrection of the text. It does so by its incorporation of 'outer' Christian myth into its examination of writing, constructing reading as a resurrection, a taking in, of Otherness. By a variety of marriages with the text, taking in words as part of a process with our own mental structures, as Jesus puts it, 'all of us are becoming virgin' (p. 63).

5

Hysterical Jung: Michèle Roberts' *The Book of Mrs Noah* and *In the Red Kitchen*

It is the task of this chapter to develop the poststructuralist implications of Jung and feminist theory which were starting to be perceptible in Chapter 4. The use of Jungian theory as the novel's structure in *The Wild Girl* means that individuation operates as a narrative myth which organises all the other myths (here of Christian and pagan religions) into a complete story. Jungian theory therefore becomes a narrative meta-myth. Both *The Wild Girl* and the previous chapter end with a series of problems about the role of Jungian ideas in representing feminist desire and spirituality. Yet, the effect of Jungian theory on literary form is, I argue, profoundly poststructuralist since it problematises the whole project of presenting a consistent, communicable ideological argument. To be precise, using Jungian individuation as a meta-myth of narrative order in the text and specifically a meta-myth of Christianity resulted in a romance between Jungian theory and Christian structures which liberated rather than contained the violence embedded in each. The Jungian idea of the shadow, the violent destructive side of individuation, provided both a site for Christian ideas of apocalypse and a place to run a counter-myth to that of identity as romance with the Other in the form of identity as hatred of the Other. The wedding of Jungian theory and Christianity in order to satisfy desire, reformulated itself as romance shadowed by tragedy. The Virgin (m)Other author, purified of shadow by her completed romance, saw the shadow return psychically and textually in the visions which conclude *The Wild Girl* and the subsequent evocation of the destruction of textual coherence in writing. Jungian theory offers *The Wild Girl* a sacrificial Christian myth of reading and writing whereby the sacrifice of the body of the text is redeemed by the virginal renewal in each distinctive subsequent reading. This is a positive construction of the myth that does not exclude a violent Other. Violence is structured by the desire to keep the myth pure at all costs. A virgin wholeness through romance with the Other is a structure shadowed by the virgin as intact because violently effacing all trace of the Other from its form.

Roberts' next two novels, *The Book of Mrs Noah* (1987)[1] and *In the Red Kitchen* (1990),[2] both examine these difficulties with the use of Jungian ideas in feminist writing and employ those difficulties as ways of representing a more complex and nuanced feminist practice. The literary texts begin self-consciously to employ post-structuralist Jung as an integral part of their ideological aims. In *The Book of Mrs Noah,* Roberts no longer pretends that feminism can be construed as a coherent movement of common feminine desire. No longer constructing women as equal victims of patriarchy, the novels are free to speculate on female erotic involvement with patriarchal power and myth, particularly *In the Red Kitchen.* This work also directly addresses the problems of using Jungian theory to represent feminist outcomes: it explores the role of the male theorist as author of texts about feminine deviance with a particular focus on Jung's tendency to objectify women into animas. *In the Red Kitchen* goes much further than *The Chymical Wedding* in reversing the medium-into-anima dynamic and offers two structures of reading: one on the male scientist model that 'murders' Otherness and one that 'hystericises' the male text to reveal the hysteria about the feminine in the male theory. Like *The Chymical Wedding, In the Red Kitchen* goes back to Jung's sources; here, his reading of nineteenth-century spiritualism. But, unlike *The Chymical Wedding,* Roberts' novel examines the problem of Jung's authority over his antecedents, in particular through her creation of William Preston who is fathered by C.G. Jung as well as by the historical William Crookes,[3] a credulous spiritualist investigator. This chapter will consider the uncited source in Jung's *Collected Works, Volume One,* in the novel's crucial displacement of Jungian theory from narrative meta-myth (authoritative as the meta-narrative organising textual structures) to criticising it as a cultural myth. Michèle Roberts has confirmed that she had read Jung's doctoral thesis as a preparation for *In the Red Kitchen.*[4] The cultural myth that the novel inscribes is still useful to feminist writing as a strategy but is important additionally as a way to examine patriarchal drives within theory. *In the Red Kitchen*'s narrative sophistication contrasts with the desire of the early novels to use Jung as a discourse external to cultural specificity. At last, Jungian theory is subjected to a historicist critique in the challenges provided by the fictional text. Chapter 2 of this book supplies relevant background information for this section.

Both *Mrs Noah* and *In the Red Kitchen* use Jungian ideas to represent the woman artist pinioned inside male master narratives such as patriarchal Christianity and the suppression of women's histories. *Mrs Noah* alone continues the attempt to use Jung as a sole narrative meta-myth, albeit in a more pluralised form, to organise narratives of feminine desire and spiritual struggle. Consequently, where *In the Red Kitchen* demonstrates two structures of reading, the murderous and the hysterical, which emphasise disjunctions and difference, *Mrs Noah*'s eccentric narrative form offers a 'guided active imagination'. Mrs Noah herself appears in the role of a benign self-doubting analyst who conducts her individuation in the sight and site of the patient-reader (all puns intended) in a redoubled attempt to divest herself of authority. It does not succeed but in a novel that embraces failure as some kind of provisional answer to the awful success of romance/tragedy in *The Wild Girl,* this failure is Mrs Noah's passport to join the Sibyls in their warring integrities as female writers. Failure, as in the inability to control or limit signifying, is here fully absorbed into Jung's deconstructive shadow in literary form. Jungian theory provides a more flexible postmodern method of constructing a narrative.

THE BOOK OF MRS NOAH

Jungian Romance and Narrative Form

Mrs Noah continues the device of the earlier novels in its similar generation of an author-narrator. However what is distinctive about Mrs Noah (as opposed to Mary Magdalen) is her comic inability to control the narrative. She travels to Venice with Noah, an academic. After a row caused by her frustrations with their relationship, including her desire for a child, she dreams herself into a 'different' Ark of women writers. Mrs Noah, by profession a librarian, mentally summons five sibyls or women writers to join her and at the last moment a male stowaway arrives, the Voice of

God, now renamed the Gaffer. All the writers are blocked and originate in the realism of the contemporary metropolis where they are burdened with children and/or husbands, lovers and financial problems. Liberated from the realism of their difficult lives to the myth of the Ark of Women, they do not become friends or a sisterly support group. Instead, Mrs Noah's lack of command over her voices (for the sibyls and the Gaffer are all Others to the narrator) is comically demonstrated by the war that erupts when she tries to get a coherent feminist line out of their heterogeneity.

> Here I am, returning to a nice warm womb full of the nourishment and sweetness of women ... and what do I find? Not only disagreement and conflict ... but also untruths. To speak is to lie ... The taking up of positions as in a war, no ambiguity allowed ... (p. 57)

The problems formulated in anguish at the end of *The Wild Girl* are restated here as comedy: the failure to achieve romantic closure becomes humour in discord. Mrs Noah pursues her project of getting to know the others or her Others by storytelling: they all tell stories without being precisely identified with any one of them. The stories chronicle female struggle within patriarchal religious history. Storytelling about Otherness in the unconscious, and spirituality, releases the speakers from fixed identities just as each of them is released from imprisonment in their blocked egos. True to Jungian theory, encounters with the Other in the unconscious promote healing and in these cases, the ability to write again. However, none of these Jungian romances with the unconscious is fulfilled in that none succeeds in completely resolving the frustrations in their writers' lives. The poor success of their quests for a whole fulfilled romantic identity seems to be an attempt to integrate the shadow into the narrative form as failure. Employment of 'failure' is the deliberate strategy of seeking the plurality and frictions of comedy to counteract the fatal dualism of romance/tragedy in the earlier novels. It is Mrs Noah who gains most from the writers' group situated within the myth of the female writers' Ark. She adopts the identity of virgin (m)Other, being now prepared to give birth to both a text and a child. Crucially, death and destruction are now part of her virgin (m)Other myth, not an external pressure shadowing it.

> The sibyls and the Gaffer have plaited a rope of stories between them. I must add mine ... A home at last: one that dissolves, is

> incomplete, and vanishes. As my child, in her time, will die. As my book, in its time, will rot. (pp. 274–5)

Mrs Noah's success is to figure art and flesh as contingent forms and to find a home in a myth in so far as it is plural and temporary. It is a philosophical response to the problems at the end of *The Wild Girl* that does not examine the problematics of leaving real oppressive structures relatively unchallenged. A poststructuralist literary form by definition can offer no universal solutions: the achievement here is the working out of the full deconstructive implications of Jungian theory in a way that *represents* the fragmenting politics of post-1970s feminism.

Three Incarnations of Jungian Theory: the Unconscious, 'Active Imagination' and the Narrative Meta-myth

Jungian ideas appear in *The Book of Mrs Noah* in threefold guise. First, the text uses the concept of the unconscious as a site of meaningful polysemic fantasy since most of the novel takes place in a dream depicted as a realm of pluralised myth. Second, Jungian notions occur in the implicit structure of reading as active imagination as Mrs Noah guides the reader. Finally, Jungian theory operates as the meta-myth structuring the text as it organises and controls narrative forms, albeit in a more pluralised version than in *The Wild Girl*.

In no sense can the text simply equal the Jungian unconscious. A writing may derive from unconscious polysemy but it cannot reproduce archetypes in their plurality because archetypes as such are unrepresentable and can only be suggested by their derivatives, the fictive and multiple archetypal images. These images themselves will have a complex relationship with their signifiers or words. The text of *The Book of Mrs Noah* is not a Jungian unconscious, but in its voyage around different articulations of feminism and spirituality it employs the concept of the Jungian plural psyche as justification for such a dangerously loose structure. In effect, this novel is a *performance* of a Jungian unconscious. What the text is performing is the interaction of unconscious polysemy with an ego (Mrs Noah) suspended in feminist difficulties about attitudes to patriarchy, childbirth and art. *Mrs Noah* performs this ego interaction with the Other in both the career of the narrator and in the implicit structuring of the reader's relationship to the text as 'active imagination'. For the reader, a model is suggested whereby writing which permits unconscious fantasy to operate in the reading process may provide a form of individuation, reconstituting subjectivity. The Jungian reading rite resurfaces. Additionally, Roberts uses 'active imagination' here as a feminist activity because of the way that fantasy is used in the text to challenge the dualistic rigidity of patriarchy. The Ark that wanders between islands becomes a wandering signifier, offering the reader an education in feminist fantasy.

> Creation starts here, in the Ark. Love actively shapes the work. My mother nourishes me with words, words of such power and richness that I grow, dance, leap. But the purpose of the Ark is that I leave it ...
>
> She points to the rainbow, umbilical cord connecting us ...
> Ark. Imagination. Body. Home. Book ... (p. 274)

To turn to the Jungian narrative meta-myth in *The Book of Mrs Noah* is to discern a structure which cannot eradicate dualism since it is still traceable in Mrs Noah's pose as the one overall narrator, different in kind from her Others, the sibyls and Gaffer. This elevation of Mrs Noah over her textuality means that the reader's 'active imagination' is guided rather than open. Nevertheless, the Jungian romantic meta-myth does try to eschew the binary form that so bedevilled *The Wild Girl*. As in the previous novel, the narrator's individuation *is* the structure of the text but instead of Jungian theory organised to depict a heterosexual couple, Mrs Noah's narrative Others are multiple. None of them represents a singular goal of her desire, the self archetype, so none of them can subordinate the Others and erect a hierarchy of voices within the text. In effect, this is what happens at the initial writers workshop: they fail to agree about art, narrative or feminism, and no leader emerges. What is on one level comedy, on another the break-up of a coherent feminist movement depicted in *A Piece of the Night*, is on yet another level an artistic strategy to make a space for multiplicity in the narrative meta-myth. On the other hand, use of the biblical Noah story with its importation of binary structures in the animals going two by two suggests that the Voice of God as Father remains fundamentally unchallenged. Just as the Jungian narrative meta-myth retains a trace of dualism in Mrs Noah's comically non-coping role as narrator, so the comic polysemous departures from the biblical frame seem to acknowledge a fundamental dependence upon it.

Similarly, the ability to represent social realism committed to radical change is limited because the social concern within the fantasy cannot be translated into drastic political action without summoning up violent shadows. Such shadows are cast by those who become animated by powerful drives as *The Wild Girl* demonstrated. In order for Jungian ideas to be plural, they must endorse relative social failure in this novel. *The Book of Mrs Noah* succeeds in offering a meta-myth of feminist desire by the way it guides the reader (after the sibyls and Mrs Noah) around images of feminist concern about oppression, art, the body, but it is a desire that is forbidden fulfilment in romance or in successful political action. The text seems to discover a kind of limit in the Jungian theory of individuation romance as a narrative form suitable for a social realism committed to real political change.

Narrative Form: Re-structuring the Shadow

Mrs Noah makes a direct attempt to overcome the problems of integrating the shadow which was such a destructive part of the classic Jungian romantic meta-myth in *The Wild Girl*. The presence of the shadow can be discerned in three ways: in the attempt to pluralise the narrative form so that there are many Others to Mrs Noah, the narrator; in the use of the Ark story as one that can hold its own darkness as part of its signifying structure; and in the conceptualising of failure.

By having many Others to the narrator (Mrs Noah summons them by thought), and by refusing to permit a hierarchy among them, the shadow or negative deconstructing side can find no stable voice. The narrators quarrel, but there is no resolution by silencing or destroying any particular narrative figure or site. By working *with* the poststructuralist implications of Jungian individuation, the literary form achieves provisional and temporary resolutions dogged by equally impermanent senses of failure and doubt. The violent configuration of satisfied romance shadowed by tragedy is superseded.

After the narrator's multiple Others, an important attempt to integrate the shadow is made through the employment of the Noah's Ark story itself. The Noah story in the Bible is the story of an apocalypse and a survival. It is the biblical apocalypse which has happened as opposed to the one that has not. In *The Book of Mrs Noah* apocalypse both has and has not happened. Mrs Noah visits an island which seems to have suffered a nuclear disaster, but since this is the realm of the unconscious represented through myths, it may also represent a fear of future possibilities.

> Oh dear. There's been an accident at the local nuclear power station. Don't panic. Nothing to worry about. The radioactive cloud hanging over the island won't stay for long: the wind will soon blow it somewhere else. (p. 185)

In *The Wild Girl*, the biblical story was rewritten as a romance of satisfied desire whose very completion seemed to summon a counter-myth of death and war. By contrast, the Noah story allows the later novel to figure apocalypse as part of its myth: it both has and has not happened; it is one of the signifieds of the Ark signifier; one site the Ark sails to. Nuclear fears which have permeated Roberts' fiction since *The Visitation* are here integrated as part of the shadow. They can now exist within the main narrative structure rather than run counter to it. Therefore the Noah myth is not allowed to solve or dissipate apocalyptic fears: it can only feature them. The rainbow *can* be made into a sign of hope for the future but it is not a promise from a transcendent being that the apocalypse won't happen (p. 101). This version of the Christian myth is a myth of *desire* for a solution to evil and death, not a form of closure.

The deployment of the shadow in *Mrs Noah* also responds to the linguistic breakdown expressed by the shadow as the abdication of meaning, opacity in writing. As in *The Wild Girl*, this shadow is intimately related to the policing of desire. The Gaffer describes the Flood as 'a sort of correction fluid' to enable him to eliminate 'perverts' and 'show the purity and beauty of married life' (p. 70). If Noah's flood is also the presence of the Jungian shadow in the narrative myth, then as in *The Wild Girl*, it is harnessed to feminist ends by being also the patriarchal erasure of heterogeneous sexuality.

Narrative Form: the Shadow in the Failure of Quests

The chief consequence of the integration of the shadow is that the quest narratives of the earlier novels (which appeared to culminate in a binary Jungian narrative of romance/tragedy), become here incompleted journeys on the road to a fulfilled romantic identity. Quests are suspended in comedy and fantasy: as feminist solutions they fail. The novel explicitly refuses romantic closure as the satisfaction of desire: '[i]f this was a romance I could give myself a happy ending ...' (p. 288). The final image of the narrator and her Others is not marriage, an achieved harmonious bonding, but an orgy, a temporary indulgence in pleasure that forms the non-realistic and momentary image of a sea-monster.

> A sea-monster, that we made between us, a creature with seven mouths sucking, seven pairs of hands caressing ... (p. 275)

Narrative plurality is capable of a temporary consummation here in contrast to the next novel, *In the Red Kitchen*, where difference will be more sharply rooted in historical specificity and social realism. *Mrs Noah*'s various stories are framed together within the structure of the rainbow. Such a plaiting of writing claims that it does not knit together smoothly enough to form a master-narrative but instead offers contingent structures including the possibilities for failure.

> The sibyls and the Gaffer have plaited a rope of stories between them. I must add mine, while the sun shines in the rain, and finish the rainbow. Add the colour that's missing. A home at last: one that dissolves, is incomplete, and vanishes. As my child, in her time, will die. As my book, in its time, will rot. (p. 274)

The novel is devoted to bodying forth contingent structures which investigate and contain shadows in writing and in myth, instead of creating virginally intact ideological forms incarnating a violent Other. It is that very contingency which allows the reader some space to be independent of the exemplary guide. *The Book of Mrs Noah* could be criticised for offering feminist protest while leaving major patriarchal ideologies in place. However, its artistic achievement is in its rainbow form that bravely integrates the notion of artistic failure into a novel using myth and non-realism to represent *desires* for real social change. By figuring Otherness as also the possibilities of failure, *Mrs Noah* aims to reduce violent projections of the shadow onto the Other without. The feminist icon of the virgin (m)Other author generated by the previous novels is modified into the virgin (m)Other wanderer; one who can wander between signifieds, including the shadow sides of textual authority (dark in restricting the reader's freedom, dark as failure that might free the reader from restrictions). *The Wild Girl* was a virgin text in its wedding with Otherness. *The Book of Mrs Noah* is an *Arki-text* in that the virgin-mother-author now wanders like the Ark between signifieds and is also an image for the reader wandering in active imagination.

In the Red Kitchen marks a departure for Roberts' artistic strategies by fragmenting rather than pluralising the writer-narrator. This move enables the text to investigate rather than reproduce the Jungian meta-myth by going back to the mothers of Jungian theory and psychoanalysis: nineteenth-century female hysterics and mediums. Working with the poststructuralist implications of Jungian theory in literary form continues but now the fiction takes a new historicist direction with the attention paid to Jung as a culturally located historical figure. *The Book of Mrs Noah* has a mythological form of the Jungian medium in the sibyl. Nor Hall's *The Moon and the Virgin* translates Toni Wolff's medium archetype for the feminine as the 'medial feminine'.[5] When discussing the medial feminine as a myth for female subjectivity, Hall explicitly associates it with the artist and offers two major embodiments: the sibyl and the wise woman.[6] The turn from the sibyl to the medium in the next novel, *In the Red Kitchen*, indicates a more critical examination and pursuit of C.G. Jung as a male architect of myths about women. *In the Red Kitchen* takes the image of the female medium as that of a creative woman dangerously subject to dispossession by translation into the deceitful fiction of the anima.

IN THE RED KITCHEN

Jung: Historical Figure and Male Theorist

In this novel Jung is an implied historical figure. His ghost hovers over the text so that Roberts can investigate the gender politics at the genesis of psychoanalysis and Jungian psychology. I shall argue that an unacknowledged source for the novel, Jung's doctoral thesis springing from his attendance at seances,[7] provides a means for both critically examining Jung in relation to gender and in re-forming the narrative meta-myth, which is here predicated upon mediumship so that it is both Jungian (in one possible interpretation of the relation between narrators) and a critique of Jungian gender definitions.

In the Red Kitchen's awareness of the problems of Jungian theory for feminism centres on the figure of the male theorist who orients himself in relation to his material in the pose of an 'objective scientist'. In Jungian notions of gender this pose leaves its mark in the drive to objectify women into animas. *In the Red Kitchen* considers the antecedent to Jungian constructions of subjectivity, the nineteenth-century medium, in order to examine the field of gender politics which became reformulated into both the male medium and female anima figures of Jungian psychology and the male analyst and female hysteria patient of psychoanalysis.[8] Challenging Jung as an historically situated male theorist (as well as using his ideas as valuable), marks a radical shift in Roberts' novels. It is a shift signalled when Minnie Preston notes the presence at a seance early in the novel of a 'Mr Charles Young, whom I understand to be writing a doctoral thesis on the psychology of the phenomena we were about to witness' (p. 48). This character takes no more part in the novel and is a textual trace of Carl Gustav Jung, whose doctoral thesis forms an important resource for the feminist investigation of male generated theories as well as for the novel's narrative forms.

In the Red Kitchen: Narrators and Mediums

In the Red Kitchen has five narrators, three of whom are linked through mediumship. Nineteenth-century Flora Milk becomes a professional medium out of financial necessity and bullies her sister Rosina into being her assistant or accomplice if, and when, she resorts to 'tricks'. Flora's spirit guide is Hattie King, who could also be the contemporary woman narrator, a cookery writer who is restoring a Victorian house (once Flora's), with her lover who is always addressed as 'you'. Flora's spirit guide could also be Hat, Pharaoh's daughter and subsequently Pharaoh in ancient Egypt who is devoted to erasing signs of her female gender so that she can rule and be immortal. The last narrator besides the resentful Rosina is Minnie Preston, a middle-class woman oppressed by childbearing. She becomes addicted to seances when Flora contacts Minnie's dead daughter, Rosalie. Minnie's husband, Sir William, is a scientist investigating occult phenomena who adopts Flora and 'Hattie' as suitable objects for his research. He is based upon the historical physicist and spiritualist investigator Sir William Crookes, whose most famous medium was working-class Florence Cook. Flora and Rosina stay with the Prestons while William conducts experiments, and the seances suggest that Minnie may be responsible for Rosalie's demise. William's 'objectivity' also permits eroticism in his relations to Flora/Hattie and he finally takes her to Dr Charcot's Salpetrière hospital in Paris where she is exhibited as an hysteric.[9] Escaping with the aid of Hattie, Flora returns pregnant to London and marries her sister's young man, George. The headstones that the contemporary Hattie finds in a London graveyard suggest that the resentful Rosina marries a wealthy benefactor, Mr Redburn, whom she contacted to complain about Flora's deceit as a medium. A major focus of the text's examination of patriarchy is the daughter's relation to the father within the structure of paternal power which effectively distorts relations between mother and daughter. Romance becomes one prominent expression of patriarchy; a romance with a father figure which does not protect the 'daughter' from exploitation and abuse.

Jungian Theory: Exploring and Challenging Patriarchy

In the Red Kitchen uses Jungian theory to both express and interrogate dualism as a founding structure of patriarchy. Contemporary Hattie has her cooking vocation announced to her in a vision which explicitly originates from a third place: the unconscious as immanent and in process with the body, not transcendent and in a dual relationship with the mind.

> The nuns would have said that a voice you hear in an empty church is either that of God or that of the Devil. It was neither of these. It was a third voice ... I saw a cavernous underground kitchen, lit by the red glare of flames ... (p. 11)

Hattie continues to operate a Jungian romance with her unconscious and the 'you' to whom she addresses her narrative. There is even a pregnancy to provide a child as a Jungian 'self' image,[10] but as in *The Book of Mrs Noah*, this Jungian romance is not permitted to culminate in satisfied desire which would structure the violent shadow of *The Wild Girl*. Not only does Hattie suffer a miscarriage, the failure expressed in *Mrs Noah*, but the strange child figure she comforts could also be a ghost, as well as a manifestation from her unconscious. Her Jungian narrative intersects with, and is critiqued by, the spiritualism at the genesis of Jungian theory.

> I couldn't think of her as a ghost. She was a real child, solid on my lap, her head pressed against my breast ... (p. 118)

Contemporary Hattie's tale is a critique of the Jungian romance of *The Wild Girl* by representing Jungian theory as an historical discourse in conjunction with its cultural predecessor. These Jungian ideas are still capable of challenging dualism even if the dualism inhabiting the theory is yet to be exposed.

By contrast, nineteenth-century mediumship in the narrative of Flora seems to be an overt display of dualism, using the ambiguous status of the feminine body as the point where opposite forces meet.

> I see the half-dead medium shudder with cold ... She is the point at which opposite charges, opposite impulses, spark and meet: life explodes into death, heat into cold, past into future ... (p. 94)

Such mediumship expresses dualism, but additionally challenges it both by its importation of the voice of the Other and by the very uncertainty of the status of the Other that it produces. The claim that the medium speaks the unadulterated voices of the dead retains the binary form of death/life even though the medium is the site of crossover in the dualistic structure. However the possibilities of the medium's Other in *In the Red Kitchen* extend to Flora's tricks and to Otherness as unconscious symptom in the employment of the term 'hysteria'. If mediumship is in part produced by the rigid gender definitions of Victorian society which depend on constructing the feminine as Other, occult, then it also confuses such a dualism in the uncertain status of its products.

Narrative Form: Mediumship, Jungian Individuation, Creative Writing

Mediumship connects the three main narrators but the narrative form includes the Other structures of Jungian individuation and female creative writing. The reader is offered three alternatives: what is summoned may be a ghost and/or a Jungian psychic Other and/or the medium could be faking so becoming a fiction-maker. The three main narrators, Hat, Flora, Hattie, are Others to each other in a complex ontological field that intertwines spiritualism, fiction composing (for varying reasons including fantasising to escape abuse) and Jungian theory. All three modes are inflected with feminism because they demonstrate how the subordinated Other is identified with the feminine in patriarchy. *In the Red Kitchen*'s medium/Jungian/female writer narrative myth is a structure that indicts patriarchy by demonstrating the patriarchal drive to exterminate Otherness as well as the structural identification of Otherness with the feminine.

Narrative Myth: Two Ontologies

The narrative myth of Jungian ideas/mediumship/female creativity also formulates the two ontological modes found in *The Chymical Wedding*'s dissection of the medium/anima drive in Jungian writing (see Chapter 3). There is the literal–metaphorical continuum applied to motifs such as the house, female body, cooking and spirits in the novel where these feature as literal objects and also as metaphors in the representations of feminine experience by the narrators. For example, contemporary Hattie's house and cooking are details of the social realism of her London life and yet also function as metaphors for her exploration of Otherness and creativity in writing. Like *The Chymical Wedding*, this ontological mode can be expressed in Jungian ideas of the unconscious and the status of spirits. To most of Jungian theory, spirits as spirits remained a possibility, but they are chiefly described as forms of the archetypal fictional unconscious. They may even be Freudian symptoms since Jung did not repudiate all Oedipal configurations. Jungian expressions of Otherness can be fluidly defined, can be metaphors of the psyche or literal spirits. However Roberts adds to Clarke's literal-metaphorical continuum deliberate fiction-making, such as Flora's tricks or Hattie's childhood fantasies, both of which are shown to derive from patriarchal pressures (Flora's being economic). The novel further considers an early Jungian text, the doctoral thesis, where Jung takes a far more rigid line on the status of spirits. This allows *In the Red Kitchen* to situate Jungian ideas historically as also partaking of the opposing ontological mode structuring patriarchal ideology. Here, we find the opposition of literal and metaphorical forms of understanding demanding that spirits be either real or metaphorical in the sense of being absolutely defined as either occult phantoms or symptoms of mental disease/fraudulent practice. I will examine the implications of Jung's doctoral thesis later. Here it is worth noting that *In the Red Kitchen* tries to recuperate the literal–metaphorical continuum that failed to offer a feminist delineation of subjectivity in Chapter 3 by adding the role of the female writer. In this novel at least, if the female medium slides into the position of the Other, she is at least represented by a female writer, one who is also suffering patriarchal oppression.

Narrative Myth: Figuring Difference and the Male Gaze

However, I am not suggesting that the problematic medium/anima oscillation of *The Chymical Wedding* is simply solved by the addition of female writer/narrators and the deletion of powerful male figures. What *In the Red Kitchen* demonstrates is the *differences* between women, apparent in comic form in *The Book of Mrs Noah,* but here far more profound differences of history, class and ethnicity. There is no question of a writers group of these five sibyls: those who are not isolated from each other in time, the Victorian group of Flora, Rosina, Minnie, are opposed in class and erotic interests. Feminism as a collective activity seems not to exist in the interests of presenting different patriarchal cultures. Indeed, the novel shows how fear of patriarchal power can drive women to identify themselves with patriarchy in the desire to expunge Otherness as other women. Hat kills her rival for her father's erotic attentions and Minnie Preston may well have killed her daughter, Rosalie. Flora's mediumship offers the Other as the accusation of the murdered daughter.

> *Mother. Smother. Mother, you smothered me. Mother, you smothered me.* (p. 94)

Roberts' exploration of female erotic involvement with patriarchy takes Freud's female version of the Oedipus complex[11] and deconstructs it as a mystification of cultural practices stemming from the structure of patriarchal power. What Freud sees as a laudable desire for the father and turn away from the mother in the cause of the establishment of heterosexuality, *In the Red Kitchen* indicts as patriarchy's cultural imposition of its structures upon hapless daughters. The daughter's subjection in patriarchy formulates her eroticism through desire and fear: power relations design her sexuality. Examples would include contemporary Hattie's childhood abuse from an uncle and Hat's desire for her father/god so that she too can gain access to immortality, to divine phallogocentrism. Similarly, patriarchy as a myth of absolute separation (such as the demand for spirits to be emphatically literal *or* metaphorical) finds embodiment in the vaunted objectivity of the Victorian scientist, metaphysically 'above' his subject. Yet, when a Victorian scientist like William studies the bodies of women, it is this myth of patriarchal objectivity that a determined 'daughter' can exploit in language permitting a shift between the desires of Victorian science and those of the Victorian scientist.

> 'I am ready to make myself available to the penetrating gaze of one such as yourself who can not be tricked! ... I am ready to face the most probing questions ...' (pp. 62–3)

Under the cover of offering herself for objective scrutiny, Flora can try to fracture the dominance of masculinist science's construction of the feminine by offering sexuality. She hopes to gain cultural and financial support but is ultimately a victim of gender and class exploitation. She is first designated an hysteric and then a fraud by both William and Minnie Preston. Sexuality does disrupt the 'objectivity' of the male scientist, but the culturally subordinated position of the feminine means that it can be redefined as female symptom of inferiority, as the hysteria to which women are prone because they are either mentally weak or morally frail and so liable to evil fantasies.[12] *In the Red Kitchen* shows patriarchy killing and abusing daughters and structuring the daughter's desire to kill the mother as a rival for the father's eros. Hat denies that she has a mother and Flora blames her mother for wanting to kill her before she was born.

It is a distinctive direction in Roberts' fiction to figure romance as a form capable of being historically structured through and against patriarchy. Romance is not only a trap it is also a possible response to fear. This suggests a new critical examination of Jungian romance which does occur in the development of William as a typical Victorian male scientist in relation to Jung's doctoral thesis. Nevertheless Jungian romance remains a positive structure for contemporary Hattie in her romance narrative addressed to 'you'. Since it is a romance and a narrative neither completed nor fulfilled, it is able to integrate the shadow as failure and death via the miscarriage and the patriarchal damage suffered by Hattie.

Narrative Myth: Women's 'Histories' and Hysteria

The novel records the loss of the sense of a collective female understanding and support which was still a potential in the sibyls writers' group in *The Book of Mrs Noah*. This loss enables the suppression of women's history to be represented in the isolation and cultural specificities of the five narrators. *In the Red Kitchen* imagines Other histories to the male stories of Egyptian rule, Victorian spiritualism and the birth of psychoanalysis. The shifting status of the narrative myth between spiritualism, the Jungian unconscious and the female writer allows the delineation of Other cultures to be constructed as fictional but also making imaginative claims on the historical. Unlike *Mrs Noah*, representations of diverse female exploitation are not sealed in fiction and fantasy but also figure an historiographical claim within the novel's form. I am not suggesting that these are 'real' histories but that the narrative myth debates the status of representations of Otherness in a way that invites the reader to greater imaginative participation beyond cultural boundaries. The narrative myth makes an ethical demand on the reader to imaginatively recover lost female history while not claiming that the novel escapes fictional status. If the narrators are mediums, Jungians and writers, then the reader is also invited to experiment by imagining varying statuses for the text. The reader is allowed to imagine these female histories as fiction but ones that make a moral claim so promoting a feminist drive within the reading experience.

When Flora is exhibited in Dr Charcot's clinic, she cannot understand the French of the male doctors, Charcot and William. However, she does hear two words that she translates as 'history' and 'women'.

> I understand one word. It recurs often enough for me to grasp it, turn it over in my hand. *Isterry*. History? And then *famm*. History and women? (p. 124)

Flora announces a major preoccupation of the novel in 'history' and 'women' but an educated reader might wonder whether she has mistaken and that the word is 'hysteria', the condition for which Dr Charcot's exhibitions were famous in their promenade of women patients. If 'hysteria' is a possible reading then it forces the reader to acknowledge a desire to overrule working class uneducated Flora in a move that aligns the reader with the coercive strategies of William in this scene. The overruling of Flora is part of the making visible of reading strategies in the novel's investigations of narrative and power. Flora in Salpetrière is the woman (artist when she is defined as creating Hattie) in male master narratives made to perform her hysteria. When hypnotised, Flora's occult powers can resemble the convulsions of the Charcot hysteric if she follows her cues.

> I copy some of the gestures of the girl in the white night-dress in the photographs. She is well-rehearsed, and, following her movements, so am I. (p. 127)

When acting the hysteric, Flora follows two models: the photographs that Charcot has created from another 'rehearsed' subject and the patriarchal structures behind the whole scene of exhibiting these female patients. *In the Red Kitchen* constructs hysteria as a patriarchal labelling of women's access to Otherness (the unconscious or spiritualism or creative fantasy) when pinioned in oppressive structures defining femininity as Other. The diagnosis 'hysteria' marks women as Other and as Other they cannot be trusted so their protests can be taken as pathological. If Flora asserts that William has abused her sexually, 'then I am nothing but a hysteric who suffers from delusions ... a wicked girl to make up such stories' (p. 130). The shift from hysteria as illness inscribing women as Other, to hysteria as symptom of woman as Other in the sense of deceitful, is contained within the discourse of hysteria when nineteenth century male physicians became liable to treat patients as if they were frauds.[13] However Flora's *performance* of an hysteric does enable her, at least, to fracture this masculinist master-narrative of nineteenth-century hysteria. She can characterise the posed photographs *differently* from male medical opinion.[14]

> The mad girl in white. But she's not mad, she's angry. (p. 130)

Jung's Medium: His Doctoral Thesis as Source

Sir William Crookes and Dr Charcot are historical personages but it is C.G. Jung who anticipates Roberts' William in providing the model of a male theorist enthusiastically attending seances but who in his writing (the doctoral thesis) was eager to collapse the medium into the hysteric. Jung's autobiography records his early fascination with spiritualism and with William Crookes in particular.

> The observations of the spiritualists ... were the first accounts I had seen of objective psychic phenomena. Names like Zoellner and Crookes impressed themselves on me ...[15]

Jung's doctoral thesis, published in 1902, is entitled 'On the Psychology and Pathology of So-Called Occult Phenomena' and in its introductory survey of cases of hysteria and sleepwalking, it cites the work of Charcot.[16] When he starts to discuss his main case history of the medium, Miss S. W., his cousin, Hélène Preiswerk (see Chapter 2), the nearest he gets to admitting his intimate involvement with her 'family romances' is to claim acquaintance.[17] Hélène Preiswerk did not produce a materialised spirit such as Crookes' Katie or Roberts' Hattie but assumed Other personalities in a trance state. Starting with the spirit voice of her grandfather, Preiswerk goes on to produce a superior feminine being named Ivenes who also claims a close connection to the Florence Cook promoted by William Crookes.

> Ivenes had to embody herself at least once in every two hundred years; apart from her, only two human beings shared this fate, namely Swedenborg and Miss Florence Cook (Crookes' famous medium).[18]

There is no evidence in Jung's text that he is the source of her reference to Florence Cook but it is notable that he describes her educational level as 'low' and her reading 'limited',[19] whereas Jung's autobiography suggests extensive knowledge of Crookes at a period prior to this doctoral investigation. Certainly, if he describes Florence Cook as 'Crookes' famous medium', he is equally constructing Preiswerk in his doctorate as *his* famous medium who can be medicalised through his writing for his own professional gain. Additionally, Jung is insistent on regarding the tales of reincarnation, the spirit world and rampant sexual adventures as 'romances', a term he repeats throughout the text.[20] The description 'romances' both conceals and seems to suggest erotic feeling between medium and male investigator. Jung preserves his pose of clinical detachment but at one point does come close to suggesting that the observer may be affecting the phenomena that he is 'objectively' studying when the seance refers to Jung's own grandfather.[21] Late in the series of seances, Preiswerk is caught cheating 'to revive the wavering belief in her supernatural powers'[22] so her 'romances' partake of the fictional. In general, the term describes the web of stories told through Ivenes, consisting of 'a vast amount of family gossip, a spate of romantic stories, piquant adventures'.[23] The 'romances' are finally used to theorise an origin for the occult phenomena in the medium's sexuality.

> Our patient's 'romances' throw a most significant light on the subjective root of her dreams …
>
> It is the woman's premonition of sexual feeling, the dream of fertility, that has created these monstrous ideas in the patient … [T]he whole essence of Ivenes and her enormous family is nothing but a dream of sexual wish-fulfilment …[24]

Jung's possible involvement in Preiswerk's eroticism is suppressed (see Chapter 2) in favour of constructing the medium as a 'patient' who can be sealed up in the male medical discourse. At first Jung suggests tentatively that mediumship may be coherent with Freud's dream theory[25] Later, he is even more accommodating to Freud in positing destinations for parts of Preiswerk's conscious personality. He explicitly cites Freud on dreams as support for his diagnosis of repressed desires.[26] The suggestive paralleling with Freud on dreams provides yet another bridge to the turning of the medium into a patient through the diagnosis of hysteria. To this early Jung, dreams are 'when we cannot help thinking hysterically',[27] and so occult phenomena defined as unconscious effects should be renamed as 'hysterical attacks'.[28]

It must be noted, as argued in Chapter 2, that the doctoral thesis is not a mere translation of the medium into an hysteria patient. As well as the parallels with Freud, later Jungian theory can be discerned in an embryonic state both in the delineation of Ivenes as a superior psychic being (prototype of the self and the teleological nature of individuation) and in the assertion of the relative autonomy of unconscious manifestations.[29]

Jung, Crookes and Sir William Preston

Jung's doctorate inhabits *In the Red Kitchen* in the thesis's prototypical formulations of Jungian romance but far more so in the figure of Sir William Preston. Preston is a Crookes[30] who becomes Jung, just as Jung may well have modelled aspects of his thesis on the renowned works of Sir William Crookes. In fact, Crookes provides the model for Preston up until the visit to Paris when Jung, the determiner of mediumship as hysteria takes over. Minnie Preston's narrative records the transition when William moves from reporting for *The Spiritualist Magazine* as did Crookes[31] to comparative investigations of hysteria which become his resignation of 'the ultimate testing of mediumship ... [to] the medical doctor and the psychologist rather than ... the physicist' (p. 144). Crookes never suggested that mediumship could be accounted for by psychology, never relinquished his faith in Florence Cook. William Preston takes on Jung's role when he starts to treat Flora as a patient. So if William is Crookes and Jung then the character is a device to imagine a primal scene of Freudian and Jungian psychology in Charcot's exhibitions, attended by Freud[32] and cited by Jung. By bringing the medium/hysteric to an amphitheatre where femininity is performed, is learned behaviour (as Flora depicts), the novel makes an explicit criticism of the scientific and objective claims of these two psychologies. It challenges Freudian and Jungian discourse by positing cultural accounts for such theories as female Oedipality and the erotic anima. For if William is also Jung, then he is not only a fictional questioning of Jung's 'objective' construction of his first patient (since the doctorate opens *The Collected Works*) but also a critique of Jungian objectivity on the feminine gender. What Jungian theory later records is not Jung's possible desire for Hélène Preiswerk but his drive to *become* Preiswerk in the way that later writings displace the feminine position from medium to anima so that male (and Jung's) subjectivity can occupy the medium role. From medium, the feminine becomes the object of the male medium. She becomes the Other voice in the unconscious, the anima as a disembodied metaphor of male subjecthood. As the early chapters have detailed, Jung then generalises from his construction of the anima to define the feminine gender as a whole. *In the Red Kitchen* fictionally exposes and criticises the construction of the anima in Jungian theory by arguing for the cultural and erotic foundations of Jung's seminal early work. It suggests that Jungian theory is built in part upon a suppressed romance that was formed within the patriarchal structure of the male writer/theorist scrutinising the female who is subordinated into a patient/object. It is a 'romance' within Jungian textuality itself in which it is impossible to distinguish the erotic from the fictional.

Hysterical Jung

By fictionally inscribing a concealed romance in Jungian ideas, *In the Red Kitchen* hystericises Jungian theory in order to suggest the hysteria inhabiting Jungian notions if the feminine. If one definition of hysteria is the failure to find a coherent subject position, then hysteria is the destiny of women in Jungian theory as they inevitably slide into the anima position. Jung's doctorate tries to confine romance to the subjectivity of his patient in order to keep its contaminating fantasy and eroticism away from his own constructed position as a theorist. Fiction can hystericise theory by exploring the Otherness of the 'romance' described by Jung in CW1, and by challenging the empirical claims of theory itself. Only by this hystericising move articulated by *In the Red Kitchen*, can the denied feminine subject position contained in the role of medium, be re-imagined. Fiction hystericises theory because it portrays the Otherness suppressed in its genesis.

To be fair to Jung, it is worth noting that Jungian theory does privilege fiction in the relation between archetypal images and archetypes and in the retention of fluidity in defining the products of the unconscious. Therefore the narrative myth of *In the Red Kitchen* is both Jungian and an hysterical version of Jung, a critique of the theory. I have already argued that the relation between the three main narrators, King Hat, Flora and Hattie, could be one of mediumship, of a Jungian 'romance' with the unconscious, or of the fictional imagination. If we take the Jungian dimension, then each is the Other of each other and frustrates dualism by the tripartite form. This is a Jungian structure which does not reproduce the mere suppression of the feminine to the anima position as in *The Chymical Wedding* since all narrators are female and, despite profound differences, are linked by patriarchal suffering. They are not animas in that they do not become subordinated Others to a masculine voice and they remain writers; female artists. The narrators first contact each Other in times of psychic need structured by patriarchal oppression, such as contemporary Hattie's fantasies of being an Egyptian princess at a time when she fears abuse. Yet these Jungian Others are also mediums, so recovering the site suppressed in Jungian masculinist 'objectivity' in CW1 and later.

They are also fiction-makers and so frustrate a potential dualism of medium/anima. In addition, these Jungian Others offer a powerful role to the female artist in resisting patriarchal definitions and exploring feminine subjectivity by hystericising male theory. *In the Red Kitchen*'s narrative myth exploits the fictional potentialities of Jungian theory while countering and critiquing the coercive gender formulations by situating them in culture and history. The novel treats Jungian ideas as an historical discourse while using them to structure possibilities for the contemporary feminist artist.

Two Models of Reading: Hysteria or Murder

In exploiting Jungian resources for the feminist artist, *In the Red Kitchen* uses Jungian ideas to offer two competing models of reading: that of reading hysterically or reading as murder. The shifting nature of the narrative myth from medium, to Jungian, to fiction-maker, a version of the literal metaphorical continuum, suggests that the reader needs to follow the myth as a guide rather than any particular narrator. Earlier I discussed how the reader is invited to overrule Flora in her translation of 'Isterry'. Flora and Minnie's narratives also disagree on the sequence of events and their interpretation. When Minnie describes her smug patronage of the poor but honest medium, Flora's narrative suggests bribery to forestall the revelation of Minnie's murder of Rosalie (pp. 90–8). Similarly there is uncertainty as to which spectral Hattie Flora encounters as a medium: the London cookery writer of the 1980s or the Egyptian princess, Hat. Also, we cannot be sure when Flora is employing tricks or when the manifestations are 'genuine'. The narrative myth suggests that we read the fragmentary and contradictory nature of the text hysterically, as a series of Other voices whose status we cannot verify. The reader can experience the inability to find a secure subject position by deciding not to privilege one narrator above an-Other. Such an hysterical reading is an advance in the reader's participation in *The Book of Mrs Noah* where the chief narrator was chosen for us in Mrs Noah. This move relegated feminist critique of patriarchal structures in other times and cultures to a subordinate position as fiction and fantasies of her Others, the sibyls and Gaffer. Thus hysterical reading of *In the Red Kitchen* is a feminist act because it is an act of solidarity with *all* the narrators, recognising their differences but suspending disbelief in their 'histories' of subordination under patriarchy. The sibyls writers group from *Mrs Noah* cannot operate in the text but can re-form in the mind of the hysterical reader.

However, the hysterical model of reading is a *choice* to employ a literal-metaphorical continuum in reading: the narrators are offering literal truth which could slide into metaphorical fantasy. The text also tempts the reader to overrule Flora, thereby asserting the superior education of one such as Minnie Preston. Minnie is ghastly rather than ghostly in her enthusiasm for class dominance and patriarchal power and this reader at least is sorely tempted to censor her self-justifying narration in favour of the more sympathetic and abused Flora. Nevertheless, if Minnie is a making visible of the ethics and power relations involved in overruling Flora, the downgrading of her narrative excises *her* victimisation under the sexual demands of William, leading to her excessive childbearing and fears of subsequent death. If the reader mutilates the text to form a coherent logical account, then that is to murder some of the Otherness in the disparate voices; a move which this novel identifies as enacting patriarchal suppression of feminine experience. Minnie Preston's role is both a critique of class oppression and a tempting of the reader to exact a reciprocal revenge. It is also an attempt to give a voice to a female child murderer who is also oppressed.

Feminist action as a collective manifestation is absent from the text of *In the Red Kitchen* but it is written into the reading practices in an attempt to address at a profound level issues of feminine cultural difference yet express a common need for support. Perhaps it is a feminism modelled as hysteria here, in the narrative myth that encourages the reading practice of hysteria, the maintaining of a shifting subject position in the processing of the text. To do otherwise is reading as the murder of the Other. To become Minnie in suppressing Flora's resonant translation of 'women and history' is also to remember Minnie's possible suffocation of Rosalie. Becoming Minnie, the text suggests, means smothering some Other voice in the novel. However, Minnie is also the difficulty of reading hysterically in maintaining imaginative participation in an Otherness which initially we may find repugnant. The reward for overcoming repugnance and reading hysterically (which does not mean ignoring the violence perpetrated by Minnie and Hat) is to see the patriarchal identified woman as also a victim; to recover imaginatively more of 'women and history', as Flora puts it.

Jungian Theory's Shadow and the Two Reading Practices

The achievement of the use of Jung in the narrative myth of *In the Red Kitchen* is in its recovery of Jung as an historical site of women and history as well as the ability to structure an hysterical text. The result is a Jungian hysterical text which incarnates otherness without forming a coherent, hermetically sealed master-narrative which would cast a destructive shadow. In making Jung hysterical, the shadow of the empirical claims of his theory, in fictionality and suppressed romances with the medium/patient, becomes a vital component of the formal expression of the text. *In the Red Kitchen* describes Jungian theory's shadow as an hysteria concealed in its own scientific and empirical claims. The novel succeeds in using this investigation of the history of Jungian ideas to offer a feminist exploration of reading strategies within a model for a feminist practices. Such a model respects difference as well as criticising a coercive and murderous form of reading which would replicate forms of power inscribed as patriarchal structures in the text itself. What *In the Red Kitchen* ably demonstrates is the ability of Jungian theory to contribute to feminist theory and feminist writing. It is a contribution made all the more potent when the resulting fiction can simultaneously subject Jungian discourse to a poststructualist and historicist critique.

Jungian Theory and the Fiction of Michèle Roberts

This chapter has considered the far more sophisticated uses of Jungian ideas for feminist purposes in two of Roberts' later novels. *The Book of Mrs Noah* developed the Jungian romantic narrative meta-myth both to test the concept of active imagination as a reading model and to investigate the notion of the shadow as a way of formulating social and textual power relations. By responding feminism's evolving understanding of difference, the novel produced a comic writer-narrator unable to control her text but who could use Jungian ideas to investigate the role of feminine creativity in both body and art. *In the Red Kitchen* represents a major artistic departure in that it fragments the writer-narrator in order to frustrate one dualistic power relation with the text (still shadowing Mrs Noah) and to situate a Jungian discourse historically so as to investigate the gender politics at its conception in the 'mothers', the nineteenth-century female mediums. The novel succeeds in delineating a narrative form that is both Jungian and a critique of Jungian theory's empirical and objective claims by its use of the seminal text of Jung's doctoral dissertation. *In the Red Kitchen* incorporates feminist practice in its narrative form by the necessary imaginative participation in Otherness and in the contrasting models for reading it offers: the hysterical or the murdering reader.

To return to the novels considered in Chapter 4, one might wonder why Roberts felt the need to develop a more critical and contingent attitude to Jungian ideas when her work always demonstrated the desire not to take Jung as a master narrative, 'fathering' her texts. This desire was apparent in three ways: the employment of female 'mediums' for Jungian ideas (*The Moon and The Virgin*, Toni Wolff), interest in the deconstructive possibilities of Jungian theory to challenge patriarchal myths and in reconceptualising the importance of the body in individuation in order to recover the despised feminine body. The early novels show Roberts using Jung to formulate an immanent spirituality, connected to bodily desires and not trancendentally separate from them. These novels desire an immanent connection to the body of Jungian writing, but do not completely succeed in expunging the traces of a transcendent Jungian authority in the fiction. Such traces are discernible in the devastating return of the shadow to frustrate feminist romance in *The Wild Girl* and in *The Book of Mrs Noah*'s inability to explode the fundamental binary form of the biblical narrative (and Jungian ideas). It is *In the Red Kitchen* which succeeds in formulating an immanent rather than a transcendent relation to Jungian ideas by participating in and breaking apart the body of his text to reveal the hysteria in the theory. Where *The Wild Girl* revealed the poststructuralist drive within Jungian literary form, *Mrs Noah* was able to make use of this drive for feminist theoretical purposes. *In the Red Kitchen* goes even further in being able to turn Jung's poststructuralism against the theory itself in an historicist construction which is also a powerful feminist critique. The anima as cultural and patriarchal masquerade is exposed. Yet, just as feminist theories have been here deployed to critique Jungian discourse, Roberts' novels also demonstrate the potential of 'hysterical Jung' to contribute to a feminist literary theories of histories/Isterries and reading. The early novels explored in Chapter 4 suggested possible Jungian feminist literary theories of writing, the body and sexuality, identity, romance and spirituality. The following chapter will examine the artistic and political implications of a determined attempt to adopt Jung as a transcendent authority. Finally, I will consider Doris Lessing's space fiction as a sophisticated investigation of colonial politics within Jungian theory.

6

Jung, Literature and Fascism: *Hopeful Monsters* by Nicholas Mosley

> The real danger signal is not the fiery sign that hung over Germany, but the unleashing of atomic energy … Will this knowledge inspire us to a great inner transformation of mind …?[1]
>
> C.G. Jung, *Essays on Contemporary Events*, 1946

It is time to look at a literary application of Jungian theory to a subject controversial in Jung's personal career: the rise of fascism in Nazi Germany. In previous chapters I have argued that Roberts' feminist fiction works with the grain of Jungian theory in developing and exploiting its poststructuralist implications. Now I want to employ an historicist approach to a text which desires Jungian ideas as a strata of unimpeachable authority, a secure metanarrative. When a literary text's subject is violence and fascism and is permeated by the desire for Jungian discourse as textual power, what then are the theoretical implications? What happens when Jungian theory colonises all aspects of a text which aims to account for histories and cultures?

Of all the novels considered by this book, *Hopeful Monsters* by Nicholas Mosley uses Jungian ideas as most authoritative and is least successful in its execution.[2] This chapter will argue that the novel is deeply flawed because it uses Jungian theory as a transcendent authority which dismisses historical and cultural specificity in a text concerned with the rise of European fascism. Whereas *The Chymical Wedding* displayed a naive faith in Jungian theory on gender, its interest in Jungian source material and notions of fictionality preclude that text from erecting Jungian ideas as a sole and stable governing authority. Michèle Roberts' creative experimentations with Jungian theory culminated in a pertinent critique of his writings, while her feminist stance with its stress on notions of gender difference, inequalities and deconstructive properties, mitigated against the early novels constructing Jung as a textual master. By complete contrast, *Hopeful Monsters* tries to use Jungian theory to evade history by offering a means of transcending differences of gender, class, culture and race which are contained in the historical record. The text provides for its author an exchange of fathers: Oswald Mosley, the British Fascist leader[3] is replaced by C.G. Jung, whose authority is transcendent in that his theories are the operating system of the novel, pretending to explain (and so marginalise) historical processes. This structure can be seen nakedly displayed in Mosley's two-volume biography of his father, *Rules of the Game, Beyond the Pale,*[4] where he quotes Jung to explain Hitler as the German psychic shadow.[5] Hitler's hypnotic power is understood as a mass projection from the repressed inferior side of the Germanic psyche, a glib explanation which, for Jung, usefully ignores cultural history. Using Jung as a transcendent authority able to explain other ideologies and comprehend historical events denies historical embodiment to Jungian discourse. It denies that the valuable concept of the shadow might apply to Jungian theory itself and, most importantly, it ignores Jung's anti-Semitic and political shadow, explored in Chapter 2. *Hopeful Monsters'* refusal to question its own Jungian structure, formed from theories of individuation, results both in the colonising of difference, and the suppressing of the body and mothering. Suppression of the body results in evocation of transcendent bodiless beings, 'angels', as the goal of individuation. These 'angels' then cast their textual shadow in the body as machine.

The hopeful monsters in this novel are the salamanders that Max, one of the two narrators, experiments upon in order to find out about the effects of the environment on reproduction and whether beauty might encourage the development of superior mutants. Subsequently, Max and his love, Eleanor, try to evade the dualism of Jungian romance/tragedy by enacting romance-as-network, a web of lovers and friends aimed at integrating shadow forces into romance. They become 'hopeful monsters' reproducing differently through the network, but their playing out of Jungian theory causes the network to resemble an individuated elite. Adopting Jung as a master-text, *Hopeful Monsters* describes the evolution of a master-race, albeit with benign and apparently non-political desires. The final hopeful monster is the reader, but the form of guided active imagination that the text offers is stifling. Since there is no evading Jungian authority, there is no evading the text's authority. The reader as hopeful monster is a colonised subject in a text that operates as a modernist desire machine.[6]

Hopeful Monsters is sincere in its narratological idealism. It genuinely desires to be a fruitful fusing of power and love which would erect a labyrinth of connections in order to provide for the 'great inner transformation of mind'[7] that Jung spoke of as the necessary evolution to avoid destruction in nuclear war. Yet in order to be hopeful, the novel concedes the necessity to supersede difference. Without difference all things can be unproblematically connected, and so all can be subject to change wrought by the potency of Jungian ideas described as wholly positive. Max works on the development of the atom bomb so, therefore, in this novel, nuclear technology is described as potentially beneficial as long as it is Jungian in stimulating mental evolution in the individuating network of love. Unfortunately, the unacknowledged and unspoken shadow side of this doctrine is that power and responsibility are safe only with an elite, here a Jungian individuation elite. Such an elite is a fusion of power and love under the transcendent authority of Jungian ideas: its shadow side is pure power that erases difference, the body, history. Just as *The Chymical Wedding* reproduced the Jungian drive to marginalise the feminine by not examining in sufficiently critical terms the move to turn mediums into animas, so *Hopeful Monsters* reproduces Jung's drive for cultural power by totally failing to consider Jung's historical and political role. The result for the individuating reader of *Hopeful Monsters'* formation of a Jungian aesthetic of power and love is the text as a colonising, machine-like body, a topic perceptible in the novel's strategies themselves.

AUTHOR AND FATHERS

Hopeful Monsters' author, Nicholas Mosley, was born in 1923, the second child and eldest son of Sir Oswald Mosley and Lady Cynthia Mosley. He was old enough to serve in the Second World War and to visit his father in his internment in Holloway prison during leaves from the front. Nicholas Mosley was never as an adult a member of any of his father's organisations and records in the biography increasing distance from his father on political and religious grounds.

> I had long since become convinced of the justness of the Second World War; I had become something of a Christian, and an anti-racialist ... The argument which I came to see with increasing passion as an area for battle was on the grounds not only that I thought his apartheid racialism ethically wrong (it seemed to me that simplification by separation was to do with death: evolution of life depended on the acceptance of ever greater connections and complexities) but that I thought his present attitudes and activities were evidence of his, and perhaps all Fascists' tendencies to self-destruction.[8]

Here Mosley affirms his principle of connectedness which informs *Hopeful Monsters* but does not allow that a connectedness without a recognition of difference is itself a structure of power which colonises the weaker vessel. The biography of Oswald Mosley contains a clue to the flawed nature of the exchange of fathers that *Hopeful Monsters* enacts, in its remark that Oswald Mosley became an admirer of Jung during the war.[9] By not treating Jung as an historical and political figure, the novel suppresses the proximity of Jungian discourse and fascist practice. The ignoring of the connections between historical Jung and contemporary fascist politics which exists in Jung's voluntary participation in early Nazi Germany[10] means that *Hopeful Monsters* attempts to exchange a biological and historical father for a transcendent textual icon of paternal power. Such a strategy occludes Jung's historical activities and his *volkisch* identity[11] linking him to Nazi culture. In an interview, Mosley situates his artistic practice most closely to Jungian theory by stating that his dense use of imagery is not arbitrary 'because I think there is some common fund of archetypal imagery (in something akin to Jung's sense) which almost everyone has and which can be tapped by these words'.[12] Significantly, when Jung is mentioned in the novel, he is mythologised, removed from historical accountability.

> Here the summer term has ended. The Wise Old Man and his Witches' Coven have all gone over the hill.
>
> By this I mean – Professor Jung has completed his seminars ... (p. 495)

Eleanor studies with Jung and eventually becomes a Jungian analyst. She writes a book which 'elaborates' Jung's ideas on alchemy (p. 540), just as Max's crucial work in physics before the outbreak of war concerns a conception of alchemy that is a clearly Jungian (but not attributed to Jung).

> Alchemists had talked as if they were concerned with the physical transformation of matter, but ... it seemed that they themselves might have felt that there was something different going on. You said 'They were trying to examine ways in which there might be connections between the inside and outside worlds ...' (p. 467)

Alchemy is used as a bonding motif in a novel structured on the premise of individuation; first of the characters and then the reader. Alchemic individuation binds the novel's discourses of philosophy, physics, art, psychology because all these become motifs in the active imagination of the characters. The novel offers a very limited definition of Jung's active imagination in order to erect a flimsy fence between the novel's strategies and Jungian theory.

> Jung and his coven of witches here advocate what they call 'active imagination' – you let consciousness go, and then messages come in from an unconscious that is said to be universal. But why should such a game between consciousness and unconsciousness be to do with reality? It seems to me that anything called 'reality' would have to be a to and fro between oneself and the outside world. (p. 497)

Hopeful Monsters' larger definition of active imagination whereby the unconscious is bonded to the world is also congruent with Jungian theory. In the first place, the image used to stimulate active imagination can come from elsewhere, such as the analyst in the analytic frame. Second, Jungian ideas speak of the unconscious becoming wedded to the world in a third form of conjunction.[13] Also, *Hopeful Monsters* is designed to provoke the individuation of the reader by positing reading as active imagination. Mosley suggests this by his comment that his imagery draws on a collective fund of archetypal imagery common to the reader. By that remark, Mosley may believe that the *content* of his images is archetypal, but if we take the strict Jungian definition of the archetype as being content free, reading as active imagination is not invalidated. A word can stand for an image offered by the analyst in the traditional Jungian analytic frame. The word provokes an image which will be shaped by the archetypal pressures and the cultural history of the reader. The action of archetypal pressures within the reader's psyche on images generated by reading is a form of active imagination and thus develops individuation. *Hopeful Monsters'* crucial flaw in its employment of active imagination is that it does not question the power implications of its relationship with the reader. Questions of power and authority are acute when a novel forms a coherent text supplying a filtered network of images to a particular ideological end in a way designed to affect the subjectivity of the reader. In this sense the Jungian reading rite can become an ideological colonisation of the reader. This flaw figures in the text itself in the absence of questioning of the analytic relation in connection to Jungian psychology. Whereas Max's mother's Freudian practice is shown through her perilous enacting of the Oedipal myth with her son, Eleanor's Jungian activities in later life are presumed to be absolutely beneficial.

STYLE, PLOT AND JUNGIAN ROMANCE IN NARRATIVE FORM

The framing plot of *Hopeful Monsters* is straightforward. The two narrators, Eleanor and Max, address their narratives to each other and carry out their Jungian sacred marriage textually and erotically, becoming legally married when Max takes Eleanor to England just before the Second World War. Both ponder the violence in their societies and in themselves. Since they are operating on Jungian principles, they aim to integrate the shadow as a way of containing and transforming violent drives. They do this in two ways: first, they refuse Jungian romance as a dualism and so integrate other lovers and friends into an affective, individuating network; and second, they meditate upon the images offered by contemporary European intellectual and political events to stimulate their active imagination. Max is the English son of a Freudian mother and biologist father, while Eleanor is the German daughter of a philosopher father and Jewish communist activist mother. Their Jungian romance produces webs of imagery throughout the novel and the individuating reader is invited to make connections. The images traverse the fields of evolutionary biology, philosophy, Einstein's science, anthropology, nuclear technology, Freudian family dynamics and finally reconfigure Christianity as Jungian romance in civil war Spain. Eleanor becomes the Virgin Mary lover of Max's Jesus Christ, which also neatly replicates Max' mother-eroticism in mythical form. It is disturbing to note that since Eleanor is half-Jewish (and therefore wholly Jewish to the Nazis who kill her mother in a concentration camp), she contrasts to Max who is not. Therefore this Jungian romance rewriting of Christianity uncannily resembles the fascist myth of the Aryan Christ, offspring of Jewish Mary and a Roman soldier, a myth that appeared to fascinate Jung at one point (see Chapter 2).[14]

What is particularly distinctive about the writing of this Jungian romance is the identical style used throughout the text. Eleanor and Max sound alike and report the words of others in their own peculiar style with constant repetition of 'I said', 'I thought'. The purpose of such uniformity is to facilitate the individuation of the reader by exposing us to imagery without the sense of a distinct personality in the way. A result can be the reader's irritation and the growing sense of being invaded by an alien voice. The uniform style makes the text monolithic, its authority inescapable. In a similar manner, the mythologising of Jung elevates him beyond questioning or resistance. Uniformity of style is particularly insidious in a text that makes demands on the reader about incorporating active imagination because it has designs on the reader's subjectivity. 'Uniformity' might also recall the precision of a machine, a topic to which I will return.

DEFINING HOPEFUL MONSTERS

If the final intention of the novel is to turn the reader into a hopeful monster, then it is worth quoting Mosley's own definition of the term and his artistic programme given in his recently published autobiography.[15]

> 'Hopeful monsters' was a term used by biologists in the 1940s to describe mutations that were on the edge of going one way or the other – either to extinction or, if some change in the environment that suited them happened to coincide, to the establishing of a new strand of life ...

> In the novels what was hopeful and sometimes monstrous about the characters was a style of mind in which they could be ironic about themselves as characters but by this be in contact perhaps with whatever it was beyond 'character' – be aware of some patterning, that is, in which human dramas, however terrible or absurd, were yet bumps and threads through a maze. This faculty of mind might be seen as some mutation …
>
> A hopeful monster being perhaps anyway less a person than a faculty of vision or of mind.[16]

Mosley's *Hopeful Monsters* assimilates this biological motif to Jungian active imagination and individuation by its textual strategies. The aim is to integrate and so make usable or positive the violent drives of the shadow. It is the 'awareness of some patterning' permeating *Hopeful Monsters* that propels this Jungian text into modernism. In effect, the novel constructs Jung as a modernist thinker whereas the other writers considered so far in this book have made more artistic capital from Jung by uncovering some postmodern implications in his work in the exploration of his fictionality and the poststructuralist challenging of his textual mastery. *Hopeful Monsters'* modernist predilections are strong. It offers a belief in a reality beyond the surface and beyond language with a faith in Jungian theory for gaining access to it. Also, the novel rewrites Christianity as a romantic myth. Jung is thereby elevated to Olympian 'objectivity' and a modernism that is designed to purify his seminal influences from historical contamination. The text aims to situate Jungian theory as an unassailable meta-narrative. Those inconvenient poststructuralist drives within the theory itself in the role of the shadow are supposed to be publicly disposed of by Max and Eleanor's 'triumph' over shadow forces. When both Jung and Mosley extrapolate from a symbolic language such as alchemy to cultural and historical events, failure to consider difference is a failure to acknowledge a historical side to theoretical and fictional discourse. The novel does allow Jung to be an historical figure (remote and offstage in his teaching of Eleanor) but mythologises him away from cultural history and fascism. Such a move is designed to protect Jungian discourse from the shadow of its drives to power. The assumption that a theory or a literary text can absolutely transcend historical forces so that it can totally explain them casts its own shadow in the suppression of Jung's political role and *Hopeful Monsters'* affective network operating as an elite.

JUNGIAN ROMANCE AND SACRIFICE IN *HOPEFUL MONSTERS*

The affective network/elite is the novel's Jungian romance meta-myth. In effect, *Hopeful Monsters* seems begin at the point reached by the end of Roberts' *The Wild Girl* in perceiving the dangers of the dualism inherent in the simple form of Jungian romance. It therefore assumes that converting the dualism into a network will integrate the shadow and solve all problems. Not only does this demonstrate an artistic unwillingness to contemplate chaos, it completely ignores the crucial dualism of reader and text which bears a structural resemblance to the analyst/patient relation in the active imagination conception of reading. Of course, such a binary form cannot be easily discarded but it can be mediated by experimenting with the form of the novel (as Michèle Roberts' later works show) to produce a less monolithic text shaping the reader. *Hopeful Monsters* may be experimental but it does not experiment with the freedom of the reader as the various voices are drawn into a single frame which eliminates their differences.

Another point where *Hopeful Monsters* diverges from previous novels considered by this book is in the matter of sacrifice. *The Chymical Wedding* subsumed sacrifice into its use of Jungian ideas by linking it with romance so that Jungian sacrifice was the sacrifice of consciousness as part of the romance with the Other, the ego sacrificing its claim to mastery of the Other. It is emphatically *not* sacrifice of an-Other. By complete contrast, *Hopeful Monsters* does not bring sacrifice into its Jungian scheme. Instead, it associates sacrifice with Fascism.

> [W]e came across a group of Nazi boys: ... they were singing their sad song – the one about blood and doom and sacrifice and death ... (pp. 120–1)

The biography of Oswald Mosley explains this further. Mosley argues that a characteristic of Fascism is that it tries most crudely to convert its political rhetoric into action. That rhetoric is much concerned with sacrifice because Fascists were obsessed with separation and death. Their superficial arguments about order are the reverse side of a rhetoric of sacrifice and a drive to death.

> Fascism is a state of mind that does not see that words are different from things ... Fascism denies that there is anything above decision and justification for decision that can judge their

> worth; it is a style by which activity seems to be a justification for itself. The drive is towards order ... if the drive to orderliness is towards death, it is still the drive that matters.[17]

Perhaps what is perceptive about *Hopeful Monsters* is that it recognises the violence always inherent in the concept of sacrifice and does not try to tame it in a particular construction of Jungian theory as *The Chymical Wedding* perilously tried to do. However, refusing to associate the violence of sacrifice with Jungian ideas is yet another means of elevating the Jungian scheme to a textual transcendence. Max and Eleanor reformulate sacrificial Christianity as Jungian romance between Max's Christ and Eleanor's Virgin Mary. Spanish civil war soldiers kill, inspired by the sacrificial rhetoric of Christianity, but Eleanor and Max avoid violent sacrifice of any kind to meet as lovers in the Jungian eroticising of Christianity. Also, at the end of the novel, a summarising narrator, Jason, assimilates individuation into knowledge of the Holy Spirit. Individuated beings have a guide into truth which takes them beyond sacrifice. He uses the revealing term 'godlike' of such beings which exposes the danger of viewing individuation as a means of raising a group into an elite network.

These ideas are incorporated into the narrative by Eleanor's father who writes that 'the age of sacrifice is over' (p. 504) as he leaves the concentration camp where he previously shared his wife's ordeal until her death. Now he is to work for the Nazis. The reader is invited to assume that Eleanor's father, along with her friend Franz, aids the Nazis so that he can be in a position to stop them making an atom bomb. Self-sacrifice would be useless by comparison. There is a practical point here about how best to oppose the Nazis but we come back to the lack of differentiation when these 'good' Germans wear Nazi uniforms and appear identical with the regime. There is an interesting parallel (not, of course, debated in the novel), with Jung's pre-war involvement with Nazi Germany and his claim that he was involved to aid Jewish analysts which he did do in a very minor way (see Chapter 2). In one way, one might want to import sacrifice back into the structures of *Hopeful Monsters* as the sacrifice of certainty, of the absolute faith in Jungian ideas, a sacrifice of the ghostly father. Were the novel to take more seriously the shadow, undoing side of Jungian theory as being capable of resisting the theory's claims to subordinate history and culture, then paradoxically Jungian discourse would survive a historicist challenge in a more intact manner.

Working with the poststructuralist possibilities of Jungian theory serves to integrate it into historicism in literary theory in a more productive fashion than merely banishing historical biases to become an external challenge to the validity of Jungian ideas as supreme authority in a text (see Chapter 5).

It is time to consider the particular erasures of difference perpetrated by the unacknowledged shadow of the Jungian romance meta-myth of the affective network: the Jungian elite. Such a shadow of a composition of an elite through individuation is perceptible in Jung's writings and is explored in Chapter 2.

TRANSCENDING DIFFERENCE

The network as a privileged class effectively suppresses class difference in the figure of Nellie, the dumb, working-class, abused child whom Max educates and who eventually becomes a Catholic nun. She bears one of the names of Eleanor and is one of the many children associated with the encounters of the major players in the Jungian romance. In the romance meta-myth with Eleanor and Max at the apex of the network, all the women can be viewed as also aspects of Eleanor, the men as images of Max. Nellie is a silent member of the network in what seems to be a cruel equation of working class and dumbness. She only speaks when she becomes a member of an enclosed order – when she accepts her fate in a sisterhood that, like the network, will allow her no power or 'voice' in its structures. The working-class surroundings of her origins in the novel are described as an alien land colonised by Max for his individuation purposes.

> I thought – These images are of a charnel house: these images are in my mind. If I am an anthropologist come to take notes of this strange tribe, what I should be doing is taking notes of states of mind. (p. 164)

The whole novel operates an erasure of cultural difference but a good example from the text is the lack of a properly maintained distinction between communism and fascism.

> Everyone has a death-wish ... in this present society a death-wish seems to take the form of an allegiance to Fascism,

> Communism; indeed those could be said to be the devouring breasts of the mother. (pp. 330–1)

I will return to this evocative mothering metaphor but here want to notice how the novel is willing to elide distinct political movements. *Hopeful Monsters* does distinguish between the two ideologies in other places but it fails to consider the historical or cultural record with any seriousness, a failure significantly glaring also in its treatment of C.G. Jung.

The colonisation of racial difference for ostensibly Jungian purposes is particularly acute in *Hopeful Monsters*. No member of the affective network is other than European in origin which makes it resemble a white elite employing other races as mere motifs for its own momentous subjectivity. Eleanor meets a man in black in the Sahara desert who saves her life and whom she considers to be her guardian angel. Naturally, he never speaks to her and although we are not told his ethnic origin, the reader is invited to connect him with the 'Moor' who makes a speech about the outbreak of the Spanish civil war at a party where Max is present. This party sets Max on a path where he will meet Eleanor in that war. Eleanor's man in black leads her to the place where German and African soldiers are embarking for Spain and there is a thematic connection to the black trombonist lover of Caroline: both objects of the women's desire are denoted by blackness and the trombonist is at the same party as the Moor; Caroline will travel to Spain with Max. I will return to Moors and the Spanish civil war, but it is noticeable that the difference of ethnicity is excluded from the network and subordinated as signs of the network's own unconscious identities and desires. There is not room in this work to go into Jung's ambiguous and often imperialist treatment of race but it is worth quoting his similar but far more overtly racist employment of 'blackness' in his autobiography when he describes his dream of a Negro.

> I took this dream as a warning from the unconscious; it was saying that the primitive was a danger to me. At that time I was obviously all too close to 'going back'.[18]

'Blackness' does not signify 'the primitive' in *Hopeful Monsters* but it is similarly marginalised as an aspect of the individuation of a white elite.

Hopeful Monsters is even more colonial in nature in its treatment of the history of the Spanish civil war but first I will return to the 'devouring breasts of the mother' and the novel's appropriation of sexual difference. Not only does Eleanor narrate in an identical style to Max but there is no registering of gender inequalities or criticism of patriarchy in the novel at all. Partly, this is achieved by the concentration on the upper middle-class status of the network/elite where women have some freedom to pursue careers while ignoring the particular cultural plight of women in other parts of society. In addition, the novel's peculiar style encourages the depiction of Eleanor's family as an anomaly. Eleanor, the only child, is favoured by her father and apparently unrestricted. At one point only in the novel Eleanor criticises the specific violence of masculinity when she describes the mad anthropologists, Rudi and Stephan 'fighting like tiny dinosaurs' (p. 311) but the simile suggests that such problems have mostly receded into the distant past. When Eleanor's father offers her yet another version of the individuated network/elite saving humanity, she fails to hear gender at all.

> [T]here is an old Jewish tradition that the real saviours of the world – those who stop the human race from destroying itself – are very few ... seven just men ...
>
> I thought, of course – Perhaps I am one of them! (p. 85)

Neither Eleanor nor her father hears that this is an elite of seven just *men*.

Of course, the refusal to acknowledge cultural gender inequalities and to examine patriarchy as a system of power is yet another example of the subordination of culture and history in *Hopeful Monsters*. The novel reconstructs patriarchy as benevolent paternalism with Jung as the seminal thinker. Unsurprisingly, the fathers of both Eleanor and Max are benign academics while the mothers provoke violence: Eleanor's communist mother draws her into political terrorism while Max's Freudian mother constellates the death drive which preoccupies her son for much of the novel. His adolescence is dominated by an eroticism textualised through mutual reading of Freudian writings on Oedipal sexuality and the perilous intertwined pleasures of death and desire. In the consequent intriguing portrait of a mother wooing her son through Freudian texts, it is unclear whether the reading of Freud shapes the energy between mother and son or explains the pre-existing dynamic. This Oedipal game culminates in mutual masturbation (p. 78) but Freudian ideas dominate Max's subsequent erotic life. He ends up taking the paternal position vis-à-vis his lover, Lilia. Max not only 'fathers' Lilia in the Jungian sense of bringing her into the affective network but years earlier helps her mother in deciding to keep the unborn Lilia when he brings the mother into the network as well. The novel stops just short of biological incest but its treatment of mothering remains ominous. The significant quotation that communism and fascism can be construed as 'the devouring breasts of the mother '(p. 331) seems to assimilate Freudian insights to the psychology of totalitarianism.

In complete and noticeable contrast to Mosley's father's culpable role in history, mothering is irredeemable in *Hopeful Monsters.* It is intimately connected to the erasure of sexual difference through the erasure of the body as a material sign of difference. Mothers provoke violence and the death drive; fathers offer companionship and intellectual stimulation on the path to individuation. Eleanor and Max reproduce differently, not bodily, but spiritually and psychologically through the affective network. Consequently their bodily sexual difference is negated as far as possible and Eleanor in particular is given a horror of biological mothering. The novel structurally equates body with mother and individuation with spirit transcending the body to form bodiless angelic beings, a point to which I will return. There is a great deal of copulation in the novel, but little sex in the sense that little is conveyed of the texture of two different bodies together. This, combined with the refusal to reproduce physically, appears to be the novel's attempt to marginalise the body and elide it with dangerous maternal forces. *Hopeful Monsters* subordinates the body's role in Jungian romance just as Michèle Roberts' work amplifies it. Eleanor and Max make a far more ethereal Mary and Christ than Mary and Jesus in *The Wild Girl.* Perhaps the comment about communism and fascism being the devouring breasts of the mother offers a clue to the text's revulsion about the biological mother: the pre-Oedipal mother is the point where the lack of differentiation germane to the novel becomes chaos with no possible self-definition, coherence or control. It is the point of Otherness within the novel's textual strategies. The relation to the mother is the opposite to the desired individuation in this text whereas the thoughtful relation to the father stimulates it. Where are the Oedipal tensions between fathers and sons in *Hopeful Monsters*? The answer is that they are transfigured by the exchange of fathers from the biological (and so potentially Oedipal) parent to the textual transcendence of C.G. Jung. A more artistically successful novel, Michèle Roberts' *In the Red Kitchen*, investigates the pre-Oedipal moment in the genesis of Jungian theory when in Jung's doctoral thesis it exists as an unbounded area of Freudian, Jungian, erotic and personal drives. *Hopeful Monsters* seeks to eradicate materiality and textuality from the body of Jungian discourse. There is a double movement in the novel: the exchange of fathers and the displacement of the horrors of bodily inheritance onto the mother. Both moves seem designed to evade the author's paternal heritage. Freudian ideas are used in *Hopeful Monsters* to carry the displacement and marginalising of mothering just as Jungian ideas structure the new, transcendent father.

Hopeful Monsters fears mothering, defining it as chaotic, dangerous, pre-Oedipal. It is a text which will permit no mothers, only erecting a transcendent father in C.G. Jung as a source of authority pretending to be immune from history. In renouncing the mother, the novel claims to renounce biology, that tie to the author's historical father which the text exchanges for the transcendent purity of a dehistoricised Jung. This transcendent, bodiless, non-historical Jung provides an authority that is deployed to suppress the mother whose bodily relation is defined as intolerable. This is done by constructing individuation as Jungian romance which is sexual, but paradoxically evades the body and bodily difference. Characters copulate like angels. Max deals with his Freudian mothering by mimicking the Oedipal myth with his child-lover, Lilia but such maternal contamination escapes biological incest to form individuation. I would suggest that this metaphorical incest be construed as 'Jungian' incest. None of this Freudian inheritance is allowed to pollute his transcendent Jungian romance with Eleanor where Oedipality has been elevated into the Christian myth: Max's Christ to Eleanor's Virgin Mary. The marginalisation of the body and the mother are the most profound means of suppressing gender difference in the novel and of constructing an elite of privileged beings not subject to cultural pressures.

If, as I have suggested, *Hopeful Monsters* is concerned with an exchange of fathers and suppression of the mother then it is the historical nature of both potential fathers that is least to be found in the novel. A text designed to marginalise the historical record defines it as an inferior discourse.

> History for the most part is made up from the public professions of politicians, but politicians are not primarily concerned with truth, so history become a statistical amalgam of special pleadings. (p. 367)

It is impossible within the confines of this book to study the momentous historical events that the novel refers to in any serious manner. However, I will give a few examples of how *Hopeful Monsters* muddles the history of the Spanish civil war in order to continue my argument about the text's use of Jungian theory to suppress painful historical matter. That painful matter, of course, is attached to C.G. Jung as well as Oswald Mosley.

The novel treats historical events as sources of motifs for the individuation of the main characters. Its most sustained historical episode is Eleanor and Max's adventures in the Spanish civil war where its specious rewriting of the colonial components of that conflict is a clear example of the dangers of a text determined to 'connect' at the expense of difference. In rearranging or ignoring the effects of colonial politics, the text's mystification results in it becoming a colonising body effacing the Other. For example, the Moor who arrives at the start of the Spanish civil war in London at a party where Max attends and the cursory mention of Moorish troops arriving in Spain, obscure, rather than convey, the historical role of such soldiers.

The standard popular account of the Spanish conflict is the Pelican edition of Hugh Thomas's *The Spanish Civil War*[19] which describes the Moorish troops, known as the *Regulares,* as the native part of the Spanish Foreign Legion formed as a colonial force to quash unrest in Spanish Africa. The Foreign Legion and the *Regulares* became known for their atrocities as they took the Fascist side. After one battle Thomas records:

> There followed a terrible retribution ... These forces behaved in the conquered territory much as if they were a victorious army living off the sufferings of the vanquished.[20]

I am not arguing that in a novel where two characters visit the Spanish civil war there needs to be a complete detailed record of actual events but that *Hopeful Monsters'* employment of Moors in this context is not only colonialist in reducing another culture and race to a psychic image, but that it also effaces a distinctive historical role. It ignores the colonial politics of the war which resulted in the peculiar dread felt by the Spanish population for the colonial Foreign Legion. It also ignores the historical role of 'Moors' on mainland Spain.[21] In addition to colonising racial difference in the treatment of the war, the novel colonises the Spanish in erasing the distinctive nature of their experience. This process becomes even more stark when the novel depicts what is identified as a fascist orator in Spain.

> The first speaker was Franco: he was a small dapper man who flung his arm up in a Fascist salute ... The third speaker I had not heard of before ... He was a small dapper figure screaming and yelling as if from his cage. Then – 'Long live Death!' (pp. 400–1)

The repetition of the description of the speakers as 'small dapper men' associates this final slogan 'Long live Death' with Franco and the general Fascist cause. It totally conceals its historical identity as the motto of the Foreign Legion, expressing its colonial brutalities.

> The Foreign Legion had a reputation for peculiar violence. Its favourite motto was, 'Long live Death'.[22]

Hopeful Monsters completely misses the intersection of colonial warfare and Spanish Fascism that Thomas describes. Not only had the most feared troops in that war learned and practised their violent regime through colonial occupation but the regular Army had a strong colonial role.[23] There are particular ironies in the fascist use of Moorish troops in the civil war. It is not only the novel which connects at the expense of difference for a particular ideological end.

Hopeful Monsters does recognise, however, the use of Christian rhetoric in Fascist violence, well documented by Thomas.[24] Franco's side claimed to be the warriors of Catholicism. When Eleanor witnesses murders she decides that the killers see her as the Virgin Mary to whom they are offering sacrifices.

> He took hold of the man in khaki by the hair; then he looked up at me. I was, yes, in my niche, like the Virgin Mary. I thought – You mean this might be some offering? Some sacrifice? (p. 362)

Christianity intersects with fascism at the node of sacrifice. As a particular narrative device, the novel attempts to recuperate the

Christian myth by using Jungian ideas to elevate it beyond sacrifice into Jungian romance. It is possible to work out which side the *Hopeful Monsters'* hapless khaki victim was on (Republican), but difficult. Just as the novel colonised the differences of race class and sex, it also colonises the history of the Spanish civil war by obscuring its colonial components and muddling its ideologies. It depicts a dehistoricised violence. *Hopeful Monsters* effaces the historical specificity of the Spanish experience just as it totally ignores the historical and *volkisch* nature of its ghostly father, C.G. Jung (see Chapter 2). The novel shares with Jung a sense of immunity from history, an irresponsibility which made Jung both comment at the end of World War Two on a general sense of European shame at concentration camps and imply his own good conscience.[25] Jung was not a Nazi but he voluntarily participated in Nazi culture and so failed to provide any of the moral leadership which he ascribes to individuation. The use of Jungian theory in this novel demonstrates the imperative for a poststructuralist (here new historicist) criticism where a fiction desires to elevate Jungian theory to a form of textual power. *Hopeful Monsters* does not advocate oppression and has a point about fascism demonstrating the dangers of positing absolute difference. However, in its creation of a white upper-class European elite it is oppressive of the Other. I now want to suggest how that Other can include the reader.

ANGELS AND MACHINES: THE JUNGIAN READER

Hopeful Monsters' adoption of Jungian individuation is an article of faith because it does not consider any possible shadow to Jungian discourse. Consequently, I would argue that the text expresses an unacknowledged shadow in individuation as elitism. As part of its suppression of difference it discounts mothering and the body. The motif that the text offers for the goal of the individuated elite is the 'angel', ageless, genderless, bodiless, motherless beings. Max finds a painting of angels whose androgyny recalls Jung's 'self' images, the goal of individuation.

> They are all three much the same; they are neither male nor female; they are all young and beautiful ... The three angels, though separate, seem to be held together by a common inner absorption ... They are serene, but they are not exactly adoring:

they know too much to be adoring: what they are in contact with is themselves. (p. 289)

This is a portrayal of individuated beings in the Jungian sense. These 'angels' have integrated the shadow of their own drives to assume power and to submit to power. They do not adore but offer serenity, an image of love integrated into power. In effect, these angels are an image of the goal of Jungian romance in the novel, an ideal model of the aesthetic scheme of the affective network. Significantly, 'angel' becomes a mode of address between Eleanor and Max. There is some cursory attempt to explore the shadow of a character becoming an angel when Eleanor in her grief for her parents imagines herself as an angel of destruction. She plans to take a pistol into a fascist gathering to exact retribution 'wearing my white overall like an angel' (p. 396). When she reaches such a gathering a man who turns out to be the husband of Eleanor's first love, Trixie, tells her she is '[l]ooking down on us like an exterminating angel' (p. 411). The man causes Eleanor to remember her former loves and she refrains from violence.

The novel does admit a shadow side to religious myths and motifs but not to Jungian ideas. Angels can be stimulants to destruction but Jungian integration of the shadow takes care of that as Eleanor finally overcomes her desire for practical revenge. Similarly Christianity can inspire violence in the Spanish civil war but Jungian romance of Max/Christ and Eleanor/Virgin Mary solves this problem. The novel's account of Jungian theory here is one that too easily 'dissolves' its poststructuralist shadow. *Hopeful Monsters* wants to present 'angels' as the goal of the hopeful monsters in the affective network. Through Jungian individuation the characters become hopeful monsters, reproducing differently so evading the body and becoming angels, beings beyond difference. Nevertheless, just as unchallenged Jungian individuation expresses its shadow as an elite colonising difference, so the unchallenged angel/self seems to incarnate its own shadow in the body as machine. Offering 'angel', a being beyond difference as the goal of individuation is another rejection of the body in the novel which seems to constellate it as a machine. If identity is ideally angelic, what is the body but a machine in which the angel self is trapped?

Hopeful Monsters makes an increasing identification between unromantic sexual desire and the machine body: sexuality mechanises the body. When Max plays his erotic games of auto-asphyxiation linked to his Freudian mother, his bodily pleasure might gain him a sense of release: 'machinery might start up again' (p. 73). Max's later affair with Mitzi in Russia has similar associations of 'machinery, music, vodka, power' (p. 267). That there might be a social dimension to desire mechanising the body is evident when Bruno takes his friends Eleanor and Trixie to a café in 1920s Germany. The café itself is essentially a machine for organising desire.

> [A]t one's table one waited for little cylinders to pop in and out of holes; all this was supposed to be to do with the satisfying of desire, even love. (p. 89)

The machine with its pump, steam, holes, messages like 'lavatory paper', is a demonstration of how the human body can become commodified, capitalised. Here the plurality of human desires is reduced to economically determined texts (invitations to sex for money). Such a machine, I suggest, could become an image of a text, the novel, mechanically organising and redefining the reader's desires. That reducing the human body to the docility of a machine is about power is also apparent in Max's citing of 'power' in connection with his mechanical encounters with Mitzi.

The body transfixed by the simplification of its desires into a machine reaches a terrible climax in civil war Spain. Here, a corpse is turned into a desire machine for money. Max pays to see his own 'hell'.

> The woman had gone to the side of the alcove and was turning the handle of what seemed to be a rack or winch; something was tightening around the throat of the figure in the alcove; I could not quite see – I felt as if there were something tightening around my own throat ... the figure in the alcove seemed to be getting an erection ... I thought ... oh – the clockwork tawdriness of hell! The body seemed to be a corpse ... (p. 380)

Max makes the connection here between the abused corpse and his own sexual experimentation with strangulation as a boy. This too evoked the body as 'machinery'. Eleanor encounters the dark side of the angel image so Max meets the lowest point of its opposite, the body as machine. Since Max situates this scene in 'hell', then his subsequent turning of the Christian narrative into a Jungian romance with Eleanor is supposed to integrate this shadow. Jungian theory provides the structuring force to reformulate Christian myths so that individuation can reverse the Fall and Eden can be re-entered. The culmination of the individuation myth of re-entering Eden in *Hopeful Monsters* occurs when Eleanor rescues Max from a castle in Spain where he was a prisoner. This reunion initiates their life together in England and fulfils the Christian narrative which they have been re-structuring as the Jungian romance of Max/Christ and Eleanor/Mary.

However, I do not agree that the body as machine is a banished nightmare. Max may feel that he has transcended his 'Freudian' birth scripts in his superior Jungian narrative with Eleanor but he merely displaces the nightmare of the machine onto the reader. First, it is worth noting Hal Foster's comments on the attraction of Fascism and modernism to machines in *Compulsive Beauty*.[26] Fascism offered a distinctive mechanised figure: the 'worker-soldier, the armoured body become weapon-machine'.[27] For some modernists:[28]

> [T]he machine held out ... the promise of creation outside woman, of identity free of difference, of self-conception without death.[29]

Self-conception might well be a potent ideal for the author of *Hopeful Monsters* but he has a textual father to aid him in C.G. Jung. The novel uses Jungian ideas as a textual machine in its drive towards an identity free of difference, reproduction without the terrifying chaos of mothering. By 'purifying' Jungian ideas of the body of history, the shadow of Jung as ghostly father, textual angel, is that of Jungian ideas structuring *Hopeful Monsters* as a modernist desire machine, part of a neo-Fascist discourse aiming to colonise the reader. The individuating reader is the ghost trapped in the text as machine, a machine designed to erase or colonise difference, to reproduce without mothers, to evade the materiality of embodiment. The way the novel uses Jungian ideas turns the text into a machine because it uses them as transcendent of textuality, infallible, non-historical and non-political. *Hopeful Monsters* seeks to reproduce the reader through individuation in reading as active imagination. It aims to offer Jungian ideas as the text's angel, transcendent and prophetic. Yet the very purity of its Jungian ideology uncontaminated by doubt or criticism colonises the reader who is subjected to its authority. In effect, *Hopeful Monsters*' Jungian authority tries to author the reader through its Jungian structures that are machine-like in the way their reproduction denies fleshly and cultural embodiment. The result is a colonised reader whom the text tries to seduce by its poetic beauty.

> There were tears on Max's cheeks: between him and Eleanor there seemed to be bits and pieces of light like a glass screen breaking. (p. 551)

The novel's proclamation of an aesthetic of power and love through a Jungian restructuring of religious narratives succeeds only in offering reading as a redemption into an initiated elite, an elite paradoxically trapped in a text as a desire machine.

HOPEFUL MONSTERS: FLAWED ACHIEVEMENT

Hopeful Monsters uses Jungian ideas as the operating system and meta-myth of the novel. Its artistic attractiveness lies in its mythologising of Jungian theory: individuation into becoming angels, active imagination into reading the text and the world, Jungian romance as a means of rescuing Christianity from the violence of sacrifice. Significantly, there is little sense of Jung's writings (unlike *The Chymical Wedding*) because the novel does not want Jung as a text but as a transcendent and phallogocentric father with the power to banish mothering and the body. The achievement of *Hopeful Monsters* lies in its use of Jungian ideas to make connections between discourses such as politics, science, philosophy, psychology, nuclear technology, art, by reducing them to the motifs of active imagination. The novel also succeeds in going beyond Jungian romance as the dualism that can produce a structure of romance/tragedy in order to explore Jungian romance as a network. Unlike the more successful treatments of Jungian ideas in Michèle Roberts' later novels, Jungian romance as a network does not penetrate narrative form which remains obstinately wedded to dualism with Eleanor and Max as the major narrators.

None the less, this is a flawed text in its attempts to be beneficial, liberating and to offer the reader a route to the transcending of destructive desires. In opposing a principle of connectedness to a Fascist one of separation and death, the novel oversimplifies ideological conflicts and ignores the danger that merely offering connections will allow a hierarchy of dominance to occur by the marginalising of weaker forces. This is enacted in *Hopeful Monsters* in the marginalising of gender, the body, culture and the colonising of race and history. Erasing of gender difference in the form of bodily experience is particularly acute in the vehement rejection of biological mothering and the assumption of Jungian theory in the urge to reproduce differently, without the troubling female body, in individuation. The process of colonising difference is made more suggestive by the novel's unacknowledged exchange of fathers: the historically and biologically linked to the author, Oswald Mosley for C.G. Jung who is erected into a transcendent authority by the occluding of his historical role in Nazism. The exchange of fathers is also effected by the displacement of the text's horror at biological parenting onto the mother so enabling fathering to enter the realm of the mythological. *Hopeful Monsters* wants Jungian theory as its angel, but it forms the text's machine-like uniformity of voice and design. The text as machine traps and colonises the very reader it tries to individuate. The novel's faith in individuation while refusing to question its Jungian source results in the Jungian romance network forming an initiated elite. Power and love, insufficiently differentiated like all else in the novel, become fused into cultural authority.

By refusing to examine or question Jungian ideas, *Hopeful Monsters* reproduces the Jungian drive for cultural supremacy discussed in Chapter 2. It wants to criticise fascism but produces an uncannily neo-fascist text in its rhetorical and coercive designs on the hapless individuating reader. Fiction again challenges Jung as literary theory. It does so here on historicist and cultural grounds which in turn detect the subordination of difference as gender, class and ethnicity, as well as the materiality of the body. This fiction unwittingly reveals a historical shadow within Jungian discourse: it constructs a Jungian textuality as complicit and coercive by failing to interrogate both the novel's and Jung's historical contingency and claims to power. In effect, *Hopeful Monsters* represents a demonstration of the *need* for Jungian theory to be construed in a poststructuralist context rather than the humanist assumption of the unproblematic transcendence of historical and political drives.

The following chapter will consider a more mature and sophisticated treatment of the authoritarian positioning of Jungian ideas in literary texts just as the previous chapter discussed an artistically successful exploration of the genesis of Jungian discourse. If colonial narratives are easily detectable within Jungian concepts then can a literary text's more poststructuralist treatment of Jungian theory also trace a postcolonial Jung? *Hopeful Monsters'* deployment of Jungian theory depicts and seeks to create reading hopeful monsters as monstrously unmothered, fathered by angels, trapped in machines. Other novels show this need not be so.

7

(Post)Colonial Jung: Doris Lessing's *Canopus in Argos*

This chapter will consider the explicit treatment of colonialism and Jungian theory in literary texts by Doris Lessing. It aims to explore a double-edged challenge to Jungian discourse on colonial grounds. Such a challenge occurs in both the tracing of colonial narratives and the potential for a resistance to colonialism within the theory. Can Lessing's more sophisticated and sceptical structuring of Jungian theory detect a postcolonial Jung?

One of the most distinctive characteristics of Lessing as a novelist is her persistent exploration of the political dimensions of literary forms. This chapter will show how her awareness of the power implications of a discourse extends to her appreciation of Jungian theory as far back as the 1960s. In particular, Lessing regards Jungian tropes as potentially complicit with colonial constructions. Despite this recognition, Jungian ideas can also be a path to esotericism for a writer equally committed to notions of mysticism and mental evolution. If Lessing diagnoses the political and esoteric as mutually implicated and embodied in Jungian theory, then I want to argue that this realisation finds its fictional expression in her science fiction novel sequence, *Canopus in Argos*.[1] These texts portray a 'good' empire of superior, highly evolved aliens (the Canopeans) battling for control of an Earth-like planet (Shikasta) with both an inferior empire (Sirius) and an evil one (Shammat). The supreme virtue of the Canopeans appears to reside in their reliance upon mental evolution and mysticism rather than brute force for their imperial domination. Does this represent Lessing's renunciation of the unequivocal criticism of colonial tropes in favour of something 'religious' or 'spiritual'? I want to argue that these novels' sophisticated deployment of Jungian theory enables a staging of both the persistence of imperialism within esotericism and a simultaneous resistance to it. The reading (w)rite first described in Chapter 3 in relation to a more politically naive work, *The Chymical Wedding*, becomes here a Jungian reading structure embedded in a textual consciousness of colonial politics. If a postcolonial Jungian theory is possible, then it must be one which can make use of the flexibility and potential poststructuralist self-consciousness of Jungian writings. Postcolonial Jung can only be realised differentiated from, but never wholly separated from, the persistence of colonial narratives within Jungian discourse.

First of all, this chapter will explore the interpenetration of the Jungian esoteric and the colonial as ways of expressing political and artistic tensions described by Lessing as early as 1957 in 'A Small Personal Voice'.[2] I will respond to a powerful essay about the authorial presence in *Canopus in Argos* by Lorna Sage.[3] My suggestion is that the concept of translation is crucial to the positioning of the reader in the first *Canopus* novel, *Shikasta*. By causing the reader to shift in the understanding of the statuses of the empires, the novel structures reading experience on a model of Jungian individuation. *Shikasta* offers a reading (w)rite that is simultaneously a perception of colonial structures of thinking. It is a criticism of the colonial trope from *within* the use of Jungian ideas for esoteric or mystical ends. Alone among the novels considered by this book, *Canopus in Argos* employs Jungian theory as always a political as well as a psychological or esoteric discourse. Lessing's sophistication in the use of Jungian ideas means that they can be utilised to explore a wider politics of representation while at the same time displaying traces of a postcolonial literary theory haunting Jungian writings.

DORIS LESSING AND JUNGIAN THEORY: COLONIAL AND ESOTERIC

Doris Lessing records an interested but not uncritical approach to Jung, considering him 'limited. But useful as far as he went'[4] in a letter to Roberta Rubenstein published in 1979, the year her space fiction sequence, *Canopus in Argos*, started to appear. As this comment indicates, Lessing was not primarily concerned with Jung. Instead, she became a student of the esoteric teaching of Sufism, particularly that version taught by Idries Shah.[5] Jung's value is enhanced for Lessing when she describes his core theories of the collective unconscious and individuation as notions of evolving consciousness occurring within the web of interacting mystical systems making up the multiplicity of Sufi thought. As early as 1964,[6] Lessing writes:

> Jung's theory of the collective unconscious is expounded by the Spaniard Ibn Rushd, was often referred to by Rumi, and 'its meaning and force are subjects of Sufi specialisation'.[7]

Jungian psychology is just one narrative in Lessing's multi-faceted Sufism which embraces alchemy, witches, Rosicrucians, the Franciscan Order, esoteric Christianity, Zen Buddhism, Yoga, the Quabbalah.[8]

To summarise, Lessing constructs Jung as contingent with esotericism as Sufism.[9] Sufism may well be a widely respected mystical discourse associated with Islam[10] but it is esoteric in its employment of guru-like teachers and indirectly accessible lore. Lessing records that the Sufism she has gained from the teachings of Idries Shah offers an education which enables the mind to reject conventional attitudes and develop higher mental faculties. Sufis believe that conscious evolution is possible and that such learning can only take place from within one's own culture. It will therefore take many different forms. To Lessing, her Sufism respects cultural difference in its teaching methods but transcends it by implication as 'Sufism is the inner secret teaching concealed within every religion'.[11] Sufism has influenced Lessing's fiction in the uses made of the teaching story to evoke altered states of consciousness,[12] in techniques of defamiliarisation to encourage alternative views of reality,[13] in transcendentalism and a revaluation of 'madness',[14] and in the use of Sufi models for teacher/disciple relationships in *Canopus in Argos*.[15] My argument will be that if Lessing subsumes Jung into Sufism in *Canopus in Argos*, the texts are nevertheless aware of the political (here imperial), dangers of a discourse transcending difference, unlike *Hopeful Monsters*. Lessing's references to Jung have included from the start a sense of a political charge to Jungian ideas. Among Lessing's earliest published comments on Jung is an acute critique of the politics of using a Europeanised system to interpret or to represent non-European realities. In reviews of books by Laurens Van der Post, she writes in 1958:

> It is no accident that the Jungians have found so much grist in the literary mills of Africa: vast spaces, hinterlands and the nameless can so easily be archetyped into sympathetic symbols.[16]

This unease becomes, in a 1961 review, the accusation of 'emphatic dogmatism'[17] in Van der Post's use of Jung as 'unsuitable for charting regions where, as the old magician knew better than anyone, every truth has a double face'.[18] We might note here Lessing's far from medical or even psychological citation of Jung as an 'old magician'. Her nascent sense of 'doubleness' will be explored below but she has not yet finished with Van der Post's Jungian projections onto a colonised landscape.

> The African landscape is still, thank God, impersonal and indifferent to man; but Mr Van der Post projects his emotions into every animal, tree, bird or human he sees, so that, identifying with the Bushmen in my own manner, I found I was in the middle of a fantasy where, hopping frantically on one leg in front of Mr Van der Post, I was shouting, 'Baas, Baas, I'm not dead yet, please don't make me into an archetype until I am'.[19]

In effect, Lessing accuses Van der Post of using Jung as a colonial discourse which (mis)translates Africa and Africans to become aspects or servants of his own psyche. Jungian psychology is described here as a mode of representation that reproduces colonial seizure by displacing meanings from the colonised and relocating them as the territories of the author. Interestingly, Lessing defines her resistance to this process as a 'fantasy', thereby acknowledging the spuriousness of her own 'identifying' with the Africans. Though aiming to challenge a colonising discourse, Lessing can only achieve this by repeating the colonial act of 'identification', even as the word 'fantasy' and comic style contain a rueful consciousness of this repetition. What is most emphatic here is Lessing's early perception of Jungian theory as complicit with colonial thinking. It is time to turn to Lessing's wider concerns with the politics of representation.

THE POLITICS OF REPRESENTATION: 'A SMALL PERSONAL VOICE'

The use of Jung to represent interior and exterior realities is always potentially a political act for this writer and feeds into Lessing's persistent concerns about representation articulated early in 'The Small Personal Voice', published in 1957. In this essay, written during Cold War terrors, the most urgent political collective identity is that constructed by the universal threat of nuclear war. This threat offers us 'the kinship of possible destruction',[20] and one which might be ignited by a 'Chairman [who] will say: "I represent the people". And the people is the brown man sitting under the tree ... the people is me.'[21] Intriguingly, the collective threat also appears to be figured in a metaphor of white colonisation: the 'Chairman' versus 'the brown man'. This structure culminates in Lessing's necessary identification with the colonised (since nuclear war is not local). I say 'appears' because we are not given the race of the 'Chairman' though the implication in 1957 is surely white and male. At the end of the same essay, Lessing makes a claim for the artist to 'represent' the people, arguing that literary form has a political extension:

> [O]ne is a writer at all because one represents, makes articulate, is continuously and invisibly fed by, numbers of people who are inarticulate, to whom one belongs, to whom one is responsible.[22]

Therefore, the term 'represent' occurs here to indicate both the Chairman's claim to power (a power so absolute that initiating nuclear war is a conceivable act of such a politician) and the novelist's commitment to her 'subjects'. It could be argued that Lessing, a British citizen who grew up in the then Southern Rhodesia, now Zimbabwe, however opposed to the regime, uses nuclear terror both to submerge her position as a white coloniser and to allow her identification with 'the people' in a politicised artistic role. Yet the contingency of these two types of 'representation', the politician/author, is irrefutable. In the Van der Post reviews, the two types of representative, the Chairman-Dictator and the author, are without any mechanism for separating themselves. It is the author who employs a colonial discourse to 'dictate' meanings to a colonised landscape: such writing is colonial appropriation and Lessing's challenge a mere fantasy that replicates the colonial act in comic self-conscious form. For Lessing, the politics of representation seem dialectically enacted by the author as a producer of a colonial discourse not finally separable from the technology (here writing) of power. 'Representing the people' cannot be an unproblematic identification with the oppressed and voiceless for the novelist. The means of representation cannot be divorced from the technologies of power, here expressed through the colonial trope. The writer is always in this sense a 'coloniser' however much she may desire to identify wholly with the 'colonised'. And if the author cannot evade the political burden of her authority, then where does this leave the reader in the politics of literary representation? As we shall see, critics have been severe with Lessing's benevolent textual imperialism.

The most overt exploration of authorial dominance and the 'doubleness' of Jungian theory in Lessing's texts is the novel sequence, *Canopus in Argos*, where she employs the perspectives of three galactic empires, Canopus, Sirius and Shammat, to interrogate a colonised 'Earth'. These novels have been frequently criticised as imperial discourses. For example, Carey Kaplan in 'Britain's Imperialist Past in Doris Lessing's Futuristic Fiction',[23] condemns Canopus as a replication and reification of British Imperialism. Most effectively, Lorna Sage in 'The Available Space', writes of Lessing's Canopeans that they are 'remarkably pure figures of power'.[24] Of the sequence as a whole, she describes the problem of 'authority' when the reader is placed in a relationship with what the author clearly considers to be superior aliens.

> They remind us that dialogue is seldom conducted between equals, and that the writer in certain crucial senses 'speaks for' and represents the reader. The reader – this reader at any rate – often feels dismissed, excluded. Or, since I'm using the term, 'colonised,' by a benevolent (and therefore even more exasperating authority ...) power struggles are not transcended but transposed.[25]

Does Lessing's science fiction show the author, at least in that genre, inevitably and 'purely' colonising the reader? Such a topos relates directly to the issue of the textual use of Jung. If Jungian theory inhabits these texts, does it do so solely as an instance of imperial thinking? My contention is that these science fiction texts utilise the 'doubleness' which Lessing detected in Jungian ideas both to reveal and criticise the colonial dimension to Jungian discourse. Jung's faith in the Otherness of the unconscious can be construed as a metaphor for imperial domination by the Other. However, apart from this tendency for Jungian theory to collapse into a colonial trope, it can also be used to suggest the possibility of an Otherness to colonial discourse itself. *Canopus in Argos*, with its galactic empires, is Lessing's most sophisticated attempt to exploit the position of the reader faced by the colonial ironies of representation where desire for solidarity with 'the brown man' is insufficiently distanced from the white dictator.

JUNGIAN ARCHETYPES IN *CANOPUS IN ARGOS*

Canopus in Argos seems to echo Jung's language about archetypes, as collective inherited potentials for meaning. He wrote of archetypes, they

> 'are not determined as regards their content, but only as regards their form and then only to a very limited degree ... Its form ... might perhaps be compared to the axial system of a crystal, which, as it were, preforms the crystalline structure in the mother liquid, although it has no material existence of its own'.[26]

These archetypal aspects recur in *Canopus in Argos*, principally by means of the super-evolved Canopeans, who are 'androgynous' (p. 142), like archetypes, and who have been 'crystallised, into forms as different as snowflakes' (p. 17). *Shikasta*'s chief Canopean representative is Johor, which means 'pearl' in Arabic,[27] a frequent Jungian sign for the archetype of the 'self',[28] an unconscious structure to which the ego becomes a subject in individuation.

However, the Canopeans cannot be 'represented' as archetypes because, as Jung's definition suggests, archetypes are unrepresentable and can be posited only from their derivatives, archetypal images. The crystalline archetype, or Canopean, can only be represented as incarnated or imaged: such images will be coloured or animated by local cultural conditions. Significantly, Canopeans are shown emerging from crystals as spacecraft: 'our crystalline sphere darting past' (p. 43). This can be a signal for the relationship of plurality and multiplicity between archetype and archetypal image since a spacecraft can obviously carry a variety of incarnations under the heading 'envoy'. Thus Canopeans visit as members of local species as Johor manifests himself as a native on Shikasta, or are born into a particular culture stripped of other identity and memory except for the crystalline imprint of the Signature from Canopus. This Canopean identity is an inner psychic one, not immediately accessible to consciousness. Canopeans born to an imperial destiny on colonised planets must discover their higher alien being within themselves by gradual realisation of their superior unconscious potentialities, a process much resembling Jungian individuation.

CANOPUS IN ARGOS

Colonial Powers and a Politicised Reading (W)rite

If the literary representing structure of the Canopeans is derived from Jung's unrepresentable crystalline archetypes incarnating in local modes as archetypal images, then these figures descend to both Shikasta and realist fiction as 'characters' bearing traces of a psychic colonisation that they can choose to ignore, as Taufiq/John does and Johor/George does not. Canopean Taufiq is born onto Shikasta as John Brent-Oxford but fails to respond to his psychic inheritance from Canopus. In effect, he refuses to 'individuate' into his archetypal/Canopean role. To deal with this defection, Johor causes himself to be born as George Sherban, who successfully individuates into his nascent Canopean potential. Johor's selected documents tell us that the main cause of fruitful Rohanda's change to broken Shikasta is a 'dis-aster' (p. 35), a fault in the stars recalling the frequent depiction of archetypes as a star-filled heaven.[30] The reader is presented with a deterministic universe, served by Canopeans as Lorna Sage's 'pure figures of power'.[31] The problem is colonial: such representation makes Canopus appear as yet another imperial trope, aiming solely at literal domination or, as Johor puts it, ensuring 'the creation of ever-evolving Sons and Daughters of the Purpose' (p. 52). Canopus, in this sense, is an exaggerated version of the Jungian principle that privileges unconscious meaning potential over a selfish, limited ego. This structure is now dangerously hardened into literal domination by an alien Other. Such a harsh stance is not softened by the Canopean method of activating unconscious paradigms within, so apparently offering choice. Johor tries to recall John Brent-Oxford (Taufiq) to his superior but unconscious knowledge, through messages from his unconscious, including dreams (pp. 106–7), but real choice is circumscribed in a dis-asterous universe.

If, as Sage suggests, the Canopeans colonise the reader by transmitting Lessing's authority, it is important to notice that in *Canopus in Argos* the reader is colonised in two senses: first, by the ideology promulgated by the Canopeans, as Sage describes, and second, by the positioning of the reader within the texts. The reader of *Shikasta* is a translator. The novel's structure, opening with a partial and non-chronological selection of documents mainly authored by Johor, is a defamiliarisation of Earth history. This is followed by a second section of Rachel Sherban's diary (sister to George/Johor), including letters and documents, written from a Shikastan perspective. Part two defamiliarises the alien reality of Johor's first section of the novel. The name 'Earth' is never used and there are virtually no terrestrial terms in the 'Canopean' part of *Shikasta*. Nevertheless, the reader is saturated with tropes and structures from Earth history and sacred literature, and so is forced to make a continual translation of this outrageously fragmented text, for example '**SEE History of Shikasta, VOLS. 2955–3015**' (p. 100). Part two does employ Earth names while eschewing 'Earth' itself, yet the charismatic presence of George, whom we know to be Johor, and the unfamiliar future setting, forces a continual retranslation into the imperial Canopean ideology of part one, especially as the reader is constantly challenged, through the sympathetic Rachel, to read beyond the realist novel to the extraterrestrial, extra-representational.

Reading as translation is inescapable but never unproblematical in this novel. By the difficulties Lessing introduces, the paucity of clues in part one, the requirement to remember the scheme of 'North West Fringes' (Europe), 'Isolated Northern Continent' (United States), and so on, the reader is forced to remain aware that she is translating between two separate ideological perceptions of reality: the Canopean empire of psyche and matter, science fictional, versus the reader's own supported by Rachel, who prefers personal relationships and writes from the domain of traditional realism. What is therefore built into the reading experience of *Shikasta* is the difficulty and impossibility of 'pure' translation between different cultural perceptions. Such a subtle and persistent friction in the reading process is substantiated by the ever encroaching presence of imperial rhetoric with its constant suggestions to the reader of a political structure. Canopus with its Colonial Service, envoys and imperial education system never allows the busily translating reader to forget the persistent colonial nature of 'spaces' within *Shikasta*. The reader is forced to become more and more aware of translation as a political act of appropriation. The novel encodes competing discourses, so by translating Shikasta into Earth, the reader is endorsing a power relationship within the text, appropriating Earth history in Shikastan terms: the reader is colonising the novel.

This manipulation into the Canopean position is further compromised by the implications of reading Shikasta as Earth. Such a reading is a transportation from the crystalline clarity of the Canopean perspective to become a citizen of Shikasta, which means a citizen of a polluted degraded planet, one who is explicitly incapable of clear thinking. Shikastans are hopelessly colonised by aliens, both biologically and psychically. We are told that pure natives, themselves reshaped by Canopus, die out in favour of the extraterrestrial Giant-native 'cross' (p. 127), and that genes from the space empires of Shammat, Sirius and Canopus have contributed to the heterogeneous stock. Translating Shikasta as Earth means assuming the identity of these colonised, polluted, hopelessly miscegenated Shikastans. The only ('unnatural') alternative is to take the role of Canopean or Shammat spy since they are all disguised in human form and may not be aware of their stella identities. Taking a non-Shikastan subject position means becoming confined to an angelic–demonic dialectic, as George the Canopean and various evil Shammat agents demonstrate. All are explicitly imperialists.

Consequently, the reader is unable to find a secure position as either a coloniser/translator of the text or as one colonised, and therefore a mentally inadequate subject of it. We are told that Canopean colonisation 'raises' natives and that it is the evil empire, Shammat, which has caused minds to degrade, but we have yet to explore whether Lessing can make a convincing distinction between the imperial discourses of the two empires. What is apparent so far is Lessing's depiction of the inescapability of the imperial trope for her readers (who need not be merely white western as *Shikasta* demonstrates) represented here in reading experience. The novel shows that the imperial trope is inseparable from the employment of Jungian theory in the representation of the Canopeans. *Shikasta* reproduces and dramatises this dynamic of the colonising/colonised reader in the description of the 'Trial of the White Races' (pp. 374–419) conveyed in the reports of the latest colonial rulers of a future 'Europe,' the Chinese.

At a time of mass starvation and overpopulation, anger at the historic cruelty of the white races reaches genocidal proportions and is focused by the drama of the mock trial. Typically, George Sherban acquires a key role as chief prosecutor for the dark races but he looks white, with only an Indian grandmother, which becomes a joke during the trial (p. 379). In fact we realise that someone, presumably George, has avoided the appearance of black/white polarisation by mixing the races on both sides and by complicating the lighting as the trial takes place at night. As throughout *Shikasta*, the reader is invited to develop other perspectives of events. In addition to the broad invitation to guess George's Canopean agency, the narrator here is a Chinese colonial official whose summaries of reports gradually force him to read his own colonial position differently from his previous complacency. Writing about the trial causes him to become conscious of an unmentionable critical analysis of his new Chinese empire with its unstated policy of population reduction by starvation and by encouraging hostility between subject races. Accounts of the trial also open up the colonising structure beyond the binary opposition of white/black, a dualism subverted in the visual presentation. While appearing to be designed to indict the white races and the white reader as coloniser, such a dualism is problematised at the end of the trial by George Sherban and his love, Sharma Patel, who present evidence of the non-white races colonising and exploiting each other. George describes the treatment of the Untouchables in India as a subject caste.

> The unspeakable treatment meted out to these unfortunate people, barbaric, cruel, senseless ... this unspeakably cruel treatment is matched for baseness by nothing the white races have ever done. (p. 414)

Some readers might dispute George's judgement here, but in context he is trying to avert the mass slaughter of all whites for oppressing all blacks. Significantly, he faces all the audience who represent all continents and races: the colonising reader is every reader even though the novel makes most visible white imperialism. It is not a move designed to eradicate all *difference* between oppressive systems and their extent. Sharma Patel, an Indian woman who has previously spoken of the inequities of white rule, endorses George: 'I, an Indian born and bred, ally myself with what our comrade has said' (p. 414). George has prosecuted the white races on behalf of the black and now the defender, John Brent-Oxford, whom the reader knows to be the Canopean Taufiq, reinforces the end of this binary opposition.

> We all know that at this time, now, there are nations, non-white nations, which dominate and subjugate by force other nations, some equally non-white, but other nations that are white. (p. 415)

This apparently uncontroversial statement must also be read in the context of the current Chinese colonisation, with the reader becoming ever more aware that this whole account is filtered or 'translated' by the Chinese official. The trial dramatises critiques of colonial power. Its 'mock' nature, overt fictional quality, makes apparent the rhetorical strategies in the representation of colonial positions. What the drama achieves is to make the term 'colonised' a shifting position within the text. George Sherban and John Brent-Oxford not only extend the possible readings of colonising and colonised beyond the dualism black and white in a fixed racist hierarchy, but also suggest the current colonised position of all present, prosecutors, defenders, audience, under the new 'Benevolent Tutelage' (p. 370) of the Chinese. Of course, the reader of *Shikasta* is aware of the additional colonial presence of the Canopeans who may be controlling this education in imperialism but we cannot be absolutely sure that they are in control *as* Canopeans, especially given John Brent-Oxford's previously detailed failures. How far do Johor and Taufiq as George and John *realise* their Canopean psychic/archetypal heritage? Do they know they are Canopeans and, if so, how much do they know? Could they be engaging in a more muddled, more Shikastan approach, effectively being mere Shikastans here? In effect, the dualistic colonial relationship between Canopeans and Shikastans is also blurred by their incarnation in a realistic text. In this realistic part of the novel we cannot be sure *where* George/Johor and John/Taufiq are between the position of coloniser as Canopean agents, and/or colonised Shikastans unaware of their imperial psychic origins. Additionally, indications of a Canopean presence remind the reader that the current supreme colonial power, the Chinese, is also colonised in the terms of the science fiction dimension of the text. The trial destabilises all possible divisions of colonising/colonised, affording the reader no single structure of colonial power.

Nevertheless, it cannot be said that the Canopean attempt to identify themselves with colonised Shikastans, taking on Lessing's authorial representative role, has completely distanced the Canopean empire from the repressive power discourse of representation. During the trial, the reality behind the British policy of 'benevolence' (p. 403) in Africa is detailed. Such a word used of British rule is perilously close to the terms 'Benevolent Tutelage', or 'Beneficent Rule' (p. 408), the euphemisms used by the Chinese to justify their empire. Contingency of British 'benevolence' and Chinese 'Benevolent Tutelage' exposes the spurious rhetoric of both empires in favour of revealing varieties of similarly autocratic harshness. The narrator of the trial, Chen Lui, tries to direct the dangerous words (and the reader) to other meanings.

> I inscribe this second word with reluctance, with the reliance on your understanding, and the reflection that the one word may have to stand for a variety of shades of circumstance. (p. 403)

This attempt to restrict the readings, paradoxically encourages unlicensed translation of colonial critiques, so much so that Chen Lui is deemed to have earned 'beneficent correction' (p. 419) until his death. Chen Lui ostensibly writes for a reader within the novel, Ku Yuang, but the external reader is drawn to question further the term 'benevolent rule' for it is that, though not in those terms, that the Canopeans claim to provide. If Chen Lui can translate his empire into an-Other culture, then the reader can translate the difference in the Canopean way: the Canopean empire is different, supposedly 'good' while both the Chinese and British oppress. But the difference, the untranslatable residue between British and Chinese cruelty and Canopean nurture, is unstable. We also see a similarity in language, in roles, while unavoidably remembering that we perceive the Canopean imperial trope from a position of degraded, muddled, colonised and colonising Shikastans. The novel allows the reading of the Canopeans as the literal, dominant empire while insisting that the reader recognises this as an act of translation not made from a neutral position, a crystalline clear vision, but from a culturally contaminated perspective. The reader is forced to recognise such a reading as a translation into the literal or the 'proper', the term preceding the literal which Eric Cheyfitz argues in *The Poetics of Imperialism*[32] is related to seizing property, and is a trope of aggressive colonisation.

> The notion of the proper, I argue, must be understood in relation to European notions of property and identity. As for the literal ... its figurative use for the notion of the proper has historically taken on a metaphysical force that naturalises writing, concealing it as technology – that is, as a form of politics.[33]

The reader colonises the text in the terms of our own fictions of cultural identity by translating Canopeans into a literal empire. This is not to argue that this is an incorrect reading, just that Lessing makes us realize it is a political reading. *Shikasta* dramatises reading as a political structure: the reader is required to perform multiple positions within colonial discourse.

Yet just as translation is invited and problematised, it is spread into other modes than the literal. This is suggested particularly by the use of fictions in imperial discourses with the Canopeans having a superior system of (Sufi) teaching stories to develop the desired cosmic consciousness. In fact fictions and metaphors are about all we have of Canopus. We are told nothing about the androgynous archetypal Canopeans apart from their incarnations as culturally specific archetypal images and the little we see demonstrated of their use of stories and metaphors in developing civilisations. Once Shikasta has fallen into individualistic Shammat, Johor tries to maintain some ghost of Canopus with his metaphor of SOWF, 'Substance Of We Feeling' (p. 96) which we are told he has devised because that is all damaged Shikastan brains can hope to retain. 'SOWF' is therefore explicitly not pure Canopean ideology but a radically diluted version for the degraded Shikastan audience and the novel's readers whether defined as 'Shikastan' or not. The perception that Canopeans are using the operating methods of Sufi teachers in stories and fictions is strengthened by the resemblances between George Sherban's education and that of Lessing's Sufi teacher, Idries Shah.[34] The sheer difficulty of literal translation into Earth concepts, its politicisation, and the persistence of Canopean fictions rather than Canopean facts means that the reader is encouraged to maintain *also* a sense of the fictionality of the Canopean empire within the experience of reading in this explicitly science fiction novel. The reader retains consciousness of the Canopeans as also fictions, a consciousness residing in the incompleteness of translation for if Shikasta is also not Earth, then we are simultaneously aware of *Shikasta*, the novel, as a fiction. Canopeans are Other voices as well as imperial agents. Such a reading structure is fostered by the constant demands for Other readings made to characters within the narrative and by the structure of the text. The problematics of reading as translation within this text means that there is always a trace of fictional self-consciousness even when the reader feels most trapped in the overlapping imperial structures.

If the Canopeans are also read metaphorically then *Shikasta* adopts an air of postmodernity, interrogating its own fictional ideology. This role is reinforced by the perception that *Shikasta* is a fictional macrocosm of Lessing's entire *oeuvre*, a meta-text, reprising long-running concerns and representative strategies in her fiction. *Shikasta* re-examines persistent Lessing themes of racial oppression, female subordination and class conflict. Also, early Lessing characters reappear redefined in science fiction, most notably Lynda Coldridge from *The Four Gated City* (1969) as a Canopean agent (pp. 226, 230–9, 431). More strikingly, in the 'case histories' given by Johor, which are like seeds for novels, some of her future fictions can be discerned. The enumeration of terrorist types anticipates *The Good Terrorist* (1985),[35] while tales of problem children suggest *The Fifth Child* (1988).[36] In addition, *Shikasta*'s imperial scheme is both a meta-text *about* Lessing's earlier and future novels but is also a cosmic macrocosm, a universe in which we may *map* the non-realist implications of her earlier fictions. The entire *Canopus in Argos* series develops a role as a fictional space of ideological empires, to form a *canopy* over Lessing's work, as well as also a textual space, reprising and extending her thematical concerns.

(POST)COLONIAL JUNG?

The encoded sense of the fictionality of the Canopeans is also supported by continuing to read envoys such as Johor as archetypal images of unrepresentable crystalline archetypes. *Shikasta* operates two poles of an unstable reading process: firstly, a reading by translating the reader into a Shikastan so under the literal authority of the Canopeans/archetypal images, and secondly, a reading aware of the resistance to translation with the Canopeans as fictional metaphors of Otherness. These readings together reproduce the Jungian structure of individuation whereby the ego makes meaning or 'reads reality' by a continual dialogue with archetypal images. The Jungian ego is conceived as imperious: it desires to translate unconscious material into its own terms, the literal, or in Cheyfitz's words, to make 'proper' the unassimilable realm of the unconscious, to translate it into the ego's property. Reading Canopus as a literal empire is a translation of unconscious Otherness into the ego's domain of understanding as our familiar history of imperialism. Therefore, when the reader of *Shikasta* is a coloniser (meaning one who is appropriating Earth political and sacred history and situating herself as a Shikastan confronting a literal Canopean empire), she is experiencing one Jungian mode of understanding. Yet it is one that is always in tension with, and inseparable from, an-Other aspect of individuation. Here, the unconscious reshapes the ego by revealing the literal translation as inadequate, as an inauthentic fantasy of dominance. In Jungian individuation, deconstruction of the ego occurs by *also* reading archetypal images as fictional, metaphorical, provisional, culturally coloured manifestations of a plural psyche not liable to conquest. *Shikasta*'s situating of the reader reproduces Jungian individuation as a way of politicising reading experience, revealing the inescapability of the imperial trope for readers within twentieth-century culture. It is also a re-cognition of the colonial forms inhabiting the Jungian structure of encounter with the Other. Moreover, it is a re-cognition which aims to develop the reader's consciousness in the manner of a Sufi teaching story. *Shikasta*'s Jungian reading (w)rite is a political and an esoteric education. The novel is therefore a challenge to the colonial component of Jungian ideas and simultaneously reveals the potential for a postcolonial Jungian literary theory. Such a theory would be one which makes use of the inauthentic nature of ego definitions when they claim to exhaust the possibilities of the Other, and of the fictive quality native to archetypal representations.

Jung's typical narrative of individuation is one of 'sacred marriage,' union with an-Other that remains untranslatable into the same.[37] The second volume of *Canopus in Argos, The Marriages Between Zones Three, Four, and Five* (1980, hereafter, *The Marriages*), seizes upon this structure and attempts to go beyond the duality of the marriage plot to explore issues of psychic and physical colonising of Other realms. The Zones start in mutual hostility, declining in fertility. The Order from the 'Providers' (p. 12), presumed to be Canopeans, is that the Queen of agrarian, utopian Zone Three, Al.Ith, must marry the king of patriarchal militaristic Zone Four, Ben Ata. This enforced union initiates beneficial movements between Zones, renewing cultures and stimulating personal individuation. However, such a positive cultural exchange is not the same as 'pure' translation, again revealed as a myth. Al.Ith asks for a dictionary over Zone Four use of the word 'love' (p. 117) but is never able completely to express her Zone Three self in her husband's land. Equally, she realises that she perceives Zone Two through the filter of her Zone Three culture: what she sees as blue may in fact be 'an iridescence of flames' (p. 236). Encountering the Other in this Jungian 'marriage' structure results in psychic process but resists a hierarchical discourse of colonial dominance. It is Zone Five, apparently the 'lowest' culture, that produces the key into the movement into the highest, Zone Two (p. 280). Interestingly, colonial hierarchy is here challenged through its replication: it persists even when denied and Lessing's obvious numbering system seems designed to make the reader more aware of it.

Like Al.Ith, exposing the impossibility of pure translation, the narrator of *The Marriages*, Lusik claims the impossibility of pure unmediated representation. Artists of Zones Three and Four produce different images for different cultural resonances. Lusik and Al.Ith are almost split Canopeans from *Shikasta*, with Al.Ith taking the incarnated role and Lusik the role of the one who makes meanings for a specific culture by creating the teaching stories. Alternatively, they can be seen as mythical projections of Lessing's two types of representative: the ruler and the author with Lusik very concerned to explore relations between the two.

> We are the visible and evident aspects of a whole we all share, that we all go to form ...
>
> I write in these bald words the deepest lessons of my life, the truest substance of what I have learned. I am not only a Chronicler of Zone Three, or only partially, for I also share in Al.Ith's condition of being ruler insofar as I can write of her, describe her. I am a woman with her (though I am a man) as I write of her femaleness ... (p. 242)

Such an argument is a statement of Canopean ideology which is written into the meta-textual nature of Lessing's science fiction. It is also a formulation of the impossibility of pure and absolute separation between narrator and ruler or author and dictator. Like the Canopeans, Lusik draws fictionality, here the constructed quality of the fable, into the reading experience. He also forces the reader to address the darker side of authorship in the use of fiction in oppressive power structures, just as Jungian individuation contains the concept of the shadow, the destructive side. To represent violent impulses is not to control them.

> Describing, we become. We even – and I've seen it and have shuddered – summon. (p. 243)

Although there is comparatively little to shudder at in *The Marriages,* issues of representation do cast a long shadow. These issues can be seen to echo anxieties articulated in 'The Small Personal Voice' in the male dictator claiming to represent the people in the political sphere and the author representing the silent in the artistic. Just as Lusik sees his role extending to a darker, autocratic shade, so Al.Ith experiences an ascent of consciousness to occupy an authorial position, if only briefly. Penetrating to Zone Two, she finds herself in the 'crystalline airs of that plain' (p. 239), clearly suggestive of the archetypal imagination. Her experience of that foreign realm can only be represented through a series of fictional images.

> Dreaming there, she believed them to be the invisible ones of Zone Two ...
>
> But the barrier between them was absolute, and this barrier was the thick clumsy substance of Al.Ith ... perhaps after all these story-tellers, or their ancestors, did see little gnarled strong men ... or at least such beings were part of the consciousness of lower Zones, to an extent that the thoughts of these minds, or the words of the story-tellers, could bring them to life – there they were now, vivid, alive, moving in Al.Ith's mind's eye, perfect and created, yet so far away, yet she could see them, and yet she might not touch them. (p. 241)

The resistance to pure translation from another culture or signifying system is carried by a proliferation of fictions just as archetypes can never be purely translated or represented but do provide a multiplicity of fictional archetypal images. These fictions can represent Otherness (and therefore other people) only as long as their plurality and full untranslatability is recognised. Otherwise, fictions or images hardened into systems of power and hierarchy dictate, take themselves literally and become frozen into oppressive imperial discourses. In *The Marriages,* Lessing examines the relations between her two figures of representation by allying Al.Ith and Ben Ata with Lusik. In the fable of *The Marriages* the rulers are embodiments of their realms, so Al.Ith and Ben Ata are extensions of Lusik, the artist as shaper, into the novel. This enables the autocratic functions of rule and the separation of rulers and subjects to be dispersed onto the Providers whose very non-appearance contributes to the fictive feel of the text. As female head of a co-operative society, Al.Ith appears the antithesis of the male dictator but it is interesting that even these ideal, 'representative' rulers have been contaminated by the threat of weapons of mass destruction. Zone Four's 'death ray fortresses' (p. 122), suggested by 'strangers' (p. 122) promote antagonism between Zones. The very language of 'death ray fortresses' plunges us into 'science fiction' and they are simultaneously revealed in the text *as* fictions, designed to intimidate and repel those 'Others' over the border. We witness a demonstration that even ideal ruler-authors cannot entirely divest themselves of the shadow side of their authority. Science fiction, as a literary form, is not without its political functions.

Similarly, in *Shikasta,* the archetypal Canopeans are an attempt to disperse Lessing's own authorship, her authority, but they find themselves in continual battle with the tyrannical empire of Shammat, clearly the hideous progeny of the white male dictator in 'The Small Personal Voice'. Shammat is different from Canopus, just the two types of representative are different but in its imperial discourse, it is not entirely separate, just as the representative author is never wholly free from the colonising, imperial shadow. Lessing's two types of representation in the early essay become two imperial discourses, the metaphorical authorial Canopeans and the literal dictatorship of Shammat: different but not separable as demonstrated by the persistence of the literal mode of understanding the Canopean empire. This literal mode of understanding Canopus draws it close to Shammat in its appearance of power. The empires exist in a Jungian trope of deconstruction between ego translation (colonising the novel into literal empires that simultaneously and ideologically colonise the reader) and archetypal representation (metaphorical, recognising the inauthenticity of translation). It is not possible to have one way of representing without a shadow of the Other. Jungian theory becomes a means of critiquing its own colonial structures while at the same time positing an Otherness to them – an Otherness not separate and outside colonialism but one that recognizes the inescapability of political fictions within any discourse. It is for this reason, I suggest, that as well as these science fictions diagnosing a colonial Jung, they also detect a Jungian contribution to postcolonial literary theory. This contribution is substantiated by a postcolonial Jungian literary theory developing the poststructuralist potential of Jungian ideas in stressing the fictional, partial and culturally implicated nature of archetypal images.

A literal reading of the Canopeans as empire of control and authority is inescapable, in addition to their roles as authors of teaching stories and as fictional archetypal images. The Shammat empire has the function of resembling and demonstrating gross difference from Canopus, offering and problematising analogy. Perhaps significantly, the Oxford English Dictionary cites 'shammat' as meaning 'excommunicated' from the Hebrew 'shammatise'.[38] Johor records that Puttiora, parent empire to Shammat, 'dismayed us more because it could only remind us of our earlier less pleasant stages of development' (p. 36). Shammat is actually peopled by the rejects of Puttiora, once its prison planet, so showing a double attempt to distance that empire from Canopus. Yet, the etymology suggests its role as that which must be cast out yet cannot be cast away, the shadow of Canopus's bright imperial body.

The reproduction of Jungian individuation in the reading process politicises this literal, dictator/fictional, author dialectic by making the reader conscious of the shadow of colonial history structuring her perceptions. Eric Cheyfitz argues that metaphor is also a colonial mode of reading, never securely separable or distanced from the literal.

> I do not agree that metaphor is a privileged place, located 'outside' of or 'beyond' or 'above' the colonial and imperial politics of language ...[39]

Lessing's use of Jung here would endorse such a conclusion while asserting the difference encoded within metaphor. If we remember that Sufi teachers, like archetypal images work with cultural material, not outside it, then Lessing's Sufi ideology clearly desires and supports the difference of metaphor to provide an alternative reading of empire, while not pretending to be outside, or to wholly escape colonial culture and structures of thinking.

It is suggestive that Al.Ith's final destination, Zone Two, is a place of 'crystalline yet liquid' (p. 237) earth, where her thoughts are 'the creatures of this unfamiliar place' (p. 238). It is a place of image: she can almost see people 'as if flames trembled into being' (p. 238) where she feels most strongly 'at home' (p. 238). Zone Two appears to be the realm of the archetypal imagination which recalls the crystalline Canopeans. Another designation of it, however, could be death. From the perspective of Zone Three it is blue, the colour of mourning in that Zone (p. 13) and Al.Ith hopes to find her dead horse Yori 'there, but a transformed and translated version of him ... so dreamed Al.Ith' (p. 242). Virtually the only use of the word 'translated' in Canopus in Argos, it is here taken back to an earlier sense of 'translated to heaven'. Only to the realm of the plural archetypal psyche can translation occur differently to the political appropriation reproduced elsewhere. Nevertheless, this difference does not take it outside the topos of colonisation explored in the whole novel series. Al.Ith's move to Zone Two is part of the cultural exchanges contained within the individuation narratives figured elsewhere as 'marriage' within this text.

THE CHALLENGE FROM LESSING'S FICTION

Lessing has dispersed her authority behind the archetypal Canopeans in order to colonise Earth history for *Canopus in Argos*. Like any imperial discourse, she gives back to the colonised (the readers) a mistranslated, ideologically biased history. Her envoys, or archetypal images, are culturally coloured by her mode of debunking religious and political myths. For example, Johor/George's early encounter with a Miriam (p. 278) reminds us that he is a Moses leading survivors to a promised land of new sacred cities by the end of Shikasta, as well as in his incarnation, suggesting Jesus. At the same time, established religions are criticised as perversions of Canopean truths. In *The Sirian Experiments*, we are told that Canopeans employ 'subtle technology' (p. 62), and as Lessing's subtle empire they embody their author's technology in individuating the readers, re-shaping interpretations. Lessing uses such Jungian ideas as archetypes, individuation and sacred marriage, to make visible the tropes of empire and colonisation that not only dominate our history but also our structures of understanding. We cannot escape reading the crystalline Canopeans as a literal empire, not securely distant from the dictator of 'The Small Personal Voice'. Yet we remain conscious that this reading is filtered by translating ourselves into Shikastans, so entering the colonising process by occupying the text. By becoming Shikastan, we are told that we pollute our vision. Thus the reader is invited to Other readings, to raise consciousness by reading Canopeans as also fictive, story-telling Sufi teachers who warn in the text of *Shikasta* against their words being 'hardened into dogma' (p. 145). This enables a recognition of *Shikasta* as

Lessing's fictional macrocosm and the possibility of reading empire differently, but not separately from the political.

Lessing's subtle empire builds on her early perception of how Jung could be used as an imperial discourse. *Canopus in Argos* explores the political potential of Jungian ideas just as it uses Jung to demonstrate the psychic persistence of politics. If Shammat is the shadow of Canopus as literal/political empire, it is part of a continual displacement of authority (from Lessing to Canopeans, Canopeans to Shammat and so on) that aims to offer a textual space to empire as metaphor, using Jungian paradigms that allow the reader to be colonised also by Otherness, to have participation through the author's representation by means of teaching story. *Canopus in Argos* draws upon Lessing's *oeuvre* where she has persistently investigated anxieties about representation, colonial politics and psychic development. Textual conflicts culminate in *Canopus in Argos,* where science fiction/Sufi techniques in-fold the tension of Otherness, of metaphor into the imperial theme. Lessing's science fiction sequence demonstrates the ability of fiction to explore the 'doubleness' in Jungian theory by both exposing political drives and revealing the more postmodern, fictional nature of the discourse itself. By interrogating colonial traces in Jungian thinking, the theory's fictional flexibility can be simultaneously deployed in the service of a projected Otherness to the reader's imperially saturated consciousness. We may trace the not unproblematic outlines of a postcolonial Jungian literary theory as one capable of a self-consciousness of its own capacity for re-producing colonial tropes. By doing so, postcolonial Jungian theory can posit an Otherness within and against our culture's imperial (pre)occupations.

Chapter 5 of this book demonstrated how Michèle Roberts' feminist use of Jung culminated in a critique of the politics of gender within his work. *In the Red Kitchen* exerted a historicist challenge to the empirical claims of Jungian theory to work as a meta-narrative of gender and psyche. Chapter 6 examined a novel which failed to respond to the political connotations of the importation of Jungian ideas as a powerful narrative discourse. As a result, *Hopeful Monsters* was doomed to replicate structures of elitism and domination. The text's very refusal to consider Jungian concepts historically made visible the cultural sediment shadowing and fracturing the theory's bid for transcendence. In this chapter, I have argued that Jungian theory is a key component in Lessing's long gestated concerns about the political dimensions of literary representation and authorial presence. *Canopus in Argos* offers the most sophisticated version of the reading (w)rite in that it uses individuation in reading structures to bring to consciousness the colonial trope haunting the modern reader. Consideration of these science fiction texts, therefore, concludes the challenge from fiction in this work in showing the profound influence of, and response to Jungian theory by this important twentieth-century writer. Such literature both employs and transforms Jungian practice within the field of literary theory as a whole. Lessing's science fiction textualises a postcolonial literary Jung just as Roberts' works assimilate his ideas to feminist literary theory in a positive as well as critical spirit. Through such novels we discern opportunities for postcolonial and feminist literary theory criticising Jung but also trace the contributions possible *to* these literary theories from Jungian texts. The final chapter of this book will survey the previous arguments regarding C.G. Jung and literary theory.

Stars signify the deterministic universe in Lessing's science fiction, sign of the Canopean empire as literal or 'proper'. Here all ultimately is the stars' property as Al.Ith muses: 'stars are what we are made of, what we are subject to' (p. 240) so it is fitting that 'Canopus' and 'Sirius' are terrestrial names for stars, thus an obvious projection, another trace of science fiction in the texts. It is not for nothing that Jung called the imagination the star in man, quoting an alchemical text.[40] The Canopeans are messengers from the stars and images from the archetypal imagination. By powerfully demonstrating how we make fictions within political and colonial tropes, Lessing's *Canopus in Argos* bids us beware how we trespass in our imaginative space.

8

C.G. Jung and Literary Theory

I started this book with the metaphor of romance in order to suggest a new relationship between the psychology of C.G. Jung and modern literary theories after poststructuralism. 'Romance' in this context is meant to describe a deconstructive intimacy between Jungian writings and literary theories in which mutual criticism and support is permissible. Theoretical approaches such as feminism and postcolonialism can make very necessary criticisms of the cultural biases deeply embedded in Jungian ideas. At the same, time I would argue that Jungian theory has been an unjustly neglected resource in the development of literary studies. This final chapter aims to review the results of the romance between Jung and literary theory posited in the foregoing pages. Such a summary should serve as an outline of both the arguments of this book and a portrayal of its 'romance'. It foresees a future expanded role for Jung in literary research.

JUNGIAN ROMANCE WITH THE OTHER

'Romance' as a metaphor has not been plucked out of nowhere to discuss deconstructive engagements with Jungian writings. On the contrary, romance is a key motif of Jungian theory which offers a distinctive delineation of the Jungian Other. Jungian romance is both literal and metaphorical. The resulting sliding of the signifier over signified is a clue to the Jungian affinity with literary theory. The core Jungian process of individuation is built upon an erotic encounter with an Other where that Other can be another person (in sexual or platonic mode) or the Other gender in the unconscious or yet another image representing Otherness. Since the Jungian unconscious is creative, autonomous and never to be fully comprehended or conquered by the ego's imperious demands, the Jungian Other is a privileged entity. This Other can only be wooed in Jungian individuation romance: it is an Other demanding an ethical relationship in a respect for its incapacity ever to be completely known to consciousness. The Jungian Other exists in a state of romance which requires the sacrifice of the ego's tendency to subordinate and control. Such a potent Other can be a valuable contribution to literary theories which recognise the textual subordination of marginalised groups. My own use of Jungian romance with the Other tries to structure the encounter between Jung and literary theory as one which stages the other discourse as the Other. In this Jungian trope, the Otherness of the 'alien' discourse enables a sacrifice of the urge to certainty and power within either literary theory or Jungian ideas. Literary theory may become permeable to Jungian contributions while Jungian texts can be thoroughly critiqued.

JUNGIAN THEORY AND DECONSTRUCTION

In the Introduction, I showed that it was broadly correct to ally Jung with humanism under an intentionalist reading. Nevertheless, a strict interpretation of the 'formlessness' of unconscious archetypes vis-à-vis their culturally inflected derivatives, archetypal images, promotes a move away from humanism towards structuralism. What has not yet been appreciated is the productive possibilities for applying Derrida's reading of Freud to Jung instead. A distinctive feature of Jungian writings is that potentials for deconstruction are overt in the text and exist alongside the most dogmatic and metaphysical statements. So Jung is frequently sceptical about metaphysical totalising tendencies in which a psychological theory (including his own) claims to comprehend all the myriad possibilities of the psyche. On the other hand, he uses the most metaphysical and logocentric language when describing his ideas. The Jungian concept of the 'self' operates as a Derridean 'supplement' which purports to originate psychic theoretical narratives. The self is the Jungian 'god-term' or logos, claiming to underpin his system. Nevertheless, Jungian psychic images can fairly be called a 'kind of writing' after Derrida because they do work on a principle of 'difference' and 'deferral' or *différance*. Archetypal images are distinguished by difference from each other and crucially defer infinitely a full and sufficient signified which would allow closure. The archetypal image can never comprehend the protean multiplicity of the archetype: its signified in the unconscious is deferred.

Jung was also able to talk about his theories 'under erasure' by describing the unknowability of the unconscious and therefore the insufficiency of 'theory'. The professionally sceptical Jung is one who allows his theory to be a metaphor which will be superseded in time by others, just as alchemy has been. He is even able to suggest the intertextuality of his discourse with alchemy by admitting that alchemical texts, not clinical 'evidence' shape and substantiate his key concepts. What is crucial here is both Jung's recognition of the spectral presence of fiction within his theory but also the readiness of Jungian writings to submit themselves to Derrida's critique. Jungian theory is ripe for deconstruction and in some ways uncannily anticipates poststructuralist thought. I have described Jungian individuation as romance but it is equally valid to draw out its deconstructive implications. Romance with the unconscious includes the sacrifice of ego claims to control. This, in turn, necessitates the sacrifice of secure signifying. Individuation romance needs a shadow side of undoing, unmaking, the loss of meaning and the acceptance of the sliding of the signifier. By applying deconstructive insights to Jungian psychology, the resulting romance produces a 'postmodern' Jung haunting his logocentrically inclined texts.

JUNG AND FEMINIST THEORY

The romance of Jungian discourse and literary theory becomes stormy at the point of the feminine. Jungian writings exhibit both misogyny and significant opportunities for feminist theoretical developments. The following pages supply an account of the arguments of this book in this contentious and very exciting area.

Jung's (Metaphysical) Language of the Feminine

Jung's constant assertion that the feminine has been wrongly neglected in western culture and particularly in the psyches of men has always caused some feminist critics to rejoice. Unfortunately the resulting 'Jungian feminism' adopts a humanist approach to

Jung and takes his descriptions of 'femininity' to be an essentialist prescription for gender; one totally independent of cultural factors. A poststructuralist approach to Jung evades this problem but let me first recap the objections to Jung's language of the feminine.

Despite (poststructurally) admitting that men can never be objective about the feminine since their own unconscious feminine side (the anima) will distort perceptions, Jung described women as unsuited for prolonged intellectual activity, dominated by erotic interests and crucially alienated from rational or spiritual perceptions. Close examination of his texts reveals a 'cultural slippage' between the anima as unconscious femininity in men and Jung's opinion of women in the world. True to his own insight, Jung is not objective or even rational about women. Jungian writings generalise from the fascinating and hypnotic anima image in the masculine unconscious to indict all women in a masquerade of femininity. Women become animas in Jungian theory; a theory thereby made hysterical in its inability to be coherent about the feminine. Given this powerful misogynistic drive, can Jung offer anything positive to feminist theory?

Jung and Feminist Theory: the Feminine in the Symbolic

It is Jung's definition of the unconscious which is the key to a more sophisticated Jungian feminist literary theory. Jung's unconscious is the creative Other to which the dependent and limited ego must develop a relationship in the deconstructive process of individuation. The unconscious is structured through archetypes as the potentials for images and psychic signifying. Archetypes are not inherited images but the inherited possibilities for certain sorts of meaning. They are androgynous, being equally capable of manifesting themselves in feminine as masculine representations. It is the unconscious as an autonomous and proactive force which promotes the formation of subjectivity in early childhood. The body and its signifiers (such as the phallus) cannot take priority over the creative unconscious. Therefore, the Jungian Symbolic is one in which the feminine must be an effective form of signifying as powerful as the masculine because the feminine is always potentially *there* in the androgyny of unconscious archetypes. The Jungian Symbolic drains Lacan's phallus of anything but a cultural meaning: the phallus is patriarchy's imposition on psychoanalytic discourse.

Individuation can now provide a dynamic narrative of feminist development for women and those whose sexual or gender identity has been repressed. Patriarchy may have injured feminine identity but romance with the Jungian Other will supply healing. The Jungian unconscious is compensatory of both ego excesses and vulnerabilities. Any marginalised subject damaged in patriarchy may look to a positive psychic Symbolic in which the feminine (for example) is an imaginative and creative force. Chapter 1 illustrated some of the possibilities of Jung's feminine in the Symbolic by suggesting that individuation could be compared to Julia Kristeva's 'subject-in-process'. Additionally, Kristeva's development of the pre-Oedipal (m)Other and abjection could be reformulated in a more productive fashion for feminine subjectivity by using Jungian notions of the 'self'.

Jungian Theory: the Feminine Body, Sexuality and Spirituality

Traditionally, the feminine body has been denigrated as the abject other to culture and patriarchal religions. Jungian theory enables the body to function as a positive partner in religious experience and signifying without excluding any gender. The body may not be assigned the position of the feminine 'other' in relation to the phallic Symbolic because neither the body nor the phallus has a privileged position in Jungian psychic signifying. Through the validation of the feminine in the Jungian Symbolic, feminist theory can discern a recoverable role for the feminine body, enabling its revaluation. In addition, it is possible to theorise a portrayal of a feminine spirituality which is immanent of the female body, not transcendentally above it.

An explicit ingredient of Jungian romance is the place assigned to sexuality in penetrating unconscious modes of signifying. Sexuality is not a necessary part of contacting the unconscious but it is a valid method of engaging with the Other. Of course, Jung expected the Other courted in sexuality to be the Other gender but the fluidity of unconscious gender and the impossibility of restricting unconscious polysemy means that homosexuality must share the positive role. Through sexuality, the body participates in the romance with the Jungian Other. Nevertheless, the body cannot govern unconscious signifying (because the Jungian Other is autonomous, creative and superior), it merely intervenes in it. Since the Jungian Symbolic is as capable of manifesting the feminine as the masculine, there can be no marginalised role for the female body. It too can penetrate the spirituality of the unconscious through Jungian romance.

Spirituality in Jungian theory is dependent upon the recognition that all experience is primarily psychic and therefore mediated by unconscious archetypes. Religious experience may or may not indicate an exterior transcendent god but it is certainly experience of archetypes in higher and spiritual modes. Therefore, spirituality in Jungian theory is an authentic mode of experience in itself. It is very emphatically not a *derivative* of sexual pleasures in bodily forms of signifying. However, sexuality, as a valid form of Jungian romance, is a genuine way of accessing the spirituality of the unconscious. The female body can participate in experiencing the Symbolic as numinous. Feminine embodiment is not only as potent as masculine embodiment in psychic signifying, it has an equal role in spirituality. Divinity may also be manifested as the feminine: patriarchy's exclusively 'father' god is dethroned. (See Chapters 4 and 5 for Michèle Roberts use of these implications within Jungian theory for feminist literary practice.)

The Anima as Phallus

So far, I have suggested two directions for feminist theorists concerned to explore Jungian texts. One is the very necessary critique of the proliferating anima in the writing which serves to veil the feminine in a masquerade. The other is the creative implications of the feminine in the Jungian Symbolic which produces interesting ripostes to Lacan, possible links with Kristeva, a revaluation of the female body and representation and possibilities for a feminine spirituality. These two directions (of feminist criticism and the building of new feminist theories) come together in the anima, and indeed spill over into an historicist investigation of the genesis of Jungian theory (see below).

I have argued that the veiling of the feminine in the anima-as-masquerade can be illuminated by linking it to Luce Irigaray's criticism of Lacan's phallus. If the phallus is what the masculine 'has' and what the feminine must 'be' for the masculine then Irigaray retorts that 'Woman' does not exist in Lacanian discourse. The feminine is a sex which is not *one* because its multiplicity cannot be reckoned in Lacanian binary logic and is *not* one because the feminine does not exist in the masculinist mirror of Lacan's writings where masculinist subjectivity merely reflects back upon itself. A place for the anima in this challenge to Lacan becomes feasible when we recall that for Jung it is the unconscious which is proactive in separating the infant from the Other and in sculpting subjectivity. For the boy-child, the major figure of the unconscious is the anima. Therefore Jung's anima acts as Lacan's phallus in being the chief signifier determining subjectivity and relations with the Other. If the anima is a phallus in this sense then we can see the anima similarly signifying the absence of 'Woman' as truly Other in Jungian discourse. The anima is what the masculine has and what the feminine must be for the masculine in Jungian individuation romance where Jung applauds the projection of the anima onto the female sexual partner. Instead of representing the 'difference' of gender in Jungian theory, the anima is a masculinist fantasy of the Same; the projection of the masculine's inferiority. The anima is a reflection of masculine subjectivity which serves to veil femininity in a masquerade.

Such criticism of Jungian writing does not deform Jung for feminist theory. I contend that in the phallic anima we have a misogynist textual drive which is open to deconstruction. Jung's feminine in the Symbolic is a recoverable product of the tempestuous romance of Jungian texts and feminist theory. Perhaps we can learn more from some of the psychic and historical traces of the anima discernible in Jung's fascination with the occult.

Mediums and Animas: Historical Feminist Criticism of Jung

Jung's first patient was his adolescent female cousin engaged in a series of seances. His subsequent doctoral thesis made much of the medium's 'romances' indicating both Jung's belief that the supernatural voices were fictional and of his diagnosis of incipient sexuality. Yet, in Jung's autobiography, he describes his own model of contacting unconscious powers very much as a medium, giving tongue to the authentic voices of the Other. We see an evolution of a gender politics in Jung's relegation of his cousin to an unreliable 'hysteria' patient and his later assumption of the medium role for himself in contacting femininity within. The female mediums of nineteenth-century spiritualism become animas in Jungian theory as the feminine takes its place as the subordinated ingredient of masculine subjectivity. The medium position is taken for the masculine in most of Jung's writings. Thus the occult strata in Jung's discourse is crucially implicated in a politics of gender.

This is not the only politics which can be discerned as a powerful drive in Jungian writings. It is time to open up Jung to other historicist challenges.

HISTORICIST CRITICISM OF JUNGIAN THEORY

In addition to a lifelong fascination with spiritualism, Jung's writings, and even more his readings, indicate his proximity to the *volkisch* discourse which formed the cultural antecedents of the Nazis. In itself, this does not indict Jung of any more than a presence in a pan-Germanic cultural movement which had both esoteric and political branches. Jung was not interested in the political *volkisch* groupings which were more directly connected with the Nazis. However, *volkisch* discourse was profoundly anti-Semitic. Evidence for Jung as an anti-Semite is ambiguous but he certainly felt free to absorb large quantities of anti-Semitic literature without repudiating its racism. Jung's personal career becomes culpable indeed when he became involved in Nazi Germany in the 1930s. See Chapter 2 for an analysis of these events. My conclusion is that Jung was not a Nazi since that definition, to me, implies specific and unambiguous endorsement of either the Nazi Party or particular Nazi policies. Instead, I suggest that Jung be regarded as a voluntary participant in Nazi Germany and his lack of public remorse for his actions after the war (despite his early recognition of the horrors of concentration camps) be taken as a profound moral flaw.

In the terms of this book, what role has Jung's cultural and political contamination in a future relationship with literary theory? In the first place we must acknowledge that those who reject Jungian ideas on moral grounds have a case, although my own opinion is that Jung was never enough of a Nazi to banish his psychology forever from academia. Jung is a powerful transmitter of romantic philosophy into twentieth century culture. For this reason, I argue against his neglect in literary studies, not because of any attraction to his personality or career.

Second, by considering Jungian theory as an historical discourse it is possible to take account of his political contamination and the drives to power within the writings. Indeed, the case can be put more strongly: if Jung is going to have a place in modern literary theory then it is essential to include an historicist approach which incorporates awareness of his politics. Chapter 6 showed the necessity of historicism in approaching Jung in textuality by examining a novel which sought to purify Jungian discourse from history, politics and power. This chapter also formed part of a larger argument about the danger of using Jungian theory as a meta-narrative in any literary work. Jung can only unite with literary theory in a deconstructive romance in which Jungian theory's drive to power as a meta-narrative of psyche or gender, is decisively frustrated.

JUNGIAN THEORY AND READER-RESPONSE

There are exciting possibilities in a new Jungian reader-response theory which can also link reading and writing with alchemy. Jung believed that the alchemy which attempted to turn lead into gold was a projection of the alchemists own individuation onto the material outer world. The actual mechanics of the projection involved a process he called 'active imagination'. This involves the taking of an image from a dream or a cultural text and concentrating upon it, so relaxing the conscious mind. The Jungian creative unconscious will then spontaneously erupt and guide fantasies. By this method, the unconscious interacts with the ego and the romance of individuation is pursued. All these concepts are crucial to a new Jungian reader-response theory.

Reader-response theory states that the meaning of a literary work is not locked away in the text but inheres in the creative engagement between text and reader. It goes further to suggest that reading reformulates the reader's subjectivity, particularly through liberating some unconscious forces. If we go back to the Jungian concept of active imagination, we could see that words on the page are one step removed from visual images. Reading a fiction will provoke mental images and these will be affected by the Jungian unconscious. In effect, to substitute a Jungian definition of the unconscious for Freud's is to argue that reading fiction promotes individuation. Thus in Jungian terms, reading fiction is a rite since the unconscious forces liberated include the sacred dimensions of archetypes. Also, reading becomes alchemy as reading becomes yet another characterisation of individuation.

Writing fiction can also be absorbed into this model. If a writer is in contact with her creative unconscious, then her writing will again be part of her individuation because the unconscious will guide the psychic signifiers. The writing of art becomes an alchemic (w)rite. Chapter 3 describes the evolution of the Jungian reading (w)rite in a novel which similarly tries to elevate Jungian theory into textual power. The result is to replicate the Jungian subordination of gender difference into the anima as mirror of masculine subjectivity. To consider the effectiveness of the reading (w)rite when not perilously masquerading as a meta-narrative, it is necessary to turn to Jung and (post)colonialism in Chapter 7.

JUNGIAN THEORY AND LITERARY (POST)COLONIALISM

Examining two science fiction novels by Doris Lessing enabled the demonstration of the Jungian reading (w)rite as a culturally sophisticated political and esoteric education of the reader. Yet, first of all we need to consider colonial Jung. Previously, I have stated that the privileged construction of the Jungian Other means that it can be invaluable to the representation of culturally subordinated groups such as the feminine and the colonial other. However, further investigation of Jung and the feminine shows that a simple application of Jungian theory is not the 'answer' to centuries of misogyny. Similarly, the colonial other is not unambiguously rescued by Jungian discourse which betrays many racist stereotypes. Crucially, it is important to stress that the autonomous Jungian Other can become literalised and hardened into an alien invasion of the conscious psyche. The delicate negotiations of precedence between ego and unconscious can in textuality be overtaken by imperial drives on either side. The ego may thwart the essential Jungian notion of its inferiority, for example by colonising the feminine for masculine subjectivity in the phallic anima. On the other hand, the Other may become a vehicle for textual power and authority which colonises the reader as well as hapless individuating characters. Again, we have Jungian theory enacting a drive for literary power as a meta-narrative: here it becomes implicated in colonialism both in portrayals in the text and in structuring a relationship with the reader. If the reader is meant to engage in the Jungian reading rite, then this represents a profound invasion of the reader's psyche if the text then claims absolute authority on Jungian grounds. As before, a more post-structuralist conception of Jungian theory mitigates these drives to power. Yes, there is a colonial narrative in Jungian discourse's claims to authority but the deconstructive romance inherent in Jungian ideas means that colonial Jung is always inseparable from a postcolonial Jung haunting the writings. Since archetypal images operate on principles of *différance* (or to put it another way, are a kind of fiction) because they can never exhaust the multiplicity of the archetype, then fiction becomes an explicit part of the colonial structure. The Other as alien invader is also the Other as fictional invader. Material for constructing archetypal images must derive from cultural perceptions so the Other in archetypal images is made up of partial fictions drawn from culture. Colonial structures in Jungian signifying are therefore as provisional and lacking in claims to authoritative 'truth' as any other archetypal imagery. The imperial Other reveals the persistence of colonial thinking still lurking in the ego, not authenticity. Scrutiny of colonial Jung reveals also postcolonial Jung in the acknowledging of the fundamental unfathomability of the Other who can only be represented to us in the material of our limited ego fictions.

Postcolonial Jung lies in the recognition of the persistent presence in Jungian theory of the fictional nature of the discourse, the spuriousness of its claims to authority in wholly comprehending or representing the Other. Therefore, a Jungian reading rite on the colonial model simultaneously makes the reader aware of the persistence of the colonial trope haunting our perceptions. Colonialism is a cultural fiction masking drives to power. Here, the value of Jungian discourse lies in its capacity for self-consciousness. Jungian theory is historically constituted, in this sense including a complicity with colonialism. Yet, its affinity with deconstruction means that it can be deployed to critique colonialism from within, an argument not pretending to be outside and transcendent of politics. It is the achievement of Lessing's science fiction to demonstrate both colonial and postcolonial Jung in textuality. Her fictions offer a politically nuanced reading rite.

JUNGIAN THEORY, POSTMODERN SPIRITUALITY AND BIBLICAL NARRATIVES

The use of Jungian ideas in literature provides concepts of postmodern spirituality in the form of religious experience independent of doctrinal meta-narratives. In turn, this enables biblical narratives to be re-formed, in particular from a feminist point of view.

All the Jungian concepts necessary for this deployment of the theory have already been described in this chapter so I will just refer to them here. Religious experience to Jung was an authentic manifestation of unconscious archetypes. It may or may not predicate an exterior transcendent god. It is most emphatically *not* the sublimation of sexuality. Nevertheless, sexuality can be a positive component in spirituality. Since sexuality can be a means of contacting the unconscious, the body can be part of the negotiation of the archetypal powers of the numinous. The body can, in this way, influence archetypal signifying, but it can never govern it because the Jungian Other is creatively superior to ego understanding.

Therefore, we are left with a genuine experience of the divine in an immanent relationship with bodily experience, not transcendent of it. Such numinosity is encased in a narrative of Jungian romance with the Other where the protean Other is now spirit. This immediate experience of the godhead or Jungian self can be made to adhere to traditional Christian narratives but need not do so. Biblical structures can be remade in Jungian theory on the model of Jungian romance with the Other where the Other is divine, gender-fluid, archetypal. See Chapter 4 for a feminist remaking of the Bible which continues to respect spirituality. A postmodern spirituality which does not disdain the body and does not require a meta-narrative is native to Jungian theory. Jungian concepts themselves are self-conscious about providing a Jungian meta-narrative, here of spirit. If we take a poststructuralist approach to Jungian romance, then the deconstructive forces of the shadow mitigate the theory's claim to account completely for the divine as the textuality of *The Wild Girl* demonstrates at the end of Chapter 4.

JUNGIAN THEORY AND LITERARY FORM

This book has explored the effect of Jungian theory on the realist form of the novel with some excursions into science fiction. Very broadly, Jungian ideas have most obvious effects in terms of structure and narration. What I would describe as the 'classic' Jungian literary form occurs in *The Wild Girl* where the narrator's Jungian encounters with her Others provides the structure of the text. This classic mode is further developed by including historicist constructions of Jungian discourse in later texts by Michèle Roberts. *Hopeful Monsters* is an example of the 'classic' form which seeks to limit the deconstructive implications of Jungian theory to content rather than acknowledge them in the novel's struggle to communicate an ideology. There, it differs crucially from *The Wild Girl*. Lessing's Jungian science fiction incorporates the historical perception of Jungian discourse in the traces of spiritualism but more significantly, it gives substance to the political dimension of Jungian ideas.

In short, Jungian theory has a poststructuralist effect on the traditional form of the novel. 'Classic' Jungian literary novels attempt to use Jung as a formal meta-narrative of structure but contain within themselves the deconstructive potentialities of the shadow as unmaking, the unravelling of stable ideas, the incapacity of form to produce communicable and absolutely coherent ideologies. Some more culturally aware fictional texts then supply a further level of challenge to Jungian theory by poststructurally exposing the cultural biases of Jung in areas such as gender, colonialism, politics, history. The resulting 'poststructuralist Jungian literary form' critiques the Jungian project in literature while exploiting its creative possibilities: it is another 'Jungian romance' of literary theory and Jung.

C.G. JUNG AND LITERARY THEORY: ROMANCE AND THE CHALLENGE FROM FICTION

I would like to end with the hope that this book has proved the value of a Jungian literary theory beyond traditional Jungian criticism and has established its potential in an age of poststructuralism. While it remains obvious that Jungian writings need the critique of feminist, postcolonial, historicist, deconstruction and postmodern theories, Jungian theory may, in turn, enrich these very discourses. Jungian reader-response tries to explain the power of imaginative literature as an architect of psyche. It is also a theory which draws alchemy and spirituality into the reading process as a rite. Its role should be assured in the developing of notions of postmodern spirituality, psychic configurations of the body and reading as a potentially sacred act.

'Romance' is the trope linking together C.G. Jung and literary theory in the sense that both partners alter and in part reconstitute the Other but neither dominates the relationship. 'Romance' here, has to be the ideal form of Jungian romance in which each sacrifices the claim to control signifying. Such has not always been the literary history of romance in its misogynist, aristocratic, homophobic and even generic forms. It is a bold argument, therefore, to try to recuperate romance in the articulation of Jung and poststructuralist theory. The challenge from contemporary fiction is to re-imagine Jung through literary textuality, to suggest deconstructive intimacies between C.G. Jung and literary theory as a romance in which the future is celebrated.

NOTES

INTRODUCTION: BEYOND TRADITIONAL JUNGIAN LITERARY CRITICISM

1. See Jos van Meurs and John Kidd, *Jungian Literary Criticism, 1920–1980: An Annotated Critical Bibliography of Work in English (With a Selection of Titles after 1980)* (Metuchen, N.J. and London: Scarecrow, 1988).
2. C.G. Jung, 'Psychology and Literature' in *Modern Man in Search of a Soul* (London and Henley: Routledge & Kegan Paul, 1933; Ark Paperbacks, 1984), pp. 175–99.
3. Richard P. Sugg, ed., *Jungian Literary Criticism* (Evanston, Illinois: Northwestern University Press, 1992).
4. Evelyn J. Hinz and John J. Teunissen, 'Culture and the Humanities: The Archetypal Approach', in Sugg, *Jungian Literary Criticism*, pp. 192–9 (p. 199).
5. For an example of Jung's tendency to collapse the archetype into the archetypal image see his discussion of the sun-wheel symbol and its recurrence in *Modern Man in Search of a Soul*, pp. 188–9.

1 JUNG FOR LITERATURE AND LITERARY THEORY

1. For Lessing's description of Jung's sense of the double face of truth see her 'African Interiors, Review of Laurens Van der Post's *The Heart of the Hunter*', *New Statesman*, 67 (27 October 1961), pp. 613–14.
2. Jung, CW11, p. 480.
3. Jung, CW6, p. 52.
4. Jung, CW9 I, p. 79.
5. C.G. Jung, *Dictionary of Analytical Psychology*, Extracted from *Psychological Types*, CW6 (London: Ark Paperbacks, 1987), p. 131.
6. Jung, *Dictionary*, p. 134.
7. Jung, CW14, pp. 465–6.
8. Jung, CW14, pp. 537–8.
9. Jung, CW8, p. 263.
10. Jung, CW8, p. 246.
11. Jung, CW16, p. 262.
12. Jung, CW11, p. 76.
13. Nancy Chodorow, *The Reproduction of Mothering: Psychoanalysis and the Sociology of Gender* (Berkeley: University of California Press, 1978).
14. For the concepts of Eros/Logos treated as being equally accessible to both genders in current British Jungian analysis, I am indebted to

Mrs Hazel Davis, a retired Jungian analyst. She conducted an informal survey of members of the British Society for Analytical Psychology on my behalf in April 1994.

15. Andrew Samuels, 'Beyond the Feminine Principle', in *C.G. Jung and the Humanities: Towards a Hermeneutics of Culture*, edited by Karin Barnaby and Pellegrino D'Acierno (London: Routledge, 1990), pp. 294–306 (p. 301).
16. Jung, CW9 ii, p. 14
17. Linda Fierz-David, *Women's Dionysian Initiation: The Villa of Mysteries in Pompeii*, translated by Gladys Phelan and with an Introduction by M. Esther Harding (Dallas, Texas: Spring Publications Inc., Jungian Classics Series II, 1988). This was completed shortly before the author's death in 1955 as *Psychologische Betrachtungen zu der Freskenfolge der Villa dei Misteri in Pompeii: Ein Versuch*, mimeographed in Zurich, Switzerland, 1957, by the Psychological Club of Zurich.
18. Fierz-David, p. 62.
19. Jung, CW10, p. 118.
20. Jung, CW17, p. 198.
21. Carol Schreier Rupprecht, 'Enlightening Shadows: Between Feminism and Archetypalism, Literature and Analysis', in *C.G. Jung and the Humanities*, pp. 279–93 (p. 282).
22. Rupprecht, p. 282.
23. Bly's mythopoetic men's movement is discussed by Andrew Samuels in his volume, *The Political Psyche* (London and New York: Routledge, 1993), pp. 183 95.
24. Samuels, *The Political Psyche*, p. 186.
25. For an explanation of 'deconstruction', see Christopher Norris, *Deconstruction: Theory and Practice*, revised edition (London and New York: Routledge, 1991).
26. David L. Miller, 'An Other Jung and An Other ...', *C.G. Jung and the Humanities*, pp. 325–30.
27. Gayatri Chakravorty Spivak, 'Translator's Preface', Jacques Derrida, *Of Grammatology* (Baltimore and London: The Johns Hopkins University Press, 1976), pp. ix–lxxxvii (p. xli).
28. Andrew Samuels, *Jung and the Post-Jungians* (London and New York: Routledge & Kegan Paul, 1985) p. 39. For Jung and structuralism, see also Paul Kugler, 'The Unconscious in a Postmodern Depth Psychology', *C.G. Jung and the Humanities*, pp. 307–18.
29. Samuels, *Jung and the Post-Jungians*, p. 40.
30. For Lacan and Jung, see Andrew Samuels, *Jung and the Post-Jungians*, pp. 40–1.
31. See, Evelyn J. Hinz and John J. Teunissen, 'Culture and the Humanities: The Archetypal Approach', *Jungian Literary Criticism*, edited by Richard P. Sugg (Evanston, Illinois: Northwestern University Press, 1992), pp. 192–9.
32. Christopher Norris, *Deconstruction: Theory and Practice*, p. 31.
33. Jung, CW18, p. 309.
34. Jung, CW15, 'Psychology and Literature', p. 85.
35. Derrida, *Of Grammatology*, p. 98.

36. Jung, CW9 I, p. 269.
37. Derrida, *Of Grammatology*, p. 15.
38. Gayatri Chakravorty Spivak, 'Translator's Preface', Jacques Derrida, *Of Grammatology*, p. xvii.
39. Spivak, 'Translator's Preface', p. xxxix.
40. Jung, *Letters* ed. G. Adler, trans. R.F.C. Hull (Princeton, N.J.: Princeton University Press, 1975), vol.1, p. 411.
41. Jacques Derrida, *Writing and Difference*, translated with an introduction and additional notes by Alan Bass (London: Routledge, 1978), p. 229.
42. Jung, CW14, p. vii.
43. Jung, CW14, p. 173.
44. Jung, CW14, pp. 555–6.
45. 'Intertextuality' is used here in the Kristevan sense. By 'intertextuality' I refer to the idea that texts of all kinds do not function as closed systems but operate within the socio-political context of their production, are generated from the writer's encounter with other texts and received through the reader's previous experience of texts. For a thorough discussion of Kristeva's intertextuality, see the introduction to *Intertextuality: Theories and Practices*, edited by Michael Worton and Judith Still (Manchester and New York: Manchester University Press, 1990), pp. 1–44.
46. Jung, CW14, p. 556.
47. Derrida, *Of Grammatology*, pp. 158–9.
48. Jung, CW14, p. 537.
49. For the violence of oppositional thinking, see Jung, CW7, p. 78, Jacques Derrida, *Positions* (Paris: Minuit, 1972), pp. 56–7; trans. Alan Bass (Chicago: University of Chicago Press, 1981), p. 41.
50. Jung, CW9 I, p. 269.
51. Jung, CW14, p. 546.
52. James Hillman, *Archetypal Psychology: A Brief Account* (Dallas, Texas: Spring Publications Inc., 1983), p. 1.
53. James Hillman is also the senior editor of *Spring: A Journal of Archetype and Culture*, published by Spring Publications, Dallas, Texas. It is the oldest Jungian journal, founded in 1941 by the Analytical Psychology Club of New York.
54. See, Edward S. Casey, James Hillman, Paul Kugler, David L. Miller, 'Jung and Postmodernism Symposium', in *C.G. Jung and the Humanities*, pp. 331–40.
55. Hillman, AP, p. 23.
56. Hillman, *Healing Fiction* (New York: Station Hill Press, 1983), p. 93.
57. Kugler, 'The Unconscious in a Postmodern Depth Psychology', *C.G. Jung and the Humanities*, pp. 307–18 (p. 313).
58. Hillman, 'Further Notes on Images', *Spring: A Journal of Archetype and Culture*, 39 (1978), 164.
59. Hillman, *The Dream and the Underworld* (New York: Harper & Row, 1979), p. 123.
60. Hillman, AP, p. 34.
61. Hillman, HF, p. 102.

62. Pre-publication blurb for Anne Baring and Jules Cashford, *The Myth of the Goddess: Evolution of an Image* (London: Viking, 1991), quoted in Samuels, PP, p. 188.
63. Estella Lauter and Carol Schreier Rupprecht, eds, *Feminist Archetypal Theory: Interdisciplinary Re-Visions of Jungian Thought* (Knoxville, TN: University of Tennessee Press, 1985).
64. Rupprecht, 'Enlightening Shadows ...', in *C.G. Jung and the Humanities*, p. 286.
65. Rupprecht, 'Enlightening Shadows ...', p. 290.
66. Julia Kristeva, *The Kristeva Reader*, edited by Toril Moi (Oxford: Basil Blackwell Ltd, 1986), p. 30.
67. Jung, CW14, p. 185.
68. For more on the concepts of the pre-Oedipal Mother and (m)Other see *The Kristeva Reader*, especially pp. 148–51, 204–6.
69. For discussion of Freud's ideas in *Moses and Monotheism* on the founding of religions and the murder of the primal father see *The Kristeva Reader*, pp. 223–4, 234–5, 261.
70. Julia Kristeva, *Powers of Horror: An Essay on Abjection*, translated by Leon S. Roudiez (New York: Columbia University Press, 1982), pp. 57–8.
71. Jung, CW14, p. 177.
72. Kristeva, POH, p. 31.
73. Fierz-David, p. 64.
74. Fierz-David, pp. 123–4.
75. Fierz-David, p. 124.
76. Andrew Samuels discusses correspondences between Lacanian theory and Jung, especially in the matter of Lacan's three orders, in *Jung and the Post-Jungians*, pp. 40–1, p. 280.
77. Jacques Lacan, 'The Signification of the Phallus', *Ecrits: A Selection*, trans. Alan Sheridan (New York: Norton, 1977), pp. 289–90. See also Malcolm Bowie, *Lacan*, Fontana Modern Masters (London: Fontana Press, 1991), pp. 122–57.
78. Luce Irigaray, *This Sex Which Is Not One*, translated by Catherine Porter with Carolyn Burke (Ithaca, NY: Cornell University Press, 1985), originally published 1977 in French by Editions de Minuit, p.129.
79. C.G. Jung, *Modern Man in Search of a Soul* (London: Ark Paperbacks, 1984), originally published 1933, p. 134.
80. Jung, *Modern Man*, p. 138.
81. CW7, p. 197.
82. Irigaray, *This Sex Which is Not One*, p. 111.
83. Fierz-David, p. 46.

2 JUNG: POLITICAL, CULTURAL AND HISTORICAL CONTEXT

1. See William McGuire, ed., *The Freud/Jung Letters*, translated by Ralph Manheim and R.F.C. Hull (London: The Hogarth Press and

Routledge & Kegan Paul, 1974). The breakdown in relations between Freud and Jung occurs between 1912 and 1914. See pp. 517–52.

2. F.X. Charet, *Spiritualism and the Foundations of C.G. Jung's Psychology* (New York: SUNY, 1993). Richard Noll, *The Jung Cult: Origins of a Charismatic Movement* (Princeton, N.J.: Princeton University Press, 1994). Andrew Samuels, 'National Psychology, National Socialism, and Analytical Psychology, Reflections on Jung and Anti-Semitism, Parts 1 and 2', *Journal of Analytical Psychology*, 37 (1992) 3–28, 127–48. A revised version of these articles appears in Samuels, *The Political Psyche* (London: Routledge, 1993), pp. 287–336.
3. *F/J Letters*, J p. 294.
4. *F/J Letters*, F p. 295.
5. *F/J Letters*, J p. 297.
6. *F/J Letters*, F p. 218.
7. *F/J Letters*, F p. 218.
8. *F/J Letters*, J p. 421.
9. *F/J Letters*, F p. 422.
10. Ernest Jones, *The Life and Work of Sigmund Freud*, 3 vols (New York: Basic Books, 1953–7), Volume 2, p. 140, citing Freud's letter to Ferenczi.
11. See C.G. Jung, *Letters, Volume Two: 1951–1961*, pp. 375–9 for a detailed discussion of what Jung meant by 'Kantian'.
12. Charet, pp. 99–100.
13. C.G. Jung, *The Zofingia Lectures (1896–99) Collected Works, Supplementary Volume A* (Princeton N.J.: Princeton University Press, 1983).
14. Kant's works concerning Spiritualism include *Universal Natural History*, 1755 and *Dreams of a Spirit-Seer Explained by Dreams of Metaphysics*, 1766, which describes spiritualist phenomena.
15. C.G. Jung, *Memories, Dreams, Reflections*, recorded and edited by Aniela Jaffe, translated from the German by Richard and Clara Winston (London: Collins and Routledge & Kegan Paul, 1963), quotations taken from the Flamingo edition of 1983.
16. Jung, MDR pp. 93–4.
17. Jung, *Zofingia*, p. 34.
18. Charet, p. 67.
19. Charet, p. 69.
20. Jung, MDR, pp. 65ff.
21. Charet, p. 36.
22. Charet, p. 37.
23. Jung, *Zofingia*, p. 32.
24. Schopenhauer, *The World as Will and Representation*, Vol 2, p. 513, quoted in Charet, p. 142.
25. Charet, p. 269.
26. C.G. Jung's doctoral dissertation, *On the Psychology and Pathology of So-called Occult Phenomena*, originally published in Leipzig 1902, now in *Psychiatric Studies, Collected Works Volume 1*, translated by R.F.C. Hull (London: Routledge & Kegan Paul, 1957), pp. 3–88.
27. Jung, CW1, p. 56.

28. Jung, CW1, p. 69.
29. Jung, CW1, p. 70.
30. Jung, CW1, p. 66.
31. See William Goodheart, 'C.G. Jung's First Patient', *Journal of Analytical Psychology*, 29 (1984) 1–34, and Charet, pp. 155–61.
32. Charet, p. 157.
33. Charet, p. 157.
34. Charet, p. 157.
35. *F/J Letters*, J p. 95.
36. Charet, p. 258.
37. Jung, MDR, p. 210.
38. Toni Wolff, 'A Few Thoughts on the Process of Individuation in Women' (1934), *Spring* (1941), 81–103 (p. 101).
39. C.G. Jung, *Septem Sermones Ad Mortuos*, privately printed 1916 and pseudonymously subtitled 'The Seven Sermons to the Dead written by Basilides in Alexandria, the City where the East toucheth the West'. It was privately printed in 1925 in an English translation by H.G. Baynes and is now available in Robert Segal, *The Gnostic Jung* (Princeton, N.J.: Princeton University Press, 1992), pp. 181–93.
40. Jung, MDR, pp. 215–16.
41. Charet, p. 267.
42. Jung, MDR, p. 217.
43. Charet, p. 265.
44. Charet, p. 266.
45. Charet, p. 265.
46. Jung, CW8, p. 101.
47. For the development of Jung's archetypal theory, see Charet, pp. 291–3.
48. Jung, CW8, p. 133.
49. Jung, 'On the Nature of the Psyche', (1947, revised 1954), in CW8, p. 183.
50. Jung, MDR, pp. 334–6.
51. Jung, MDR, p. 209.
52. Jung, MDR, p. 208.
53. Jung, MDR, p. 187.
54. Charet, pp. 242–4.
55. Diana Basham, *The Trial of Woman: Feminism and the Occult Sciences in Victorian Society* (London: Macmillan, 1992), p. 108.
56. Basham, p. 7.
57. Basham, pp. ix, 2.
58. Basham, p. 108.
59. Basham, p. 108.
60. Wolff, p. 101.
61. *F/J Letters*, J p. 421.
62. Noll, p. 75.
63. Noll, pp. 76–8.
64. Noll, p. 133.
65. Noll, p. 69.
66. For more on Theosophy, see Noll, pp. 64–9.

67. Noll, p. 66.
68. Friedrich Max Muller's solar interpretation of myths is discussed by Noll, pp. 81–2.
69. Noll, p. 85.
70. For details of Haeckel's introduction of the 'Aryan Christ' myth, see Noll, pp. 85–6.
71. Noll, pp. 77–8.
72. On the similarities between Jung and Diederich, see Noll, pp. 86–8.
73. Noll, p. 107.
74. For a detailed discussion of the *volkisch* and sun worship elements of Jung's *Wandlungen und Symbole der Libido* (1917), see Noll, pp. 109–30.
75. Noll, p. 81.
76. Noll, p. 240.
77. C.G. Jung in Aneila Jaffe, *C.G. Jung: Word and Image* (Princeton, N.J.: Princeton University Press, 1979) p. 75, quoted in Noll, p. 242.
78. For Jung's constant attempts to rewrite Christianity see *Aion* (CW9 II), *Psychology and Religion* (CW11).
79. Noll, p. 88.
80. Noll, p. 209.
81. Jung, *Seminars on Analytical Psychology* (1925), published 1989 CWB, p. 96, quoted in Noll, p. 213.
82. Noll, p. 214.
83. Jung, *Seminars on Analytical Psychology* (1925), published 1989 CWB, p. 98, quoted in Noll, p. 214.
84. Noll, pp. 124–5.
85. Noll, p. 237.
86. Jung, Letter, 26 May 1923 to Oskar Schmitz (1873–1931), *Letters 1, 1906–1950*, pp. 39–40, quoted in Noll, pp. 134–5.
87. Jung, 'Wotan' (1936), first published in *Neue Schweizer Rundschau* (Zurich) 1936, now in *Essays on Contemporary Events, Reflections on Nazi Germany*, German edition 1946, published in England (London: Kegan Paul Trench Trubner, 1947), Ark paperback edition introduced by Andrew Samuels, 1988. *Essays* now in CW10, pp. 177–243.
88. Jung, Wotan, *Essays*, p. 11.
89. Jung, Wotan, p. 17.
90. Jung, Wotan, p. 12.
91. Jung, Wotan, p. 16.
92. Noll, p. 103.
93. Jung, 'Adaptation, Individuation, Collectivity', (1916) CW18, p. 453, quoted in Noll, p. 249.
94. Jung, CW7, p. 237.
95. Jung, 'Introduction: the Fight with the Shadow' in *Essays on Contemporary Events*, pp. 1–9, originally a broadcast talk at the BBC, November 3 1946. First published in *The Listener* (London), XXXVI (1946), No. 930, 615–16. Now also in CW10, pp. 218–26.
96. Jung, *Essays*, p. 4.
97. Noll, p. 130.
98. Noll, pp. 73–4.
99. Noll, p. 72.

100. Freud to Ferenczi 1913 quoted in Jones, Volume 2 (1955), p. 149, quoted in Samuels 1, 8–9.
101. Jung, 'The State of Psychotherapy Today', published 1934 in *Zentralblatt fur Psychotherapie*, now in CW10, pp. 157–73.
102. Jung, CW10, p. 166.
103. Jung, CW10, pp. 165–6.
104. Jung, CW10, p. 165.
105. See Samuels 1, 8 quoting Jung CW10, p.166, Jung CW10, p.533.
106. Samuels 1, 6–7.
107. Samuels 1, 11.
108. Samuels 1, 10–11.
109. Vincent Brome, *Jung: Man and Myth* (London: Macmillan, 1978), pp. 219–20 and Samuels 1, 7.
110. Jolande Jacobi, *The Psychology of C.G. Jung* (London: Kegan Paul Trench Trubner, 1942), p. 33.
111. Jung, *Seminars on Analytical Psychology* (1925), published 1989 CWB, p. 133.
112. Samuels 1, 19.
113. Samuels 1, 19.
114. Samuels 1, 20–1.
115. Jung, CW10, p. 13.
116. Samuels 1, p. 20.
117. Jung, *Essays*, p. 6.
118. See Noll, pp. 259–60.
119. Andrew Samuels' introduction to *Essays* (1988 edition), p.vii.
120. Samuels 1, 11.
121. Jung, CW10, p. 166.
122. Jung, *Essays*, p. 52. This essay was first published as 'Nach der Katastrophe', *Neue Schweizer Rundschau* (Zurich) n.s., XIII (1945), 67–88.
123. Jung, *Essays*, p. 52.
124. Jung, *Essays*, p. 4.

3 A JUNGIAN READER THEORY: ALCHEMY AND *THE CHYMICAL WEDDING* BY LINDSAY CLARKE

1. C.G. Jung, CW12, p. 482.
2. For an introduction to alchemy, see Titus Burckhardt, *Alchemy: Science of the Cosmos, Science of the Soul*, trans. William Stoddart (London: Stuart & Watkins, 1967), especially pp. 11–22.
3. Burckhardt, p. 12.
4. Burckhardt dismisses 'depth psychology' as a complete explanation for alchemy, pp. 8–9.
5. Jung's views on alchemy have been influential on writers such as Alan McGlashan in *The Savage and Beautiful Country* (London: Chatto & Windus, 1966), and his influence is considered in A.J. Harper, 'Mysterium Conjunctionis: On the Attraction of "Chymical

Weddings"', *German life and Letters*, 47, pt 4 (1994), 449–55. This article contains an appreciative discussion of Jung's alchemy in Lindsay Clarke's *The Chymical Wedding*.
6. Wolfgang Iser, *The Act of Reading: A Theory of Aesthetic Response* (London and Henley: Routledge & Kegan Paul, 1978).
7. Iser, pp. 26–7.
8. For complete explanations of 'ideation', 'image building' and 'repertoire', see Iser, pp. 137–48.
9. Iser, p. 148.
10. Iser, p. 150.
11. Iser, p. 139.
12. Iser, p. 157.
13. Iser refers to Freud, pp. 158ff.
14. For Jungian 'active imagination' see Chapters 1 and 2 and the Glossary. For 'reading (w)rite' see the Glossary.
15. Iser, p. 147.
16. Iser, p. 212.
17. Jung CW14, p. 526.
18. See Jung, *Memories, Dreams, Reflections*, recorded and edited by Aniela Jaffe, trans. Richard and Clara Winston (London: Collins and Routledge & Kegan Paul, 1963), p. 210.
19. Richard Wilhelm sent Jung the Chinese alchemy text of *The Secret of the Golden Flower* in 1928, which stimulated his interest. See MDR, p. 195.
20. See Chapter 2 and Jung's 'Individual Dream Symbolism in Relation to Alchemy' (1936) and 'Religious Ideas in Alchemy' (1937) now both in CW12, pp. 39–223, pp. 225–472.
21. Burckhardt, pp. 15–16.
22. Burckhardt, p. 18.
23. See note 19.
24. Nathan Schwartz-Salant, *Jung on Alchemy* (London: Routledge, 1995), introduction, p. 20.
25. The adept in Jung is male with a *soror mystica* (mystic sister) assistant. See CW14, p. 153.
26. Burckhardt, p. 151.
27. Lindsay Clarke, *The Chymical Wedding, A Romance* (London: Jonathan Cape, 1989). Page references are incorporated into the chapter.
28. See Andreae, Johann Valentin, *The Hermetick Romance or The Chymical Wedding of Christian Rosenkreutz*, translated by E. Foxcroft of Kings College (London: A. Sowle, 1690). Lindsay Clarke could have consulted a copy in Cambridge University Library.
29. Many references to Andreae's *The Chymical Wedding of Christian Rosenkreutz* in Jung's *Collected Works* are in CW14, *Mysterium Conjunctionis*. See p. 43, note 19 (refers to the Foxcroft translation), p. 194, p. 232 Jung quotes the motto of *The Chymical Wedding*, p. 293, note 136, p. 295 discusses 'transformations', p. 304, p. 305 on the 'two-faced goddess', p. 330, p. 351, p. 435, note 248, p. 461 on the sea journey, p. 513.
30. Jung, CW14, p. 330.

31. Mary Anne Atwood, *A Suggestive Inquiry into the Hermetic Mystery with a Dissertation on the more Celebrated of the Alchemical Philosophers Being an Attempt Towards the Recovery of the Ancient Experiment of Nature* (London: Trelawney Saunders, 1850), reprinted with an introduction by Leslie Wilmshurst (London: J.M. Atkins, 1918), this edition reprinted by Yoga, 1976.
32. Jung, CW16, p. 294.
33. M. Esther Harding, *Psychic Energy: Its Source and Its Transformation*, with a foreword by C.G. Jung, Bollingen Series X (USA: Bollingen Foundation, 1948, second enlarged edition, 1963), pp. 453–4.
34. Jung, CW14, p. 11.
35. Jung, CW12, p. 482.
36. See Chapter 1 for discussion of Jungian theory's weaknesses on gender.
37. Diana Basham, *The Trial of Woman: Feminism and the Occult Sciences in Victorian Literature and Society* (London: Macmillan, 1992), p. 108.

4 ROMANTIC VIRGINS: JUNG AND FEMINIST NARRATIVE IN THE EARLY NOVELS OF MICHÈLE ROBERTS

1. Michèle Roberts, *The Wild Girl* (London: Methuen, 1984), quotations taken from the paperback edition of 1985. All further references are incorporated into the chapter.
2. Discovery of 'Jungian Feminism' occurs between the writing of *A Piece of the Night* (1978) and *The Visitation* (1983). This was later confirmed by Michèle Roberts in a telephone call on 9 July 1994. By 'Jungian feminism' Roberts principally refers to Nor Hall, *The Moon and The Virgin: A Voyage Towards Self-Discovery and Healing* (London: The Women's Press, 1980).
3. Michèle Roberts, *A Piece of the Night* (London: The Women's Press, 1978). All further references are incorporated into the chapter.
4. Michèle Roberts, *The Visitation* (London: The Women's Press, 1983). All further references are incorporated into the chapter.
5. Michèle Roberts, 'The Woman Who Wanted to Be a Hero', *Walking on the Water: Women Talk About Spirituality*, eds. Jo Garcia and Sara Maitland (London: Virago Press, 1983), pp. 50–65.
6. 'The Woman Who Wanted to Be a Hero', p. 62.
7. Jean Radford, 'Women Writing', first published in *Spare Rib*, 76, (November 1978), later published in *No Turning Back, Writings from the Women's Liberation Movement 1975–1980,* edited by Feminist Anthology Collective (London: The Women's Press, 1981), pp. 259–64, p. 261.
8. See, Jacques Lacan, *Ecrits: A Selection,* trans. A. Sheridan (New York: Norton, 1977). At the time of writing *A Piece of the Night*, Roberts had read no Lacan but secured a female transmission of male authority by ringing up female academic friends for short lectures over the phone. See, Rosemary White, 'Michèle Roberts: An Interview with

Rosemary White', *Bête Noire*, 14/15 (1994), 125–40, p. 127.

9. Toni Wolff, 'A Few Thoughts on the Process of Individuation in Women' (1934), *Spring* (1941), 81–103, and *Structural Forms of the Feminine Psyche*, translated by Paul Watzlawik (Zurich: Privately printed for the C.G. Jung Institute, Zurich, July 1956).
10. Michèle Roberts, 'Outside My Father's House', *Fathers: Reflections By Daughters*, ed. Ursula Owen (London: Virago Press, 1983), pp. 103–11.
11. 'Outside My Father's House', p. 110.
12. Nor Hall, p. xiv, preface.
13. See, C.G. Jung, CW9 I, p. 87, n. 3.
14. Hall, p. 140.
15. Hall, pp. 154–5.
16. For a discussion of Jung on transcendence, see *Jung and Christianity: Faith, Feminism and Hermeneutics*, edited by Robert L. Moore and Daniel J. Meckel (New York: Paulist Press, 1990), especially Murray Stein's chapter, 'C.G. Jung, Psychologist and Theologian', pp. 3–20.
17. 'Child' does not always mean 'self' in Jung. It can stand for childishness or immaturity. However child means unconscious potential leading on to the self. The Christ child in the womb and the divine or golden child are self images. See Jung, CW12, p. 180, n. 125 and CW11, p. 441. 'Virgin birth' can signify the genesis of the 'self' in CW9 I, p. 166.
18. Jung, CW13, p. 259 links the pearl in Christ's parable to alchemical symbolism and thence to individuation and the symbolism of the self.
19. Jung, CW9 I, p. 160. The pearl stands for the child as self.

5 HYSTERICAL JUNG: MICHÈLE ROBERTS' *THE BOOK OF MRS NOAH* AND *IN THE RED KITCHEN*

1. Michèle Roberts, *The Book of Mrs Noah* (London: Methuen, 1978). All further references are incorporated into the chapter.
2. Michèle Roberts, *In the Red Kitchen* (London: Methuen, 1990). All further references are incorporated into the chapter.
3. Roberts' acknowledged source for Sir William Preston is Sir William Crookes in Alex Owen, 'The Other Voice: Women, Children and Nineteenth-century Spiritualism', in *Language, Gender and Childhood*, edited by Carolyn Steedman, Cathy Urwin and Valerie Walkerdine (London: Routledge & Kegan Paul, 1985), pp. 34–73. Sir William Crookes' was a physicist and spiritualist investigator who made famous a working-class medium called Florence Cook. She materialised a spirit named 'Katie King'. These figures become Sir William Preston, Flora Milk and Hattie King respectively in *In the Red Kitchen*.
4. Michèle Roberts confirmed in a phone call on 9 July 1994 that she had used Jung's doctoral thesis on a series of seances as a source for *In the Red Kitchen*.

5. Nor Hall, *The Moon and the Virgin, A Voyage Towards Self-Discovery and Healing* (London: The Women's Press, 1980), pp. 32–5.
6. Hall, p. 173.
7. Jung's doctoral thesis, *On the Psychology and Pathology of So-Called Occult Phenomena*, originally published in Leipzig 1902, now in *Psychiatric Studies, Collected Works Volume 1*, translated by R.F.C. Hull (London: Routledge & Kegan Paul, 1957), pp. 3–88.
8. By the century's end (when Jung was attending seances) what was previously characterised as occult phenomena in women was more likely to be 're-framed' as hysteria or fraudulent tricks. Freud learnt hypnosis from Charcot in his famous hysteria clinic and applied it to his own patients in the early days. See Owen, p. 67, quoting Frank Podmore, *Modern Spiritualism: A History and a Criticism*, vol. 2 (London: Methuen & Co., 1902), pp. 323–4.
9. Roberts' acknowledged source for Charcot is Elaine Showalter, *The Female Malady: Women, Madness, and English Culture, 1830–1980* (London: Virago Press, 1987). For details of the historical career of Charcot, pp. 147–55.
10. For Jung's self image as a divine child, see CW12, p. 166. For Christ as a self image, see CW12, pp. 18–19 and *Aion*, CW9 II. Virgin birth stands for birth of the self (as divine child) in CW9 I, p. 166.
11. For Freud's discussion of the daughter's desire for the father, see *The Pelican Freud Library, Volume 7, On Sexuality: Three Essays on the Theory of Sexuality and Other Works*, translated from the German with the general editorship of James Strachey, compiled and edited by Angela Richards (London: Pelican Books, 1977), pp. 371–8.
12. For a comprehensive history and discussion of the varying definitions of hysteria see *Hysteria Beyond Freud*, essays by Sander L. Gilman, Helen King, Roy Porter, G. S. Rousseau, Elaine Showalter (Berkeley, Los Angeles, London: University of California Press, 1993).
13. See Owen, pp. 66–7. Showalter notes Charcot's advance in arguing that hysteria was a genuine illness and the patients were not fraudulent, p. 147.
14. Showalter records that hysterics were not listened to by Charcot. She describes the recorded dreams of 'Augustine' as containing, 'fire, blood, rape, hatred of men, revolution and escape', p. 154, strongly suggestive of female anger.
15. Jung, MDR, p. 103.
16. CW1, pp. 9–10.
17. CW1, p. 39.
18. CW1, p. 36.
19. CW1, p. 18.
20. Jung calls the spirit stories 'romances' in a section headed 'The Romances', pp. 36ff, see also pp. 38, 39, 69.
21. CW1, p. 56.
22. CW1, p. 43.
23. CW1, p. 38.
24. CW1, pp. 69–70.

25. CW1, p. 56.
26. CW1, pp. 77–8.
27. CW1, p. 67.
28. CW1, p. 65.
29. CW1, p. 66.
30. Crookes never relinquished his belief in the genuine manifestation of 'Katie King' by Florence Cook. Yet by the century's end, definitions of hysteria or fraudulent tricks were more often applied to female mediums. See note 8.
31. See Owen, p. 65, quoting William Crookes, 'The Last of Katie King', *Spiritualist*, (5 June 1874). Reprinted in full in M.R.Barrington, ed., *Crookes and the Spirit World* (London: Souvenir Press, 1972), pp. 137–41.
32. Showalter on Freud studying with Charcot and later praising his work, pp. 147–8. It is also worth noting Freud's major break with Charcot's methods in abandoning hypnosis and listening to patients as Charcot conspicuously did not. See Showalter, p. 154.

6 JUNG, LITERATURE AND FASCISM: *HOPEFUL MONSTERS* BY NICHOLAS MOSLEY

1. C.G. Jung, *Essays on Contemporary Events, Reflections on Nazi Germany*, foreword by Andrew Samuels (London: Ark Paperbacks, 1988), pp. 89–90.
2. Nicholas Mosley, *Hopeful Monsters* (London: Martin Secker & Warburg limited, 1990), p. 288. All citations taken from the Minerva paperback edition of 1991. Further references are incorporated into the text.
3. For details of the career of Oswald Mosley see the biography by Robert Skidelsky, *Oswald Mosley* (London: Macmillan, 1975).
4. Nicholas Mosley, *Rules of the Game: Memoirs of Sir Oswald Mosley and Family* (London: Secker & Warburg, 1982), *Beyond the Pale: Memoirs of Sir Oswald Mosley and Family* (London: Secker & Warburg, 1983). All citations are taken from the one volume paperback edition of 1992.
5. Mosley's biography, p. 336.
6. For an exploration and definition of 'modernism' see, David Lodge, *The Modes of Modern Writing: Metaphor, Metonymy and the Typology of Modern Literature* (London: Edward Arnold, 1977).
7. Jung, *Essays*, pp. 89–90.
8. Mosley's Biography, pp. 568–9.
9. Mosley's Biography, p. 304.
10. See Chapter 2 for Jung's career in Nazi Germany.
11. See Chapter 2 for an explanation of *volkisch* and for Jung's cultural proximity to neo-fascist esoteric sources.
12. See John O'Brien, 'An Interview with Nicholas Mosley', *The Review of Contemporary Fiction*, William Gaddis/Nicholas Mosley Number, 2, No. 2 (1982), 61.

13. The three forms of conjunction are: 1) the sacred marriage of genders in the unconscious, 2) psyche and body, 3) psyche and world. See Chapter 1 and the Glossary.
14. Given the uncanny replication of the Aryan Christ motif, it is intriguing that this construction takes place at the site of a fascist opportunist erasure of difference in the Spanish civil war by the use of Moorish troops against the Republicans. The use of Moorish troops by Fascists (the so-called Christian side) is particularly ironic in the Spanish context where there is a long history of a Moorish presence in Spain with crusades by Christendom against African and Islamic states in the medieval period. See, Bernard F. Reilly, *The Medieval Spains* (Cambridge: Cambridge University Press, 1993), pp. 51ff.
15. Nicholas Mosley, *Efforts at Truth* (London: Secker & Warburg, 1994).
16. Mosley, *Efforts*, pp. 328–9.
17. Mosley, Biography, p. 212.
18. Jung, MDR, p. 302.
19. Hugh Thomas, *The Spanish Civil War* (Great Britain: Eyre & Spottiswoode, 1961), using the revised Penguin Books edition of 1965.
20. Thomas, p. 123.
21. See note 14 about the historical ironies in the Fascist use of the Moors in Spain.
22. Thomas, p. 87.
23. Thomas, pp. 86–7.
24. Thomas, p. 242.
25. Jung, *Essays*, p. 52.
26. Hal Foster, *Compulsive Beauty* (Cambridge, M.A.: MIT, 1993).
27. Foster, p. 136.
28. Foster argues that one project of Dada and Surrealism was as a critique of the fascination of some aspects of modernism with machines. See Foster, pp. 125–53.
29. Foster, p. 152.

7 (POST)COLONIAL JUNG: DORIS LESSING'S *CANOPUS IN ARGOS*

1. The *Canopus in Argos* series consists of the following: *Canopus in Argos: Archives, Re: Colonised Planet 5, Shikasta* (Great Britain: Jonathan Cape, 1979), citations taken from the Grafton edition of 1981, *Canopus in Argos: Archives, The Marriages Between Zones Three, Four and Five* (Great Britain: Jonathan Cape, 1980), citations taken from the Grafton edition of 1981, *Canopus in Argos: Archives, The Sirian Experiments* (Great Britain: Jonathan Cape, 1981), citations taken from the Grafton edition of 1982. *Canopus in Argos: Archives, The Making of the Representative for Planet 8* (Great Britain: Jonathan Cape, 1982), *Canopus in Argos: Archives, Documents Relating to the Sentimental Agents in the Volyen Empire* (London: Jonathan Cape,

1983). All further references are incorporated into the chapter.
2. The essay, 'The Small Personal Voice', first appeared in *Declaration* (London: MacGibbon & Kee, 1957), pp. 11–27 and was reprinted in Doris Lessing, *A Small Personal Voice: Essays, Reviews, Interviews,* edited by Paul Schlueter (New York: Alfred A. Knopf, 1974), pp. 7–25. All citations are taken from the Flamingo reprint of 1994.
3. Lorna Sage, 'The Available Space', in *Women's Writing: A Challenge to Theory,* edited by Moira Monteith (London: Harvester Press, 1986), pp. 15–33.
4. Doris Lessing in a letter to Roberta Rubenstein quoted in Rubenstein's volume, *The Novelistic Vision of Doris Lessing, Breaking the Forms of Consciousness* (Urbana, Chicago, London: University of Illinios Press, 1979) pp. 230–1.
5. Lessing's definition and attitude to Sufism, a mystical system associated with Islam, and her teacher Idries Shah is most comprehensively explicated in her article, 'If You Knew Sufi ...', *Guardian* (8 January 1975), 12.
6. Doris Lessing, 'An Elephant in the Dark', *Spectator,* 213 (18 September 1964), 373.
7. 'An Elephant in the Dark', 373.
8. 'An Elephant in the Dark', 373.
9. See, Phillis Sternberg Perrakis, 'Sufism, Jung and the Myth of the Kore: Revisionist Politics in Lessing's *Marriages*', *Mosaic: A Journal for the Interdisciplinary Study of Literature,* 25, pt 3 (1992), 99–120.
10. See, S. Kumar, 'Sufism in Doris Lessing', *Punjab University Research Bulletin (Arts),* 14 (1983), 167–79.
11. For Lessing's developing accounts of her relation to Sufism see, 'An Elephant in the Dark', 'If You Knew Sufi' and 'What Looks Like An Egg and Is An Egg?', *New York Times Book Review,* 77 (7 May 1972), 6, 41–3.
12. See Nancy Shields Hardin, 'Doris Lessing and the Sufi Way', *Contemporary Literature,* 14 (1973) 565–81, and 'The Sufi Teaching Story and Doris Lessing', *Twentieth Century Literature,* 23 (October 1977), 314–26.
13. See Ann Scott, 'The More Recent Writings: Sufism, Mysticism and Politics', in *Notebooks/Memoirs/Archives: Reading and Rereading Doris Lessing,* ed. Jenny Taylor (London and Boston: Routledge & Kegan Paul, 1982), pp. 164–90.
14. See, Kumar.
15. See, M. Patricia Mosier, 'A Sufi Model for the Teacher/Disciple Relationship in *The Sirian Experiments*', *Extrapolation: A Journal of Science Fiction and Fantasy,* 32, pt 3 (1991), 209–21.
16. Doris Lessing, 'Desert Child, Review of Laurens Van der Post's *The Lost World of the Kalahari*', *New Statesman,* 56 (15 November 1958), 700.
17. Doris Lessing, 'African Interiors, Review of Laurens Van der Post's *The Heart of the Hunter*', *New Statesman,* 67 (27 October 1961), 613–14.
18. 'African Interiors', 613.
19. 'African Interiors', 613.
20. 'The Small Personal Voice', p. 13.

21. 'The Small Personal Voice', p. 14.
22. 'The Small Personal Voice', p. 24.
23. Carey Kaplan, 'Britain's Imperialist Past in Doris Lessing's Futuristic Fiction', in *Doris Lessing: The Alchemy of Survival*, edited by Carey Kaplan and Ellen Cronan Rose (Athens: Ohio University Press, 1988), pp. 149–58.
24. Sage, p. 30.
25. Sage, p. 31.
26. C.G. Jung, CW9 I, p. 79.
27. Peter Caracciolo, 'What's in a Canopean Name?', *Doris Lessing Newsletter* 8, no. 1 (1984), p. 15.
28. Jung, CW9 I, p. 160.
29. Sage, p. 31.
30. Erich Neumann, *The Origins and History of Consciousness*, translated by R.F.C. Hull (London: Routledge & Kegan Paul, 1949), pp. 437–8.
31. Sage, p. 30.
32. Eric Cheyfitz, *The Poetics of Imperialism: Translation and Colonisation from The Tempest to Tarzan* (New York, Oxford: Oxford University Press, 1991).
33. Cheyfitz, p. xviii.
34. George Sherban's education is distinguished by a variety of unusual teachers, a year working on a farm, and visits abroad to experience different cultures, all aspects of the education of Idries Shah according to Lessing in, 'If You Knew Sufi ...'.
35. Doris Lessing, *The Good Terrorist* (London: Jonathan Cape, 1985).
36. Doris Lessing, *The Fifth Child* (London: Jonathan Cape, 1988).
37. Jung, CW14, p. 469.
38. *The Oxford English Dictionary*, describes 'Shammat' as deriving from 'shammatize' meaning excommunicated or anathematised in Hebrew. See *The Compact Edition Of The Oxford English Dictionary, Complete Text Reproduced Micrographically*, Volumes 1–3 (Oxford: Oxford University Press, 1971), volume 2, p. 2768.
39. Cheyfitz, p. 108.
40. Jung, CW12, p. 277.

Bibliography

JUNG AND RELATED WORKS

Barnaby, Karin and Pellegrino D'Acierno, eds, *C.G. Jung and the Humanities: Towards a Hermeneutics of Culture* (London: Routledge, 1990).

Bernheimer, Charles and Claire Kahane, eds., *In Dora's Case: Freud, Hysteria, Feminism* (New York: Columbia University Press, 1985).

Bowie, Malcolm, *Lacan*, Fontana Modern Masters (London: Fontana Press, 1991).

Brome, Vincent, *Jung: Man and Myth* (London: Macmillan, 1978).

Charet, F.X., *Spiritualism and the Foundations of C.G. Jung's Psychology* (New York: State University of New York Press, 1993).

Chodorow, Nancy, *The Reproduction of Mothering: Psychoanalysis and the Sociology of Gender* (Berkeley, Los Angeles, London: University of California Press, 1978).

Freud, Sigmund, *The Standard Edition of the Complete Psychological Works of Sigmund Freud*, translated from the German under the general editorship of James Strachey, in collaboration with Anna Freud, assisted by Alix Strachey and Alan Tyson, 24 vols. (London: The Hogarth Press and the Institute of Psycho-Analysis: 1953–74).

Freud, Sigmund, *The Pelican Freud Library, Volume 7, On Sexuality: Three Essays on the Theory of Sexuality and Other Works*, translated from the German with the general editorship of James Strachey, compiled and edited by Angela Richards (London: Pelican Books, 1977).

Fierz-David, Linda, *Women's Dionysian Initiation: The Villa of Mysteries in Pompeii*, Translated by Gladys Phelan and with an Introduction by M. Esther Harding (Dallas, Texas: Spring Publications Inc., Jungian Classics Series II, 1988). This was completed shortly before the author's death in 1955 as *Psychologische Betrachtungen zu der Freskenfolge der Villa dei Misteri in Pompeii: Ein Versuch*, mimeographed in Zurich, Switzerland, 1957, by the Psychological Club of Zurich.

Gilman, Sander L., Helen King, Roy Porter, G. S. Rousseau and Elaine Showalter, *Hysteria Beyond Freud* (Berkeley, Los Angeles, London: University of California Press, 1993).

Goodheart, William, 'C.G. Jung's First Patient', *Journal of Analytical Psychology*, 29 (1984), 1–34.

Hall, Nor, *The Moon and the Virgin, A Voyage Towards Self-Discovery and Healing* (London: The Women's Press, 1980).

Harding, M. Esther, *Psychic Energy: Its Source and Its Transformation*, with a foreword by C.G. Jung, Bollingen Series X (Princeton, N.J.: Bollingen Foundation, 1948, second enlarged edition, 1963).

Hillman, James, 'Further Notes on Images', *Spring: A Journal of Archetype and Culture* (1978), 164.

Hillman, James, *The Dream and the Underworld* (New York: Harper & Row, 1979).

Hillman, James, *Inter Views: Conversations Between James Hillman and Laura Pozzo on Therapy, Biography, Love, Soul, Dreams, Work, Imagination and the State of Culture* (New York: Harper & Row, 1983).

Hillman, James, *Archetypal Psychology: A Brief Account* (Dallas, Texas: Spring Publications Inc., 1983).

Hillman, James, *Healing Fiction* (New York: Station Hill Press, 1983).

Hinz, Evelyn J. and John J. Teunissen, 'Culture and the Humanities: The Archetypal Approach', in *Jungian Literary Criticism* edited by Richard P. Sugg (Evanston, IL: Northwestern University Press, 1992), pp. 192–9.

Irigaray, Luce, *This Sex Which Is Not One*, translated by Catherine Porter with Carolyn Burke (Ithaca, New York: Cornell University Press, 1985), originally published 1977 in French by Editions de Minuit.

Jacobi, Jolande, *The Psychology of C.G. Jung* (London: Kegan Paul Trench Trubner, 1942).

Jaffe, Aniela, *C.G. Jung: Word and Image* (Princeton, N.J.: Princeton University Press, 1979).

Jones, Ernest, *The Life and Work of Sigmund Freud*, 3 vols (New York: Basic Books, 1953–57).

Jung, C.G., *The Collected Works of C.G. Jung, vols. 1–20, A and B*, edited by Sir Herbert Read, Michael Fordham MD, MRCP, Gerhard Adler PhD, translated by R.F.C. Hull (London: Routledge & Kegan Paul, 1953–91).

Jung, C.G., *Modern Man in Search of a Soul* (London: Kegan, Paul, Trench, Tubner, 1933; Ark Paperback, 1984).

Jung, C.G., *Essays on Contemporary Events, Reflections on Nazi Germany*, German edition 1946, published in England (London: Kegan Paul Trench Trubner, 1947; Ark Paperback edition introduced by Andrew Samuels, 1988).

Jung, C.G., *Memories, Dreams, Reflections*, recorded and edited by Aniela Jaffe, translated from the German by Richard and Clara Winston (Great Britain: Collins and Routledge & Kegan Paul, 1963).

Jung, C.G., *Analytical Psychology: its Theory and Practice, The Tavistock Lectures*, foreword by E.A. Bennet (London and Henley: Routledge & Kegan Paul, 1968).

Jung, C.G., *Letters: 1906–1961*, edited by Gerhard Adler and Aniela Jaffe, translated by R.F.C. Hull, 2 vols (Princeton, N.J.: Princeton University Press, 1973–5).

Jung, C.G., *C.G. Jung Speaking*, edited by William McGuire (London: Thames & Hudson, 1978).

Jung, C.G., *Aspects of the Feminine*, translated from the German by R.F.C. Hull (London: Ark Paperbacks, 1986).

Kristeva, Julia, *Powers of Horror: An Essay on Abjection*, translated by Leon S. Roudiez (New York: Columbia University Press, 1982).

Kristeva, Julia, *The Kristeva Reader*, edited by Toril Moi (Oxford: Basil Blackwell, 1986)

Kugler, Paul, 'The Unconscious in a Postmodern Depth Psychology', in Karin Barnaby and Pellegrino D'Acierno, eds, *C.G. Jung and the Humanities: Towards a Hermeneutics of Culture* (London: Routledge, 1990), pp. 307–18.

Lacan, Jacques, *Ecrits: A Selection*, trans. A. Sheridan (New York: Norton, 1977).

Lauter, Estella, and Carol Schreier Rupprecht, eds, *Feminist Archetypal Theory: Interdisciplinary Re-Visions of Jungian Thought* (Knoxville, TN: University of Tennessee Press, 1985).

McGlashan, Alan, *The Savage and Beautiful Country* (London: Chatto & Windus, 1966).

McGuire, William, ed., *The Freud/Jung Letters*, translated by Ralph Manheim and R.F.C. Hull (London: The Hogarth Press and Routledge & Kegan Paul, 1974).

Moore, Robert L. and Daniel J. Meckel, *Jung and Christianity: Faith, Feminism and Hermeneutics*, edited by Robert L. Moore and Daniel J. Meckel (New York, Mahwah: Paulist Press, 1990).

Neumann, Erich, *The Origins and History of Consciousness*, with a foreword by C.G. Jung, translated from the German by R.F.C. Hull, Bollingen Series XLII (Princeton N.J.: Princeton University Press, 1954).

Noll, Richard, *The Jung Cult: Origins of a Charismatic Movement* (Princeton N.J.: Princeton University Press, 1994).

Rupprecht, Carol Schreier, 'Enlightening Shadows: Between Feminism and Archetypalism, Literature and Analysis', in Karin Barnaby and Pellegrino D'Acierno eds., *C.G. Jung and the Humanities: Towards a Hermeneutics of Culture* (London: Routledge, 1990), pp. 279–93.

Samuels, Andrew, *Jung and the Post-Jungians* (London, Boston and Henley: Routledge & Kegan Paul, 1985).

Samuels, Andrew, Bani Shorter and Fred Plaut, *A Critical Dictionary of Jungian Analysis* (London and New York: Routledge, 1986).

Samuels, Andrew 'Beyond the Feminine Principle', *C.G. Jung and the Humanities: Towards a Hermeneutics of Culture*, edited by Karin Barnaby and Pellegrino D'Acierno (London: Routledge, 1990), pp. 294–306.

Samuels, Andrew, *The Political Psyche* (London and New York: Routledge, 1993).

Schwartz-Salant, Nathan, *Jung on Alchemy* (London: Routledge, 1995).

Segal, Robert, *The Gnostic Jung* (Princeton, N.J.: Princeton University Press, 1992).

Van Meurs, Jos, and John Kidd, *Jungian Literary Criticism, 1920–1980: An Annotated Critical Bibliography of Work in English (With a Selection of Titles after 1980)* (Metuchen, N.J. and London: Scarecrow, 1988).

Wolff, Toni, 'A Few Thoughts on the Process of Individuation in Women' (1934), *Spring* (1941), 81–103.

Wolff, Toni, *Structural Forms of the Feminine Psyche*, translated by Paul Watzlawik (Zurich: privately printed for the C.G. Jung Institute, Zurich, July 1956).

FICTIONAL WORKS

Clarke, Lindsay, *The Chymical Wedding, A Romance* (London: Jonathan Cape, 1989).

Lessing, Doris, *The Four-Gated City* (Great Britain: MacGibbon & Kee, 1969).
Lessing, Doris, *Canopus in Argos: Archives, Re: Colonised Planet 5, Shikasta* (London: Jonathan Cape, 1979).
Lessing, Doris, *Canopus in Argos: Archives, The Marriages Between Zones Three, Four, and Five* (London: Jonathan Cape, 1980).
Lessing, Doris, *Canopus in Argos: Archives, The Sirian Experiments* (London: Jonathan Cape, 1981).
Lessing, Doris, *Canopus in Argos: Archives, The Making of the Representative for Planet 8* (London: Jonathan Cape, 1982).
Lessing, Doris, *Canopus in Argos: Archives, Documents Relating to the Sentimental Agents in the Volyen Empire* (London: Jonathan Cape, 1983).
Lessing, Doris, *The Good Terrorist* (London: Jonathan Cape, 1985).
Lessing, Doris, *The Fifth Child* (London: Jonathan Cape, 1988).
Mosley, Nicholas, *Hopeful Monsters* (London: Martin Secker & Warburg, 1990).
Roberts, Michèle, *A Piece of the Night* (London: The Women's Press, 1978).
Roberts, Michèle, *The Visitation* (London: The Women's Press, 1983).
Roberts, Michèle, *The Wild Girl* (London: Methuen, 1984).
Roberts, Michèle, *The Book of Mrs Noah* (London: Methuen, 1987).
Roberts, Michèle, *In the Red Kitchen* (London : Methuen, 1990).

LITERARY CRITICISM AND THEORY

Basham, Diana, *The Trial of Woman: Feminism and the Occult Sciences in Victorian Society* (London: Macmillan, 1992).
Caracciolo, Peter, 'What's in a Canopean Name?', *Doris Lessing Newsletter*, 8, pt 1 (1984), 15.
Cederstrom, Lorelei, *Fine-Tuning the Feminine Psyche: Jungian Patterns in the Novels of Doris Lessing*, American University Series, Series IV English Language and Literature Vol. 99 (New York, Bern, Frankfurt am Main, Paris: Peter Lang, 1990).
Cheyfitz, Eric, *The Poetics of Imperialism: Translation and Colonisation from The Tempest to Tarzan* (New York and Oxford: Oxford University Press, 1991).
Cleary, Rochelle, 'What's in a Name? Lessing's Message in *The Marriages Between Zones Three, Four, and Five*', *Doris Lessing Newsletter*, 6, pt 2 (1982), 8–9.
Derrida, Jacques, *Of Grammatology*, translated by Gayatri Chakravorty Spivak (Baltimore, MD: Johns Hopkins University Press, 1977).
Derrida, Jacques, *Writing and Difference*, translated with an introduction and additional notes by Alan Bass (London: Routledge, 1978).
Derrida, Jacques, *Positions* (Paris: Minuit, 1972); trans. Alan Bass (Chicago: University of Chicago Press, 1981).
Fishburn, Katherine, *The Unexpected Universe of Doris Lessing: A Study in Narrative Technique*, Contributions to the Study of Science Fiction and Fantasy number 17 (Westport, CT and London: Greenwood Press, 1985).
Hardin, Nancy Shields, 'Doris Lessing and the Sufi Way', *Contemporary Literature*, 14 (1973), 565–81.

Hardin, Nancy Shields, 'The Sufi Teaching Story and Doris Lessing', *Twentieth Century Literature,* 23 (October 1977), 314–26.

Harper, A.J., 'Mysterium Conjunctionis: On the Attraction of "Chymical Weddings"', *German life and Letters,* 47, pt 4 (1994), 449–55.

Iser, Wolfgang, *The Act of Reading: A Theory of Aesthetic Response* (London and Henley: Routledge & Kegan Paul, 1978).

Kaplan, Carey, 'Britain's Imperialist Past in Doris Lessing's Futuristic Fiction', in *Doris Lessing: The Alchemy of Survival,* edited by Carey Kaplan and Ellen Cronan Rose (Athens: Ohio University Press, 1988), pp. 149–58.

Kumar, S., 'Sufism in Doris Lessing', *Panjab University Research Bulletin (Arts),* 14, pt 2 (1983), 167–79.

Lodge, David, *The Modes of Modern Writing: Metaphor, Metonymy and the Typology of Modern Literature* (London: Edward Arnold, 1977).

Maslen, Elizabeth, 'Doris Lessing: The Way to Space Fiction', *Doris Lessing Newsletter,* 8, pt 1 (1984), 7–8, 14.

Mosier, M.Patricia, 'A Sufi Model for the Teacher/Disciple Relationship in *The Sirian Experiments', Extrapolation: A Journal of Science Fiction and Fantasy,* 32, pt 3 (1991), 209–21.

O'Brien, John, 'An Interview with Nicholas Mosley', *Review of Contemporary Fiction,* William Gaddis/Nicholas Mosley Number, 2, No. 2 (1982), 58–79.

Perrakis, Phillis Sternberg, 'The Marriage of Inner and Outer Space in Doris Lessing's *Shikasta', Science Fiction Studies,* 17, pt 2 (1990), 221–38.

Perrakis, Phillis Sternberg, 'Sufism, Jung and the Myth of the Kore: Revisionist Politics in Lessing's *Marriages', Mosaic: A Journal for the Interdisciplinary Study of Literature,* 25, pt 3 (1992), 99–120.

Radford, Jean, 'Women Writing', in *No Turning Back, Writings from the Women's Liberation Movement 1975–80* edited by the Feminist Anthology Collective (London: The Women's Press, 1981), pp. 259–64.

Rubenstein, Roberta, *The Novelistic Vision of Doris Lessing, Breaking the Forms of Consciousness* (Urbana, Chicago, London: University of Illinois Press, 1979).

Sage, Lorna, 'The Available Space', in *Women's Writing: A Challenge to Theory,* ed. Moira Monteith (Brighton: The Harvester Press, 1986), pp. 15–33.

Seligman, Dee, ed., *Doris Lessing, An Annotated Bibliography of Criticism* (London and Westport, CT: Greenwood Press, 1981).

Scott, Ann, 'The More Recent Writings: Sufism, Mysticism and Politics', in *Notebooks/Memoirs/Archives: Reading and Rereading Doris Lessing,* ed. Jenny Taylor (London and Boston: Routledge & Kegan Paul, 1982), pp. 164–90.

Spivak, Gayatri Chakravorty, 'Translator's Preface' to *Of Grammatology* by Jacques Derrida (Baltimore, MD: Johns Hopkins University Press, 1977).

Sprague, Claire, *Rereading Doris Lessing, Narrative Patterns of Doubling and Repetition* (Chapel Hill and London: University of North Carolina Press, 1987).

Sprague, Claire, ed., *In Pursuit of Doris Lessing, Nine Nations Reading* (London: Macmillan Press, 1990).

Taylor, Jenny, ed., *Notebooks/Memoirs/Archives: Reading and Rereading Doris Lessing* (Boston, London, Melbourne, Henley: Routledge & Kegan Paul, 1982).

White, Rosemary, 'An Interview with Michèle Roberts', *Bête Noire,* 14/15

(1994), 125–40.
White, Rosemary, 'Five Novels as History: The Lives and Times of Michèle Roberts' Prose Fiction', *Bête Noire*, 14/15 (1993), 144–57.
Worton, Michael, and Judith Still eds, *Intertextuality: Theories and Practices*, (Manchester and New York: Manchester University Press, 1990).

SUPPLEMENTARY MATERIAL

Allen, Paul M., *A Christian Rosenkreutz Anthology*, compiled and edited by Paul M. Allen (New York: Rudolf Steiner Publications: 1968).
Andreae, Johann Valentin, *The Hermetick Romance or The Chymical Wedding of Christian Rosenkreutz*, translated by E. Foxcroft of Kings College (London: A. Sowle, 1690).
Atwood, Mary Anne, *A Suggestive Inquiry into the Hermetic Mystery with a Dissertation on the more Celebrated of the Alchemical* Philosophers *Being an Attempt Towards the Recovery of the Ancient Experiment of Nature* (London: Trelawney Saunders, 1850), reprinted with an introduction by Leslie Wilmshurst (London: J.M. Atkins, 1918; repr. Yoga, 1976).
Barrington, M. R., ed., *Crookes and the Spirit World* (London: Souvenir Press, 1972).
Burckhardt, Titus, Alchemy: *Science of the Cosmos, Science of the Soul*, translated from the German by William Stoddart (London: Stuart & Watkins, 1967).
Foster, Hal, *Compulsive Beauty* (Cambridge, MA: MIT, 1993).
Holmyard, E.J., *Alchemy* (Harmondsworth: Penguin Books, 1957).
Klossowski De Rola, Stanislas, *Alchemy: The Secret Art* (London: Thames and Hudson, 1973).
Lessing, Doris, 'Desert Child, Review of Laurens Van der Post's *The Lost World of the Kalahari*', *New Statesman*, 15 November 1958, 700.
Lessing, Doris, 'African Interiors, Review of Laurens Van der Post's *The Heart of the Hunter*', *New Statesman*, 27 October 1961, 613–14.
Lessing, Doris, 'An Elephant in the Dark', *Spectator*, 18 September 1964, 373.
Lessing, Doris, 'What Looks Like an Egg and is an Egg?', *New York Times Book Review*, 7 May 1972, 6, 41–3.
Lessing, Doris, 'The Small Personal Voice', in *A Small Personal Voice, Essays, Reviews, Interviews*, edited and introduced by Paul Schlueter (New York: Alfred A. Knopf Inc., 1974; repr. Flamingo, 1994), pp. 7–25.
Lessing, Doris, 'If You Knew Sufi ...', *Guardian*, 8 January 1975, 12.
Lessing, Doris, *Under My Skin, Volume One of my Autobiography, to 1949* (London: HarperCollins Publishers, 1994).
McLean, Adam, ed. with an Introduction and Commentary, *The Chymical Wedding of Christian Rosenkreutz*, translated by Jocelyn Godwin (Grand Rapids, MI: Phanes Press, 1991).
Mosley, Nicholas, *Rules of the Game, Sir Oswald and Lady Cynthia Mosley 1896--1933* (London: Martin Secker & Warburg, 1982).
Mosley, Nicholas, *Beyond the Pale, Sir Oswald Mosley and Family, 1933–1980* (London: Martin Secker & Warburg, 1983).

Mosley, Nicholas, *Rules of the Game, Beyond the Pale, Memoirs of Sir Oswald Mosley and Family* (London: Martin Secker & Warburg, 1992, 1993).
Mosley, Nicholas, *Efforts at Truth* (London: Secker & Warburg, 1994).
Owen, Alex, 'The Other Voice: Women, Children and Nineteenth-Century Spiritualism', in *Language, Gender and Childhood*, edited by Carolyn Steedman, Cathy Urwin and Valerie Walkerdine (London: Routledge & Kegan Paul, 1985), pp. 34–73.
Owen, Alex, *The Darkened Room: Women, Power, and Spiritualism in Late Nineteenth Century England* (London: Virago Press, 1989).
Oppenheim, Janet, *The Other World, Spiritualism and Psychical Research in England, 1850–1914* (Cambridge: Cambridge University Press, 1985).
Podmore, Frank, *Modern Spiritualism: A History and a Criticism*, vol. 2 (London: Methuen, 1902).
Redgrove, S., *Alchemy: Ancient and Modern* (London: William Rider & Son, 1911).
Reilly, Bernard F., *The Medieval Spains* (Cambridge: Cambridge University Press, 1993).
Roberts, Michèle, 'Outside My Father's House', in *Fathers: Reflections By Daughters*, edited by Ursula Owen (London: Virago, 1983), pp. 103–12.
Roberts, Michèle, 'The Woman Who Wanted to Be a Hero', in *Walking on the Water: Women Talk About Spirituality*, edited by Jo Garcia and Sara Maitland (London: Virago, 1983), pp. 50–65.
Roberts, Michèle, 'Write, she said', *The Progress of Romance: The Politics of Popular Fiction*, edited by Jean Radford, History Workshop Series (London and New York: Routledge & Kegan Paul, 1986), pp. 221–35.
Skidelsky, Robert, *Oswald Mosley* (London: Macmillan, 1975).
Showalter, Elaine, *The Female Malady: Women, Madness, and English Culture, 1830–1980* (London: Virago Press, 1987).
Thomas, Hugh, *The Spanish Civil War* (Great Britain: Eyre & Spottiswoode, 1961; repr. Penguin, 1965).

Glossary: Principal Jungian Terms

Words in **bold** indicate Glossary entries.

Active imagination is the term Jung gave to his therapeutic method of asking a patient to fantasise spontaneously upon an image, usually a dream image. By this method, **unconscious** material may be brought into consciousness and thus **individuation** is promoted. Active imagination is the opposite of conscious invention: it is a method of surrendering the direction of fantasies to the Other or the unconscious. Most often, active imagination indicates the use of the subject's unconscious image from a dream, but Jung argued that cultural or artistic images could also be employed.

Alchemy is defined by Jung as a projection of the individuation process onto the chemical operations performed by the alchemist. He interpreted alchemy texts as demonstrating the projection of unconscious activities and alchemists as unwitting self-analysts. Alchemists developed symbols and Jung regarded these as enabling psychological transformations similar to the role of dreams in his psychology. In his view, alchemists used chemical operations and symbolic language to stimulate their own individuation so that they could reach the 'gold' of union with the divine or self archetype. Other key Jungian alchemical terms include the **nigredo**, the stage of blackness, death, being trapped in matter before the processes of alchemy liberate the spirit or unconscious, and **Mercurius**, a major figure of the potential powers of the unconscious for Jung. As a figure for the unconscious, Mercurius is androgynous, a container of opposites, a trickster and akin to the dark side of Christ or a devilish figure.

Anima to Jung means a feminine figure for unconscious complementarity in the psyche of a man. In that this locates a feminine mode in the subjectivity of the masculine gender, denoting a bisexual unconscious, it is a helpful concept. However, at times, Jung uses his own unconscious anima as a model for designating female subjectivity as 'more unconscious' than males. A complication occurs through Jung's introduction of two principles, Eros/

Logos where Eros denotes relatedness and feeling with Logos as a motif of spiritual meaning and reason. Jung aligned feminine consciousness with Eros and masculine subjectivity with Logos. A female's contrasexual image in the unconscious is masculine, the **animus** which becomes a problem when the animus is the carrier of the masculine Logos principle so implying that women have an indirect access to reason. Contemporary British Jungian Analytic practice tends to discount the animus with its connotations of male authority, to regard men and women as having equal potentials for Eros and Logos, and to consider unconscious images as more fluidly gendered. In this way, a woman can have feminine Others (animas) as well.

Archetypes are inherited structuring patterns in the unconscious with potentials for meaning formation and images. They unrepresentable in themselves and evident only in their manifest derivatives, archetypal images. Archetypes are containers of opposites and so are androgynous, equally capable of manifesting themselves as either gender or non-human forms. The archetype is a psychosomatic concept linking body and psyche, instinct and image. Body and culture will influence the content of archetypal images but not govern them as archetypes are the structuring principles of an autonomous psyche. Archetypes are not inherited ideas or images. When actually called upon to define archetypes, Jung insisted that they were not inherited contents. He used the helpful metaphor of a crystal to describe archetypes themselves as existing in a solution which could then crystallise out into various archetypal images. Jung's archetypes exist in the tradition of Platonic Ideas and Kant's *a priori* categories of perception.

Archetypal images are the visible representations of archetypes which can never account for the multifarious potential of the archetype as such. Consequently, archetypal images have a metaphorical connection to the archetype, or I have argued, a fictive relation. They are 'fictional' not because archetypal images are completely arbitrary but because they are always creative yet provisional and partial images of a greater unrepresentable complexity.

The Jungian **ego** is the centre of consciousness concerned with the sense of a personal identity, the maintenance of personality and the sense of continuity over time. However, Jung considered the ego as something less than the whole personality as it was constantly interacting with more significant archetypal forces in the unconscious. The ego is perceived as responsive to the demands of the self as superior ordering principle of the psyche as a whole. In itself, the ego is a limited and inauthentic fiction of personality without acknowledgement of the superior creative Other in the unconscious. Jung tended to equate the ego with consciousness in his writings.

Individuation is Jung's term for his concept of subjective processes whereby the ego is continually deconstructed by the archetypal processes of the unconscious. I use the term 'deconstruction' because the ego is constantly made, unmade and remade by the teleological forces of the Other. Even 'meaning' in the ego is subject to dissolution and reconstitution by the Jungian Other. Dreams are a record of individuation which is teleological, directing consciousness towards conjunctions with the unconscious (sometimes taking the metaphor of sacred marriage) leading towards the ego becoming a satellite of the governing archetype of the self. The aim of analysis is to facilitate individuation which, if operating properly, will heal psychic wounds since the psyche is autonomous and self-regulating, with the unconscious performing a compensatory relation to conscious excesses. Although Jung viewed individuation as an essentially common psychic process to be encouraged by analysis if not properly functioning, at times he seemed to suggest a more elitist conception in which a more consciously pursued individuation could develop superior beings, at least in moral terms. Individuation could involve three stages of conjunction with unconscious forces: firstly, with the Other gender in the unconscious, then of psyche with body and thirdly, of psyche with the outer world.

Reading (w)rite is a term coined in this book to signify a concept whereby Jungian active imagination is absorbed into reading and/or writing fiction. If active imagination relies upon spontaneous unconscious fantasies in the processing of images, then the same idea could apply to images provoked by words or groups of words. The more fictional or poetic a text, the more the active imagination might apply because of the greater scope for images likely to stimulate unconscious fantasies. If reading fiction can be construed as active imagination, then reading enters the individuation process in the continual re-forming of subjectivity: it becomes a rite of the subject. Similarly, if writing fiction occurs when the writer desires to romance the Other, to be open to fantasy images from the unconscious before choosing words, then writing also becomes a (w)rite of individuation. Romance and sacrifice occur in the reading (w)rite in the romantic commitment to the Other and the sacrifice of ego control, the desire to possess all meanings, exhaust all signifieds. When writing, sacrifice also occurs because words inevitably have more fixity than the images they may be in response to, so that some sacrifice of the Other occurs in what I have called the violence of signifying. If Jung's conception of alchemy is used (as projected active imagination) then the reading (w)rite could be characterised as reading or (w)riting alchemy.

Religious experience in Jungian ideas is distinctive because to Jung all experience is mediated through the psyche and its inherited structuring principles of archetypes. Consequently, transcendence is located in the psyche and is a property of the supreme governing archetype of the self. Therefore to Jung, religious experience is indistinguishable from intimations of the self, allowing for a concept of religions which could harmonise with external religions (especially when Christ is named a self image) but could also validate religious experience without an external transcendent God. It is not reducible to a mythologising of bodily drives. Religious experience is also accessible in Jungian ideas through bodily experience in the sacred marriage. Archetypes are containers of opposites and androgynous so that it is impossible to exclude the feminine from the divine.

Sacred marriage is both a metaphor and a description of a pivotal Jungian event: the momentary union of the ego with the unconscious when the unconscious is characterised by the Otherness of the Other gender. The momentary conjunction is part of the process of individuation when the ego becomes subjected to the transcendent and numinous powers of the self. Sacred marriage is a metaphor when it is a matter of consciousness interacting with a figure for the Other gender in the unconscious. However sacred marriage can become corporeal when the unconscious is accessed through sexuality. Because the body is connected to psyche but does not govern it, bodily experience can be a route to autonomous numinous archetypal experience. The sacred marriage becomes a bodily, unconscious and, in Jungian terms, religious rite. Jung interpreted sexual metaphors of alchemy as his form of sacred marriage. The concept of sacred marriage is important for Michèle Roberts' use of Jung and may make future contributions to feminist theory.

The **self** is the supreme governing archetype of the unconscious to which the ego becomes subject in individuation. Jung frequently described self images in dreams in circular or mandala forms. He argued that Christ functioned as a self image in Christianity and that birth of the self in the unconscious was analogous to the divine virgin birth of Christ. A child is not always a self image: it can stand for childishness, immaturity, but the Christ-child or child of a virgin birth has the divine touches of authentic intimations of the self. Michèle Roberts' novels draw on this. The self is not merely divine light; it also comprehends the shadow and darkness so positing a crucial bonding between Christ and anti-Christ, the essential structuring of shadow as interior to self and psyche.

The **shadow** is the archetypal forces of blackness, reversal or undoing. Intrinsic to the idea of a compensatory relation between ego and unconscious, the shadow is that which is denied in conscious personality. Consequently the shadow could be figured as the potential evil within every personality. Jung warned that the shadow needed to be brought into a relationship with conscious personality lest repression caused it to swell in power and break out in neurosis or violence.

The shadow is not some dynamic independent force for evil but is part of the principle of oppositions underpinning the Jungian psyche. It is part of the multifarious conception of archetypes so is the reverse of their structuring, meaning making function, a reversal within the very processes of signification itself. As Jung puts it, the less the negative inferiority of the shadow is recognized as integral to psychic structures, the more powerful an opposition it forms. Intrinsic to the deconstructive elements of Jungian thought, the shadow is the unmaking of the constant creativity of the psyche.

The Jungian **unconscious** is a key contribution of Jung to psychology and is fundamental to all developments of Jungian theory. Like Freud, the term unconscious denotes both mental contents inaccessible to the ego and a psychic arena with its own properties and functions. The Jungian unconscious is superior to the ego and exists in a compensatory relation to it. It is the locus of meaning, feeling and value in the psyche and is autonomous, not subject to bodily or external (for example spiritual) governance. It is not, however, completely separate from the body but offers a third place between that perennial duality, body and spirit. Body and culture influence unconscious contents (archetypal images), but the unconscious is autonomous and so not *subject* to either force. This means that the Other gender can be encountered in the unconscious and that a gender hierarchy based on the body is not coherent with Jungian thought. The unconscious is structured by archetypes which are hypothetical inherited structuring principles, only manifested by their derivatives, archetypal images. These archetypal images are intrinsically unable to comprehend the essential heterogeneity of the archetype. The unconscious operates teleologically in compensating for ego excesses or damage and in subjecting the ego to the superior forces of the governing archetype of the self in individuation.

Index

Page references in **bold** indicate more detailed entries

The manufacturer's authorised representative in the EU is Springer Nature Customer Service Centre GmbH, Europaplatz 3, 69115 Heidelberg, Germany. If you have any concerns regarding our products, please contact ProductSafety@springernature.com

Printed and bound by CPI Group (UK) Ltd, Croydon, CR0 4YY

31/10/2025

01988966-0013